Doing Interview-Based Qualitative Resear

For many students, the experience of learning about and us..._
be bewildering. This book is an accessible step-by-step guide to conduc.....
based qualitative research projects. The authors discuss the "hows" and "whys" or
qualitative research, showing readers the practices as well as the principles behind
them. The book first describes how to formulate research questions suited to qualitative
inquiry. It then discusses in detail how to select and invite research participants into a
study and how to design and carry out good interviews. It next presents several ways to
analyze interviews and provides readers with many worked examples of analyses. It also
discusses how to synthesize findings and how to present them. *Doing Interview-Based
Qualitative Research* equips readers in disciplines such as psychology, sociology,
education, counseling, nursing, and public health with the knowledge and skills necessary to embark on their own projects.

Eva Magnusson is Professor Emerita of Psychology and Gender Studies at Umeå
University in Sweden.

Jeanne Marecek is William R. Kenan Professor Emerita of Psychology at Swarthmore
College in the USA.

Their book *Gender and Culture in Psychology: Theories and Practices* was published by
Cambridge University Press in 2012.

Doing Interview-Based Qualitative Research

A Learner's Guide

EVA MAGNUSSON AND JEANNE MARECEK

Umeå University and Swarthmore College

CAMBRIDGE
UNIVERSITY PRESS

CAMBRIDGE
UNIVERSITY PRESS

University Printing House, Cambridge CB2 8BS, United Kingdom

Cambridge University Press is part of the University of Cambridge.

It furthers the University's mission by disseminating knowledge in the pursuit of education, learning and research at the highest international levels of excellence.

www.cambridge.org
Information on this title: www.cambridge.org/9781107674707

© Eva Magnusson and Jeanne Marecek 2015

A catalogue record for this publication is available from the British Library

Library of Congress Cataloguing in Publication data
Magnusson, Eva, 1947–
Doing interview-based qualitative research : a learner's guide / Eva Magnusson, Jeanne Marecek.
  pages cm
ISBN 978-1-107-67470-7 (paperback)
1. Qualitative research. 2. Social sciences – Research. I. Marecek, Jeanne, 1946– II. Title.
H62.M23576 2015
001.4′2–dc23

2015016411

ISBN 978-1-107-06233-7 Hardback
ISBN 978-1-107-67470-7 Paperback

Contents

1 Introduction

People continually reflect on themselves and their worlds, and they are continually called upon to give accounts of themselves. People have hopes, fears, reasons, intentions, and values, and they may experience times of satisfaction, confusion, and demoralization. The premise of this book is that researchers ought to and can study these matters. In this book, we give readers the conceptual framework and practical tools to do so.

We have written this book for students and researchers who are new to qualitative research. We have been doing qualitative research for more than two decades. Each of us has taught courses on qualitative research for many years and supervised such research in a variety of contexts. We have taught psychology students, medical students, students in interdisciplinary programs such as gender studies, and social science researchers new to this type of research. We have also jointly conducted seminars on research methods in several countries and for scholars from many backgrounds. And we have written about theories and practices of gender research (Magnusson and Marecek, 2012). This book draws on all of these experiences as teachers, supervisors, and researchers. Our hope is that readers of this book will become adept and judicious practitioners of the research methods that we present.

mugnesson and marecek (2012) call it interpretative research, with the goal of its methods to

Introducing interpretative research

Before we proceed, we pause to introduce a key term. For the types of research methods you will learn here, the term qualitative research is the term most commonly used. However, we use the term *interpretative research*. We have chosen this term because it is both more precise and more descriptive. Interpretation is at the heart of the research methods we describe in this book. The goal of these methods is to understand – that is, to interpret – the meanings that people ascribe to events and actions, how they make these meanings their own, and how they negotiate these meanings in interactions with other people. The term interpretative research thus forthrightly proclaims the central purpose of the research as well as the central activity of the researcher.

Another reason why we use the term interpretative research is that it sidesteps the many misunderstandings that surround the term qualitative research. To take a prime misunderstanding, qualitative research and quantitative research are often set in opposition to each other. That opposition rests on the notion that the fundamental distinction between qualitative and quantitative research is whether or not a research project uses numbers (i.e., quantities). It takes only a moment's reflection to demolish that notion. On the one hand, most research – whether qualitative or quantitative – aims at least partly at some kind of estimates of some kind of quantities. On the other hand, in any research project, whether qualitative or quantitative, the researcher must make numerous qualitative judgments in the course of the project.

The research methods that we present in this book are grounded in certain assumptions about people and about what researchers can learn about people. Qualitative researchers (or, as we will call them from now on, interpretative researchers) think of people as always located in social contexts and as continually engaged in making sense of their experiences. The expression "making sense" refers to how people imbue things and events with meaning and, by doing so, make them understandable. Interpretative researchers are interested in people's ways of making sense of their activities, experiences, and relationships and how they plan and act in accord with these ways of making sense. We return to the topic of meaning-making later in this chapter.

The interpretative research methods that we include in this book have another feature in common. They direct attention to how people are situated in social contexts of several kinds. People are positioned within societal hierarchies and structures, and they are part of organizations, institutions, and social groups. Social contexts such as these set the frames for personal meaning-making. Indeed, people form meanings and modify them in the course of interactions within these social settings. These social formations can be thought of as interpretive communities that share a culture, that is, a patterned set of ways of understanding the world. We take up the topic of context and culture later in this chapter.

Interpretative researchers hold that the best way to learn about people's meanings and meaning-making is to listen to people talk about their experiences in their own way and in their words. People's own words afford the best access a researcher can have to how they understand their experiences. As you might guess, interpretative researchers rarely administer questionnaires and scales to their research participants because these instruments compel participants to respond to a limited array of alternatives that have been set by the researcher. For interpretative research projects, loosely structured interviews that bring forward the participants' stories, memories, worldviews, and beliefs are far more useful. We devote a good portion of this book to helping you learn to do such interviews.

A good way to start to learn about interpretative research is to read about research projects. Therefore, we provide descriptions of several research projects throughout the book. We begin here with brief descriptions of five interpretative studies.

Living with agoraphobia. Agoraphobia is a psychiatric condition in which the sufferer experiences severe anxiety and even panic attacks and as a result is confined to home. Lisa Capps and Elinor Ochs, two researchers in the USA, collected and analyzed an extensive set of interviews with a woman with long-standing agoraphobia so severe that it kept her housebound. In the interviews, the woman told many stories about her anxieties and her panic attacks. The researchers came to see that she used a consistent story organization as she told these stories. This story organization adhered closely to psychiatric theories that emphasized locations (e.g., heavy traffic and tight spaces) as the triggers of panic attacks. This emphasis restricted the content of the stories to themes of helplessness and irrationality. By closely analyzing the stories, the researchers showed that there was another possible way of reading them. This reading featured the woman's difficulties in communicating with others, in particular her difficulty in asserting her needs and wishes to her husband (Capps & Ochs, 1995b).

Black racial identities. Andrea Dottolo and Abigail Stewart, two researchers in the USA, studied interviews with middle-aged Black people and White people who had grown up in a medium-sized city in a Midwestern state in the USA and had remained residents there. In the interviews, these individuals were asked to recollect experiences in which racial identity and race relations were salient. The analyses focused in detail on experiences of racial discrimination, which were described by many of the Black participants. For both Black men and Black women, such negative experiences often involved contact with the police. Thus, as the researchers noted, a common element of Black racial identity for these individuals was the expectation of racial discrimination (Dottolo & Stewart, 2008).

Stories of serial migration. Serial migration refers to a pattern in which parents migrate and their children follow several years later. Ann Phoenix, a researcher in England, interviewed adults who had experienced serial migration from the Caribbean to Great Britain when they were children. Phoenix found that the adult narrators told about their childhood experiences in ways that enabled them retrospectively to construct "adequate" childhoods in spite of having childhood experiences that were nonnormative according to Western ideals of family life and child development (Phoenix, 2008).

Negotiating about proper masculinity. Nigel Edley, a researcher in England, analyzed group interviews with young British men in their mid-teens. The interviews, which concerned a wide variety of everyday topics, brought up controversial matters such as sexual behavior and excessive drinking. Edley's analysis pinpointed how the young men placed themselves and one another in more or less "troubled" speaking positions during the course of the conversations. Such positions influenced participants' chances of being heard and taken seriously in the discussions (Edley, 2001).

Negotiating about proper femininity. Dawn Curry and her colleagues, a group of researchers in Canada, interviewed young teenage girls who participated in activities that were atypical for girls in their local context. These activities included studying science, skateboarding, and choosing to wear "uncool" clothes and hairstyles. Some of the girls explicitly presented themselves as being opposed to conventional "girlie"-ness. The researchers were interested in how this subset of girls talked about their opposition to "girlie"-ness. The researchers found that this subset of girls grounded their resistance to the rules of conventional femininity in a generalized discourse of rational individualism, not in feminism (Currie, Kelly, & Pomerantz, 2006).

These studies indicate the breadth of topics and issues that interpretative researchers study. The summaries also show some of the types of conclusions that interpretative researchers draw from their research, as well as the scientific contributions such research can make. Because of the specific interest in understanding people's meaning-making by studying their own words, interpretative research contributes some types of knowledge that researchers find difficult to acquire by other methods. For example, interpretative research contributes useful knowledge about how people experience important events in their lives. See, for instance, the study of agoraphobia. Interpretative research also contributes useful knowledge about people's everyday practices, and how people make sense of those practices in the wider contexts of their lives. See, for instance, the study of girls who engaged in atypical leisure activities. And interpretative research contributes knowledge about how the societal and cultural context is implicated in and shapes people's ways of understanding themselves and others, thus making links between macro structures and micro processes. See, for instance, the study of African Americans' experiences of racial discrimination. Interpretative research can also contribute practical knowledge about what people's talk accomplishes in everyday interactions: how talk serves to place speakers and listeners in more or less comfortable positions in an interaction, as well as conveying content. See, for instance, the study of young men's group conversations.

Interpretative research methods have always had an important place in such disciplines as sociology, anthropology, education, and psychology. Like all scientific methods, interpretative methods are disciplined ways to obtain and organize knowledge. They are based on systematic observation. They are transparent: that is, researchers can clearly and precisely describe the procedures they used. This enables others to evaluate the soundness of the work or to repeat it. Like other forms of research, interpretative research generates knowledge that is provisional and subject to modification.

The theoretical framework for the book: some building blocks

The research approaches in this book all focus on people as they are situated in their sociocultural worlds and the ways that they make meaning of their lives. Here we describe some of the key concepts in those approaches.

Culture

We use the word culture to refer to the shared meanings, views of the world, moral visions, and practices that together make up a way of life for a social group. Elements of such shared meanings, views of the world, and practices often are so commonplace for members of a group that they are invisible *as meanings*, etc.; they are taken as "just the way things are." Culture is more than just the sum of the shared meanings, views of the world, and practices of a social group, however. At the same time, it is also the framework within which members of that group understand themselves and others (Bruner, 1986). This means that the cultural framework of a social group may limit the ways in which people are able to understand themselves and others (Shweder, 1991).

Two central components of culture are *worldview* and *ethos* (Geertz, 1973). A worldview is a model of how things are; this includes assumptions about people's resources, faculties, and capabilities. Ethos refers to moral, affective, and aesthetic aspects of life, including assumptions and values about what a person should be or become, and about what constitutes the good life.

The image of culture as a framework might be read to imply that culture is something that exists outside individuals. This would be a misrepresentation of a complex reality: On the one hand, it is people who create cultural frameworks, and therefore there could be no culture apart from the individual. On the other hand, there could be no individuals apart from culture. Culture is an integral part of each individual in a social group.

Meaning

We use the terms meaning and meaning-making when we write about how people understand themselves and the world around them. Let us consider the multiple senses in which people use the term meaning in everyday talk. Looking up "meaning" in a dictionary or thesaurus yields many different shades of meaning and scores of synonyms. Roughly speaking, there are four general senses of the word "meaning":

One sense is the message conveyed by a certain statement or the gist of an account. Some synonyms are substance, content, import, and point (as in "get to the point"). An example is "What is the meaning of that sentence?"

The second sense is the intention that is implied in a statement. Some synonyms are implication, spirit, sense, and tenor. An example is "I could get the meaning of his argument."

The third sense is the interpretation of an account. Some synonyms are explanation, analysis, and understanding. An example is "What could be the meaning of his dream?"

The fourth sense is the significance of what is said. Some synonyms are moral (as in "moral of the story") or lesson. An example is "The meaning of the parable is 'Love thy neighbor'."

All these senses of the term meaning come into play as we look closely at personal meaning and meaning-making in this book. Meaning is central to the book because meaning-making is a central human activity. In daily life, people continually impose personal meanings and order on the world. These meanings are connected to their sense of themselves, their previous experiences, and their expectations and plans. This is true moment to moment as well as on a larger timescale. People give meaning to their present activities and experiences and to their previous experiences on the basis of where they feel their life is going and where they want it to go. Therefore, meaning-making is connected to people's intentions. On the one hand, what people want to achieve in a particular situation to a large extent determines the sense that they make of that situation. On the other hand, the meanings of the world and of themselves that people bring to a situation serve as templates for action, which influence their plans, choices, and decisions in that situation (Bruner, 1990).

Personal meaning-making is not simply personal, however. As we noted in the section about culture, the resources for meaning-making are provided by culture. These resources both enable meaning-making and restrict the pool of available meanings. This means that the framework of culture simultaneously makes events knowable in some ways and not knowable in other ways. Moreover, personal meanings are always explicitly or implicitly negotiated with other people. It is such negotiations that determine which meanings will be dominant and which will be marginal in a particular context. Such negotiations are often characterized by unequal power relations among those involved; the power to influence which meanings will be dominant is seldom distributed equally.

Talk and language

Most of what people do when they make meanings, negotiate about meanings, and use cultural resources in their meaning-making happens in language. People talk about what they have done and why; they discuss with others how a thing should be understood; they think about what things mean to them; and they often have cause to write down their arguments. And so on. Language is omnipresent in people's lives. But language is present in more than one way. On the one hand, people use language to express their personal ideas, wishes, or experiences. On the other hand, language to a great extent shapes how it is possible for people to express these ideas, wishes, or experiences.

It is not surprising that language should have this dual character, if you consider how children acquire language. When children are born, they enter a language environment that existed long before their birth. In this environment, they interact with people, they are spoken to, and they gradually learn to speak, all within the framework provided by the words and categories that these people use. People are in such language environments for their whole lives (Billig, 1996). Therefore, neither words nor their meanings can ever be purely "personal" or idiosyncratic. Speakers have to use already-existing words and expressions that they share with others in order to make themselves understood by these others. At the same time, word use certainly is often "personal," in the sense that a speaker creates a unique twist on shared words and meanings. Even the most idiosyncratic twists, however, need to be expressed in a language that can be understood by listeners (Kirschner & Martin, 2010).

Talk does more than express and shape personal experiences. Talk is also used to perform actions – to get things done (Edwards, 1997). For instance, in conversations with others, people do not use talk just to recount their experiences and opinions; they also use talk to do things like justify their actions or call others to account (Edley, 2001; Wetherell, 2001). People can also use talk to bring across a communicated meaning *in a certain way* to a listener, to present themselves *in a particular light*, or to make a certain activity seem either worthwhile or pointless. This facet of talk is often referred to as "talk-as-action."

Interviews

Interviews – that is, face-to-face conversations structured by the researcher – provide an effective way to gather material that speaks to interpretative researchers' interests and goals. This is so because in a research interview, the interviewer asks the participant to explain herself and her world, and the participant has the task of telling the interviewer what she knows in a way that can be understood by an outsider. Interviewing is therefore a good way to locate clues to people's personal and cultural meanings that would be difficult to find in any other way (Quinn, 2005). Interviews can yield full and rich accounts of how people see the world, what sense they make of it, and what concerns they bring to their lives. The talk that an interview conversation yields also is a window onto the linguistic and cultural resources that are available to the speaker, and that the speaker uses to make the world intelligible.

Our aims for the book: bringing practice and theory together

We have several aims for this book. Our first aim is that, after finishing the book, readers shall have gained competence in doing interpretative research. This includes how to develop research questions; decide about and contact participants; design interview guides and carry out interviews; select analytic procedures and carry out several kinds of analyses; and draw conclusions and write about projects. To fulfill this aim, we describe the concrete strategies and steps in each phase of a research project. In particular, we describe in close detail different ways of analyzing interview talk. This emphasis is deliberate; beginners usually find the analysis to be the most difficult part of an interpretative research project.

Our second aim is that readers shall acquire a working acquaintance with the distinctive goals of interpretative research. To accomplish this aim, we provide close-ups of the kinds of knowledge that different types of interpretative research yield; we combine these close-ups with detailed descriptions of specific projects.

Our third aim is that readers will develop an appreciation of the theoretical and epistemological commitments of interpretative researchers. Research methods are not "theory-neutral" tools but always part of larger theoretical frameworks. To fulfill this aim, we are careful to situate methods within their theoretical frameworks.

Our fourth aim is that readers will gain knowledge of how the theoretical frameworks inform the practical aspects of interpretative research. To fulfill this aim, we elaborate in detail the view of research participants as socially and culturally situated meaning-makers. We also describe in detail the view of interview talk as giving a unique set of clues about people's ways of understanding themselves and their worlds.

Many research approaches are compatible with the theoretical premises of interpretative research. Newcomers to interpretative research often find it difficult to know where to begin, because there are so many different methods on offer, such as narrative analysis, discourse analysis, phenomenological analysis, grounded theory, thematic analysis, and more. And, to make the beginning more difficult, researchers have developed several variants of all these approaches. This proliferation of methods and variations means that the methods are not so clearly delimited – or definable – as a learner might wish.

As teachers and supervisors of undergraduate and postgraduate students, we have repeatedly witnessed the confusion and uncertainty that the multitude of approaches creates. We have come to believe that beginners can best get a grip on research methods by becoming thoroughly familiar with some basic principles of interpretative research and how those principles guide practical choices about methods. This conviction has informed the way we wrote this book. We have distilled a number of premises and assumptions that underlie the set of interpretative research approaches that we describe. We describe the central theoretical principles of each approach and present them in ways that we have found are accessible to beginners. And we present and work through the procedures of these approaches in detail.

The road map for the book

In this chapter, you have learned what we mean by "interpretative research" and you have read short descriptions of a few studies. We have briefly introduced the theoretical framework of the interpretative research approaches that the book presents. And you have seen what we aim to achieve with the book and our strategies for achieving these aims.

Chapter 2 offers an in-depth acquaintance with several projects that used interpretative methods and with some of the deliberations of the researchers as they worked on the projects. Material from some of these projects serves to illustrate analytical procedures in later chapters.

We then turn to the practical steps involved in preparing and planning studies and gathering interviews. Chapter 3 describes the first steps involved in planning an interpretative research project. It introduces the research journal as an essential tool for planning and keeping track of your work; it describes strategic ways to read the research literature and learn from other researchers; it considers how to assess the feasibility of a project; and it begins a discussion about how to develop and refine one's researchable questions. This discussion is continued in later chapters.

Chapter 4 takes up the many choices to be made about the participants in a project. It presents the principle of purposive selection of participants, including decisions about the number of participants. It also discusses how to contact and enlist potential participants and how to set up the interview situation. Finally, it reviews the ethical guidelines governing interview research.

Chapter 5 describes in detail how to construct an interview guide. It begins by introducing the format of the semi-structured interview. It describes the open-ended questions used in such interviews. In the chapter, we pay close attention to helping learners draw the crucial distinction between research questions, that is, the questions that guide the research project, and interview questions. The chapter gives advice about how to compose interview questions and follow-up questions for the different segments of an interview.

Chapter 6 presents the principles and practices for conducting interviews in an interpretative research project. It gives an overview of the phases of a semi-structured interview. It also presents practical interviewing techniques for typical interview situations, as well as a discussion of unusual and complicated situations. It discusses the relationship between the interviewer and the participant, as well as the specific demands on the interviewer in that relationship. Finally, the chapter describes how to pilot-test the interview guide.

Chapter 7 briefly sets the stage for the chapters to come, which detail several analytical procedures. It describes procedures necessary to produce high-quality and detailed transcripts of the interviews. It then turns to the topic of assessing the quality of interpretative research projects. It presents a set of criteria that are commonly used to judge such projects.

The next four chapters take up specific analytic procedures. Our aim has been to present each in sufficient detail and with sufficient clarity to enable readers to embark on their own analyses. The analytic procedures in these chapters are linked by a common framework, although they offer quite different ways of examining interview material.

Chapter 12 takes up the matter of preparing a written report of a research project. It discusses what ought to be included in such reports, as well as the accepted format for organizing the material. We then turn attention to how the material should be presented, taking up briefly such matters as writing style, the use of illustrative examples, and the ethical requirement to conceal participants' identities.

The book closes with a brief epilogue.

2 Some examples of interpretative research

One of the best ways to learn about interpretative research is to get acquainted with some actual projects. In this chapter, we describe five projects. Our intention is to show what the researchers were interested in, how they specified what they wanted to study in order to make it researchable, how they gathered their material, some examples of analyses, and some findings that the projects yielded. The projects we describe concern diverse topics, locales, and peoples: childrearing practices in the USA and Taiwan; repeated re-hospitalizations of people in the USA who had severe mental illnesses; how heterosexual couples in the Nordic countries make sense of gender-equal practices in daily life; Canadian women's accounts of their depressive experiences; and the spiral of suicide-like behavior among adolescent girls in Sri Lanka.

We have two reasons for presenting these projects. First, we want to give a sense of what interpretative research is like; for instance, how such projects might be structured and the kinds of questions that researchers can answer. Second, we use some of these projects as examples when we describe different ways of analyzing interviews. Before you read further, let us point out that these five studies do not cover all types of interpretative research. The selected studies illustrate some possibilities of such research, not all such possibilities.

As you will see, two of the project descriptions in this chapter stem from studies in which one of us was the researcher. We do not include these studies because they are necessarily the best examples of interpretative research, but rather because we have full knowledge of all the details, including details that normally are not described in research articles. (Quite a lot of what goes on in research is omitted in research publications.) Furthermore, we have extensive material from these studies, including, for example, interview transcripts, our research journals, and unpublished reports.

In the project descriptions, we discuss four key components:

1. **The researcher's knowledge interests.** The term *researcher's knowledge interests* refers to the overarching topic or issue that a researcher is interested in learning more about (such as "depression and gender" or "deliberate self-harm among adolescent girls"). Knowledge interests often arise from real life: from the researcher's everyday experiences, concerns, and commitments or from the experiences of a social group that the researcher has closely observed. A knowledge interest is sometimes motivated by social justice concerns. Typically, knowledge interests are formulated in rather general or abstract terms and therefore not directly researchable.

2. **The researchable questions that the researcher developed for the project.** In order to be able to design a study, researchers have to develop one or more *researchable questions* on the basis of their knowledge interest. (We use the term "researchable questions" instead of the more common "research questions" to emphasize that the questions must be formulated in such a way that they are amenable to empirical investigation.) To develop researchable questions, the researcher needs to make decisions about the theoretical framework of the study, the specific context for the study, the specific types of people to study, the methods for gathering material, and the analytical procedures.

3. **How the researcher gathered material for the project.** Here, we describe briefly how the researchers went about gathering their interview material. This includes deciding which kinds of people to study and designing and carrying out the interviews.

4. **Examples of analyses and findings in the project.** We end each project description with examples of some of the analytical strategies that the researcher used and some of the findings. For readers who want more details about the projects, we give references to the original published reports.

Self-esteem as folk theory: comparing mothers in Taiwan and the USA

1   The researcher's knowledge interest

This example describes the work of a research group based in the USA and led by cultural psychologist Peggy Miller (Peggy Miller, Su-hua Wang, Todd Sandel, & Grace Cho, 2002). The research group was broadly interested in uncovering the local folk psychologies of child development in both the USA and Taiwan and in comparing the childrearing and disciplinary practices that parents employ. As Miller and her colleagues assert, a "culture-inclusive understanding of child development cannot be achieved without taking into account parents' folk theories about children and child-rearing" (p. 210). Such folk theories are closely related to childrearing practices; indeed, they inform and motivate most of the actions of caregivers. In the study described below, the researchers were specifically interested in the concept of self-esteem. They noted that in the USA, experts and laypeople alike have come to view self-esteem as crucial for the development of a wide array of psychological strengths and capacities, a significance it did not assume at earlier points in time and that it does not assume in many societies elsewhere.

2   The researchable questions that the researcher developed for the project

We focus on two of the researchable questions that the research group formulated, both of which addressed "the meanings and practices associated with self-esteem and with the larger folk theory in which it is embedded" (Miller et al., 2002, p. 212). These questions were as follows: What are the meanings that European-American and Taiwanese mothers associate with the idea of self-esteem? What are the local folk theories that contextualize the idea of self-esteem or that offer alternative formulations of the goals and values of childrearing?

3   What the researcher did to gather material

The multicultural and multilingual team performed their study in two large rural towns, one in the Midwest of the USA and the other in a rural area of Taiwan. Household organization and childcare arrangements differed considerably between the two locales, as did the larger economic and social features of the communities. For example, in the USA, all the primary childrearing was carried out by mothers; in Taiwan, grandmothers often played this role while mothers worked in the agricultural fields. Consequently, the researchers needed to adjust their data-gathering approaches for each site.

The larger group from which the researchers selected their potential participants consisted of women who were caregivers for three-year-old children. The recruitment of participants differed between the two sites. Mothers in the USA were recruited through a university participant pool; in Taiwan, caregivers were located through introductions by the researchers' elder relatives. The interviewing process also differed. Participants in the USA were familiar with the idea of being interviewed and they had a template of an interview ready at hand. That template involved, for instance, a time and space set aside for the purpose of the interview. By contrast, the Taiwanese participants were not accustomed to the formal question-and-answer format of an interview or to the idea that interviews should occur in a private place. As a result, in Taiwan, interviews were more like conversations; they took place while other activities were ongoing; and passersby and other household members sometimes joined in. At each site, sixteen caregivers (mothers in the USA and a mix of mothers and grandmothers in Taiwan) of three-year-olds were interviewed.

The interview protocol identified topics for conversation rather than a specific list of questions. These topics included childrearing goals and values, strategies for promoting the child's development, modes of disciplining a child, sources of childrearing information, and the caregivers' ideas about children's shame, pride, and self-esteem. The interviewers deliberately refrained from mentioning self-esteem directly until late in the interview conversation. This enabled the researchers to observe whether and how caregivers spontaneously wove the concept of self-esteem into their accounts of raising children.

4   Examples of analyses and findings in the project

In their analysis of the interview material, the research group focused closely on their researchable questions. First, what were the meanings given to the term self-esteem or, in Taiwan, its Taiwanese or Chinese approximations? Second, what were the caregivers' folk theories of childrearing, especially those that pertained to self-esteem? The examination of *what* was said in relation to those topics was complemented by an examination of *how* things were said, that is, of distinctive features of the interview interactions. In these analyses, sharp contrasts emerged between the Taiwanese caregivers and the mothers residing in the Midwest of the USA.

The analysis uncovered many differences in meaning-making (i.e., folk theories) about self-esteem in children's development and childrearing. We give only a few examples. Not surprisingly, many of the US mothers spontaneously mentioned self-esteem and associated words like self-respect, self-confidence, and self-worth before the interviewer mentioned them. Mothers in the USA invoked these terms repeatedly in responding to a range of questions about their child and their childrearing practices. This was not true for the Taiwanese caregivers. For a start, neither Mandarin Chinese nor Taiwanese (the two languages spoken in Taiwan) contains a word that is equivalent to the English word self-esteem. The interviewers instead had to resort to a seldom-used word that could be roughly translated as "self-respect-heart/mind." Fewer than one-third of the Taiwanese participants spontaneously used this word during the interview prior to it being introduced by the interviewer. Furthermore, no mother in the USA had difficulty understanding the meaning of the term self-esteem. In Taiwan, by contrast, in roughly half the interviews, it was not possible for the interviewer and the participant to establish common ground around the meaning of the expression "self-respect-heart/mind." Also, the mothers in the USA readily attributed a profusion of positive developmental outcomes to self-esteem – happiness, psychological resilience, achievement, and mental health. By contrast, caregivers in Taiwan proffered far fewer thoughts about self-esteem. Those who had things to say were concerned about negative consequences of overly high self-esteem, such as a tendency to be easily frustrated in the face of difficulty or to be rebellious.

Repeated hospitalizations for severe mental disorders in an American community

1   The researcher's knowledge interest

Larry Davidson is an American psychologist whose general knowledge interest focuses on how recovery from severe mental disorders such as schizophrenia is connected to membership in the broader community. He has, for instance, carried out studies that used several different social engagement strategies such as peer support and forms of community outreach to engage people with severe psychiatric disorders. Davidson is critical of traditional views of schizophrenia that promote a stereotype of people with schizophrenia as little more than empty shells of what they used to be. He has argued that such views discourage clinicians from seriously trying to reach people diagnosed with schizophrenia, and that these views also convey to such persons that there is nothing they can do to recover (Davidson et al., 1997, 2001a, 2001b). Davidson points to research showing that people with schizophrenia do improve over time and that their own efforts to cope with the disorder are important factors in improvement.

For the study we describe here, Davidson and his co-workers formulated a specific knowledge interest about what it is that drives the problem of frequent re-hospitalizations of people with severe mental disorders. When the researchers read the research literature, they found that existing explanations and attempts at prevention all focused on factors internal to the individual person, and were based in what they called "the deficit and dysfunction model of treatment" (Davidson et al., 2000, p. 165). That is, these explanations were almost exclusively conceived within a narrow medical model and focused on the signs and symptoms of the disorder. Davidson and his team of clinicians initiated a program to prevent re-hospitalization based on this model of individual psycho-pathology. However, they soon found that although people enjoyed taking part in the program's activities while they were inpatients, the frequency of re-hospitalization after they had been discharged did not decline. This sobering realization led Davidson and his team to reconsider what re-hospitalization means to the individual person with schizo-phrenia and whether these meanings could have anything to do with the failure of their program.

2   The researchable questions that the researcher developed for the project

The researchers decided to interview people diagnosed with schizophrenia who were classified as recidivists (that is, those who had had two or more hospitalizations in the last year). Their first researchable question concerned the participants' experiences of re-hospitalization: how the re-hospitalizations had come about, and what functions they served in participants' lives, as described in the participants' own words. The second researchable question developed from the analysis of the first and focused on what the experiences of re-hospitalization that the participants described meant for the participants, as opposed to what they might mean for the researchers. To begin to answer the second research question, the researchers had to move away from thinking in terms of whether the experiences that their participants described fitted into the researchers' theoretical preconceptions about recidivism. To be able to make this move, the research-ers chose to combine phenomenological analysis with a participatory approach to analyzing the interview material.

3   What the researcher did to gather material

The larger group from which the researchers selected their participants consisted of patients who were suffering from severe mental illness and who had experienced repeated hospitalizations. The researchers recruited twelve patients suffering from schizophrenia who had taken part in the earlier program to prevent re-hospitalization. They interviewed each patient once, using what the researchers described as an open-ended phenomenological interview format. In the interviews, the researchers asked each participant to think back to the most recent re-hospitalization episode and to describe the experiences that led up to the re-hospitalization, that happened during it, and that followed it. They also asked the participants to describe their experiences of taking part in the prevention program, and about what they would find more useful than the earlier program. The interviews were audio-recorded and transcribed verbatim.

4   Examples of analyses and findings in the project

The researchers began the analysis by reading the interview transcripts of the participants one at a time and categorizing recurrent themes in each participant's descriptions of his or her experiences. The purpose at this stage was to arrive at a synthesis of each interview that placed the themes that recurred in the interview into the time-context of the participant's ongoing life. Only after all the interviews had been thoroughly categorized one by one and the researchers had agreed upon each synthesis did the researchers compare the analyses across the participants. They were then able to identify themes that all participants shared and themes that they did not share. The researchers then convened a group of participants and presented the analysis to them and asked for their feedback. The researchers summarized their findings from the analyses, including the feedback from the participants, into four main themes, which we describe briefly here. (For details, see Davidson et al., 1997, pp. 774–777.)

Attractions of the hospital: Contrary to the expectations of the researchers, the participants did not have a desire to avoid re-hospitalization. Rather, the participants described numerous attractions that the hospital held for them. These attractions made returning to the hospital a thing to wish for instead of a thing to avoid at all costs. Participants described the hospital as a place where they were safe, where they could rest, where they were fed, and where they could have privacy.

Impoverished community life: The participants' descriptions of life outside the hospital were in stark contrast to how they described their time in the hospital. What was especially stark was their descriptions of lack of support from friends or family outside the hospital and, in many cases, of total social isolation.

Powerlessness, fatalism, and apathy: The participants described a nearly total lack of control over possible relapses and over problems in their daily lives, such as poverty, unemployment, homelessness, and living in a dangerous environment.

Disconnection from mental health services: The participants described the treatments given by mental health professionals as providing little or nothing useful to them when it came to dealing with the problems they experienced in their lives. In fact, the participants did not even seem to see the treatments as "treatment," but rather as various exercises that they had to go through, but which had no relevance to, or impact on, their lives.

This study was part of a larger project that included efforts to reform outpatient treatment for persons with severe mental disorders. The researchers and clinicians went on to put what they learned from the research to practical use. They report briefly about that work in Davidson et al. (1997). See also Davidson (2003) and Davidson et al. (2000, 2001a, 2001b).

The spiral of suicide-like behavior among adolescent girls in Sri Lanka

1   The researcher's knowledge interest

Jeanne became interested in culture-specific aspects of suicide when she was working in Sri Lanka, a small country off the south coast of India. Sri Lanka was then in the midst of a dramatic and unexplained spiral of suicides; indeed, by the mid-1990s, the official statistics recorded the highest rate of suicide in the world. Speculations about the causes of this rise were rife in the popular press, but most of the purported causes (such as "poverty," "war," and "labor migration") were not consistent with the available facts. Other than counting the number of deaths and which lethal means were used, little social scientific work had been done.

For a number of years, Jeanne had worked with voluntary grassroots organizations concerned with suicide prevention. That work enabled her to have conversations with key informants from those organizations as well as with local doctors and psychiatrists. She learned that people in Sri Lanka (whether doctors, community workers, or members of the general public) understood suicide in a distinctly different way than she had been trained to do as a clinical psychologist in the USA. These differing understandings of suicides could be called folk theories or culture-specific narratives. Such folk theories – whether in the USA or in Sri Lanka – offer ways of explaining suicidal acts when they occur. They also serve as templates that guide future suicidal acts. That is, they indicate to members of a culture when a suicidal act is a suitable response, what it might serve to communicate to others, and how others ought to respond in the face of suicidal threats, suicidal acts, or actual deaths. In most Western countries, the dominant cultural narrative of suicide usually centers on psychiatric disorder, depression, and hopelessness. By contrast, the dominant narrative of suicide among professions and laypeople in Sri Lanka makes no reference to psychiatric disorder, long-standing depression, or self-denigration. The narrative that prevails among Sri Lankans focuses on acute interpersonal conflict (such as a family altercation, being publicly insulted, or losing face or honor), anger, and vengeance. Individuals who have engaged in suicidal behavior are not thought to need psychiatric or psychological care and do not receive it.

The official focus on fatalities had overlooked the large number of people who had survived a suicidal act, even though the number of such individuals was many times higher than the number who died. To gain a more detailed and complete picture, Jeanne and Chandanie Senadheera, a Sri Lankan psychologist, studied medical and police records over a decade. Those data showed a dramatic recent increase in the number of adolescents who had engaged in suicidal behavior; in the most recent years, nearly all (over 99 percent) survived. Nearly all these episodes involved swallowing poison or overdoses of medicine. The records also showed that, year after year, girls accounted for nearly 75 percent of these cases (Senadheera, Marecek, Hewage, & Wijayasiri, 2010). Because of Jeanne's long-standing commitment to studying the lives of women and girls, she was especially interested in the special risk that girls seemed to experience. This led her to acquire a specific knowledge interest in the cultural context and dynamics of adolescent girls' suicidal acts in Sri Lanka.

2   The researchable questions that the researcher developed for the project

With Chandanie Senadheera, Jeanne devised a set of researchable questions. Among them were these: How do girls who had engaged in suicidal acts portray those acts in their own words? What are the specific contexts for girls' suicidal behavior? How do they and their families understand ("make sense of") what had taken place? Do they draw on the dominant narrative of suicide and, if so, how is it modified in light of their age and gender? What are the repercussions (if any) that a suicide episode might later have for girls among their kin and in the broader community? Jeanne and Chandanie anticipated that the answers to these questions would uncover not only the cultural meanings related to suicide, but also the ways that local norms regarding femininity and (female) adolescence came into play in the circumstances preceding the suicidal act and in its aftermath.

3   What the researcher did to gather material

The larger group from which Jeanne and Chandanie selected their participants consisted of adolescent girls who had engaged in suicidal acts, and the mothers of those girls. Chandanie was on staff at a hospital where many girls were admitted after they had engaged in suicidal acts, and she had access to these girls. In this context, Jeanne and Chandanie interviewed girls admitted for medical care following an episode of suicidal behavior, along with their mothers. (Because suicidal behavior is not regarded as a psychiatric problem, the care for patients who have engaged in suicidal acts – even those involving high-lethality means – is strictly limited to biomedical treatment.) Girls admitted to hospital following a suicidal act do not represent the entire universe of girls who engaged in suicidal acts. Two subsets are left out – those who died and those who did not seek medical treatment. There were no practical ways of gaining information about girls in either of these groups. Luckily, data gleaned from hospital records showed that both groups are very small.

When an adolescent girl was admitted for self-poisoning, Chandanie waited for medical clearance and then approached her to ask if she was willing to take part in an interview study and to have her mother be interviewed as well. Nearly all those who were invited agreed. Chandanie then approached the girl's mother to seek permission to interview her daughter and to invite her to be interviewed. The interviews were conducted separately and in private. Altogether, twenty-two pairs of mothers and daughters, nearly all of whom were Sinhalese, took part. For both the girl and her mother, one interview took place in the hospital. In some cases, a second interview took place a month later at the family home.

Jeanne and Chandanie wanted to gather detailed and reflective stories about the suicidal act, what preceded it, and what transpired afterward. To obtain such stories, they relied on semi-structured interviews to enable the participants to tell their stories in their own way and in their own words. Chandanie carried out all the interviews in Sinhala, the participants' mother tongue. She began the interview with an open-ended question that did not "pull for" one or another kind of story (for example, a story about events, or about feelings, or about psychiatric symptoms). The question was simply "What happened?" If necessary, Chandanie prompted participants to flesh out the story. After the participant concluded her account, Chandanie asked about specific elements that had not been included. In addition, she asked mothers and daughters to envision what would happen when the girl was discharged from the hospital. At the interview that took place a month later, she began by asking the participant to again tell the story of "what happened." That interview also asked the participants to describe what had transpired in their families and communities since the girl had returned home.

All the interviews were audio-recorded and transcribed. They were translated by a professional bilingual translator and then checked by Chandanie (who is also bilingual). In working on the analyses together, Jeanne and Chandanie often had recourse to the audio-recordings to clarify matters of interpretation, translation, and nuance; for example, to ascertain whether something had been said ironically or humorously.

4   Examples of analyses and findings in the project

In the first phase of the analysis, Jeanne and Chandanie looked at girls' answers to the question "What happened?" The girls described in lengthy detail negative and hurtful interactions with other people (most often, their parents or elders). The girls framed the suicidal acts as a direct and swift response to those actions, undertaken with little deliberation or consideration of alternative courses of action. The accounts seldom mentioned the girls' feelings, emotional states, or motives.

The arrangement of the suicidal acts strongly suggested that they were expressive acts directed toward others. In virtually all cases, they took place in the girl's home while several family members were present. As the girls themselves said, there was very little premeditation – sometimes only minutes, sometimes a few hours. After they had consumed poison or an overdose, most girls quickly informed a family member about what they had done. In some instances, the girls dramatically swallowed pills or poison in full view of others in the household (Marecek & Senadheera, 2012). One implication of these findings is that researchers would do well to re-conceptualize these acts as "suicide-like behavior" or as "acts that serve to put the idea of suicide into someone else's mind." It is misleading to call them or think of them as "suicide attempts" (a term that builds in the assumption that the person intended to die). Another implication is that the suicide-prevention programs designed for adolescents in American and European contexts, which focus on "early warning signs" and "depression awareness," are likely to be of little use in the Sri Lankan context.

In the second phase of the analysis, Jeanne and Chandanie focused on the gendered aspects of suicide-like behavior. If such behavior is expressive, what is being expressed? And why are the usual means of communicating, like speaking, insufficient or unavailable? As daughters, adolescent girls are expected to adhere to norms of obedience and familial piety. Moreover, the research literature on femininity and gender ideology in Sri Lanka points out that, by tradition, girls who have reached puberty but are not (yet) married are subject to stringent norms regarding sexual purity, modest demeanor, and segregation from men (D'Alwis, 1995); violating these norms jeopardizes one's marriageability and the family's honor. Nowadays, however, girls are faced with a new set of norms that encourage advanced education and preparation for paid work and with emerging ideas about romantic love (Lynch, 1999).

These cultural ideologies threaded through the girls' accounts of their suicide-like behavior. Most of the girls lived in tight-knit rural communities, with many kin near at hand; their actions were continually under scrutiny. Nearly all the accounts made reference to breaches of sexual respectability in one form or another. Most stories involved sharp reprimands, often accompanied by physical assaults, by angry parents or elders who had learned of an infringement (or suspected infringement) of the norms of sexual respectability. Few girls described arguing with a parent, disputing a mistaken accusation, or pleading extenuating circumstances. Such actions would have violated another set of norms concerning respect for elders and proscriptions on women's anger. Following the logic of the girls' accounts, the suicide-like behavior was a response to parental anger, perhaps the only possible response. (As one girl said, "It wasn't a foolish thing to do; it was the *only* thing I could do.")

The third phase of the analysis looked at *how* girls said what they said. One example is what Jeanne and Chandanie called a pattern of "disavowed agency." They observed that girls seldom elaborated on any thoughts and feelings in relation to how they came to swallow poison or overdoses. Girls said they had acted rashly, without thinking, and after only brief deliberation, if any. ("I saw the bottle of insecticide on the window sill and I drank it.") Some girls relied on passive-voice constructions. ("Pills got bought" or "The insecticide got swallowed.") Such "disavowed agency" is perhaps not surprising in light of the gender and generational norms because it sidesteps questions of moral culpability for anger directed at one's parents. The stories that girls' mothers told, however, readily identified their daughters' suicide-like act as an outburst of anger. Many described it as "willful" or "disobedient" and "stubborn." Examples of the analyses from this project appear in later parts of our book. See especially Chapter 9.

Heterosexual couples in the Nordic countries forming their identities within and against gender equality ideologies

1 The researcher's knowledge interest

This example is taken from a study in which Eva and her co-workers interviewed women and men in couples about their daily lives with children (Magnusson, 2005, 2006, 2008a, 2008b). One of Eva's general knowledge interests is the relation between ideology and practice in daily life, such as the contrast between official gender equality policy and propaganda and people's agreement with these policies on the one hand, and on the other hand their everyday practices, which are often not so gender-equal. This contrast is of special interest in the Nordic countries (Denmark, Sweden, Norway, Finland, and Iceland), which are known as the most gender-equal countries in the world (NOSOSCO, 2011). National politics and government policies in these countries reflect long-standing commitments to reduce inequality and asymmetries between men and women in spheres of life such as access to and payment for paid work, the care of small children, and access to healthcare. Eva was interested in how it is that even in countries where national policies strongly endorse and promote such change, movements toward equality in family life are slow. Her specific knowledge interest in this study was how heterosexual couples *as couples*, and the men and women within couples, made sense of the ideologies and cultural messages that surrounded them, and how the men and women interacted with each other while doing so. She was also interested in how they organized their daily lives and how they, within their different cultural contexts, explained their ways of organizing. "Made sense of" and "explained" mean both how they understood the ideologies and put them into practice (or not) in their lives, and how they understood themselves and their partners as women, men, fathers, mothers, partners, and workers.

2   The researchable questions that the researcher developed for the project

One of Eva's researchable questions was: What are the cultural understandings and ideologies related to equality, femininity, masculinity, motherhood, and fatherhood that inform the men's and women's accounts of themselves as mothers, fathers, spouses, partners, and workers? A second researchable question was: How do couples vary in their ways of relating to (acquiescing to or subverting) dominant cultural understandings of these issues? Work on the first two researchable questions led Eva to develop a third researchable question about "talk-as-action" in the couple interviews. That is, she was interested in what the partners in the couples achieved with their talk beyond conveying information. She studied, for instance, how talk between the partners was used to achieve relational goals, and how the couple used certain terms and forms of talk to convey a particular image of themselves as a couple to the interviewer.

3   What the researcher did to gather material

The larger group from which Eva selected participants consisted of married or cohabiting women and men with children in Denmark, Finland, and Sweden. The types of couples were chosen to match the modal family: a man and a woman who were biological parents of the children they were raising. The selection of couples was carried out such that it resulted in similar distributions of educational levels, ages, numbers of children, and children's ages, as well as residential patterns (large cities, towns, rural communities) across the three national groups. The reason for using these categories for selection was that earlier research had shown differences between couples who were differently located in relation to the categories. The researchers used their own networks to reach couples with whom they were not acquainted, and who fit the distribution of characteristics that the study aimed for. The participants were all white and of Danish, Finnish, or Swedish ancestry.

Eva's research assistants interviewed thirty couples, ten each from Denmark, Finland, and Sweden. All interviews were conducted in the couples' homes and in their native language. Both partners were present throughout the interview. The interviews were semi-structured with open-ended questions. Most questions were not directed specifically to either of the partners; either was free to answer.

The interview guide contained questions about practical issues in the daily organization of life, such as the most common household chores and personal leisure time, and about decision-making and responsibility related to these matters. The couples were also asked to describe in detail an ordinary working day, and they were asked who was responsible for each of ten common household and childcare tasks. The interviewer used prompts to encourage the participants to elaborate their answers if that seemed necessary. The participants were encouraged to bring in their own topics, and there was time for reflections and discussions about the issues they brought up. The couples regularly availed themselves of these opportunities. The interviews were audio-recorded and transcribed verbatim. The interviews that were conducted in Finnish were translated into Swedish by the Finnish interviewer. Because Eva is fluent in Swedish and Danish, the Danish interviews did not have to be translated.

4   Examples of analyses and findings in the project

As her first analytic step, and in order to structure the material, Eva looked at how the thirty couples replied to the questions about who was responsible for each of ten common household and childcare tasks. She found that a third of the couples shared equally or very nearly equally. In another third, the woman did a few more of the chores than the man. In the remaining third of the couples, nearly all of the tasks fell to the woman. There were no clear differences in the shape of this distribution among the couples from the three countries.

In her next analytic step, Eva followed up this distribution of chores by comparing the direct responses to the interview questions in the three groups of couples. A pervasive overall pattern emerged where the couples in which the woman did most of the housework and childcare stood out as different from the rest of the couples. There were many differences, but here we focus only on one of them, which is related to Eva's second researchable question. She found that the couples in which women did nearly all the housework and childcare insisted that they had never had any discussions with their partner about how to allocate housework tasks. Their traditional allocation, they usually said, had just happened that way, "by itself." Some couples explained that this was the *natural* way to organize things (i.e., that it was in tune with biological or psychological differences between men and women). In these couples, then, adherence to a traditional gender ideology seemed to be taken for granted and to be something that should not be questioned. These couples also portrayed conflict as potentially endangering a marriage. In contrast, the couples who had an equal distribution of housework and childcare described a history of negotiations about their sharing that had in some cases escalated to conflict. However, they portrayed these conflicts as benign and as something to be expected. Not surprisingly, these couples questioned traditional gender ideology.

The next set of analyses focused on how some of the differences between the equally sharing couples and the couples in which women did most of the housework related to the researchable questions. Eva first studied how the two groups of couples drew upon ideologies and cultural meanings about gender equality, femininity and masculinity, and parenthood during the interviews. To take just one example of the many findings related to this: The couples in which women did most of the housework and childcare talked about inequalities (such as the husband's greater access to leisure activities) as normal or natural. Such "naturalizing" talk did not appear in the couples who shared equally. Another example: When describing how they had allocated paid work, leisure, childcare, and housework, the unequally sharing couples talked about the woman's time and labor in ways that made her time and labor seem much more negotiable than her husband's. Also, several of these couples used a language of "male–female differences" to explain their unequal sharing of housework and childcare. Further analysis showed that in these couples, "sex-difference talk" drew attention away from any suggestion of power differences. In contrast, the couples who shared equally did not talk in terms of sex differences, nor did they talk in terms of "natural" inequalities or asymmetries.

Eva's third set of researchable questions and analyses focused on "talk as action," that is, what people achieve by their talk. This interest is based on the observation that, while talking about a factual topic unrelated to themselves, people often indirectly present themselves as a certain (e.g., good) kind of person, and someone else as a different (e.g., less good) kind of person. These types of indirect "presentations" also often serve to set up power relations between people (see Chapter 10). In one analysis of talk-as-action, Eva studied the details of how the men and women talked to each other when they were specifically discussing their own and others' gendered arrangements. To exemplify: Some of the men told stories about other men whose wives had demanded that they do "too much" housework. It was said that the men who featured in those stories were now about to divorce their wives because of these demands. When Eva analyzed the details of these stories, she found that they could convey at least two different messages. First, by telling such stories about "other men" and their wives, a man could let the interviewer know that his wife was not one of those excessively demanding women. Second, these stories could also, and at the same time, be read as cautionary tales, indicating to the speaker's wife that if she were to make too heavy demands for his participation in housework, he might divorce her.

The analyses we have described in this section mainly focused on the narratives of the men and women who did not share housework and childcare equally. In her project, Eva also analyzed the narratives of the equally sharing couples (see Magnusson, 2006). Examples of analyses in this study will appear in later parts of our book, especially in Chapters 10 and 11.

Canadian women's medicalized accounts of depression

1   The researcher's knowledge interests

This study was done by the Canadian psychologist Michelle Lafrance (2007). Its focus was on how women who had had episodes of clinical depression told about and understood these episodes in retrospect. The study particularly looked into the ways of understanding "depression" that the women used in their narratives. For Michelle Lafrance, women's experiences and understandings of depression form an overarching knowledge interest. Another overarching knowledge interest was the cultural forces that surround depressed women: for instance, the institutional power of medicine to shape how people in Western countries understand psychological distress. Lafrance had noticed in her earlier research that although most of the women with previous episodes of depression put forward difficult life experiences as the explanation of their depressive episodes, some seemed to prefer biomedical explanations. She became interested in the possible consequences of such preferences. To learn more, she reviewed earlier research about the consequences of different explanations of psychological distress. She found much evidence that biomedical explanations, by focusing on biological factors internal to the person, depoliticize people's suffering. This focus masks the impact of people's living conditions.

In the study we describe here, Lafrance formulated a specific knowledge interest: How are dominant biomedical explanations of depression maintained – or contested – in women's ways of understanding their depressive episodes after they recover? Meaning-making was central to her study in three ways: First, she was interested in women's ways of telling about and making sense of their psychological distress. Second, she was interested in the role that culturally dominant meanings of depression, such as biomedical explanations, played in individual women's ways of making sense of their depressive episodes. And third, she was interested in the personal, social, and possibly political consequences of adhering to biomedical explanations of depression.

2   The researchable questions that the researcher developed for the project

To make her knowledge interest researchable on an individual level, Lafrance decided to study the details of the interviews of women who favored a biomedical explanation of their depressive experiences. She developed three researchable questions to ask about the interview material. The first was: What were the details of the biomedical explanations that these women drew on in their accounts? The second was directed at details of the women's talk as they drew upon biomedical explanations. She looked, for instance, at features of grammar, of metaphor use, how personal agency was featured or not, and how the speaker came to be positioned through these features. The third researchable question developed as she analyzed for the first two questions: How well (or badly) did the women's depressive experiences fit with the biomedical model?

3   What the researcher did to gather material

The larger group from which Lafrance selected her participants consisted of women who had been depressed at least once in their lives and had been prescribed antidepressant medication at that time. She recruited participants by advertising in the local newspaper in the Canadian province where she worked. She also distributed flyers throughout the community. For this study, she analyzed interviews with eight women who had given biomedical explanations of their depressive episodes. These women were a subset of the total number of women she interviewed about depressive episodes. The interviews were semi-structured. Lafrance had decided on a number of topics (or interview items) that all interviews addressed. These topics included the participant's understandings and experiences of depression, how she had managed when she was depressed, and how she eventually became well. The interviews were structured around these topics, but Lafrance also encouraged participants to bring up topics or questions of their own.

During the interviews, Lafrance paid special attention to her participants' use of words to describe their experiences, and she often asked them to elaborate upon their choice of words. If a participant varied in her choice of words during the interview, Lafrance pointed that out and explored this variation with her. Lafrance audio-recorded all interviews and transcribed them in full.

4   Examples of analyses and findings in the project

Lafrance was interested both in how her participants made use of existing biomedical explanations of depression and in the specific ways that these explanations enabled them to understand their own depressive experiences. She therefore chose a discursive approach that combined fine-grained analysis of speech with analysis of how larger cultural understandings make personal experiences understandable in certain ways.

In the first phase of her analysis, Lafrance identified the large patterns of cultural meaning that informed the women's accounts. She found that when the women talked about depression as a biomedical condition, they drew on two such cultural meanings. The first framed depression as a diagnosis, that is, as a condition that has been given a name and exists as an independent entity. The second cultural meaning equated depression to "real" physical illnesses and thus brought it into the domain of medicine. In her interviews, these two cultural meanings together made depression equivalent to a "real illness." These meanings thereby imparted to depression some measure of the type of legitimacy that characterizes physical illnesses. As the last part of this analytic phase, Lafrance looked at the specific rhetorical and linguistic strategies in the women's talk that achieved the legitimizing. She found an abundance of strategies in the women's talk that enhanced the legitimacy of their depressive experiences as real illness and as a biomedical one.

In the next phase of the analysis, Lafrance identified several instances when the biomedical explanations had only limited power to legitimize depressive experiences. She noted, for instance, that the lack of visible evidence of "illness" made medical legitimacy hard to achieve. This put the women in an uncomfortable position. If they could not find objective ways to prove that they suffered from a biomedical condition, they seemed to risk having to concede that their suffering was their own fault. Lafrance concluded that such constant threat of illegitimacy forces sufferers to keep negotiating – and accommodating to – biomedicine's assumptions about "real" illnesses and biomedical language when they account for their depression (Lafrance, 2007).

In conclusion: what unites interpretative research?

As we mentioned in the introduction to this chapter, the studies we have presented here give only a partial picture of interpretative research. However, these studies illustrate many characteristics of interpretative research. As a conclusion to this chapter, we summarize these characteristics. In later chapters, we discuss them in detail.

1. The researchable questions in the projects focused on meaning-making, that is, the ways in which people experience and make sense of their worlds, events in their worlds, other people, and themselves. In Chapter 3, you will learn how to develop such researchable questions.

2. Interpretative researchers expect to revise and refine their original researchable questions as they learn more about their research topics. This refining process is a central feature of interpretative research. It was also typical of the studies described in this chapter.

3. In the projects we described, the researchers purposively composed study groups that were suited to help them address their researchable questions. The researchers drew on the research literature for indications of the range of experiences and the categories of people who might have had the experiences they were interested in. In Chapter 4, we describe details of the procedures for selecting participants.

4. All the studies used interviews. Interviews, including moderated group discussions, are the most common way to gather data for interpretative research. An important benefit of interviewing is that participants will be trying to, and expected to, explain themselves to the interviewer, who is necessarily an outsider to the participants' personal experiences. In Chapters 5 and 6, we describe in detail how to construct interview guides and formulate open-ended questions, as well as how to conduct interviews in interpretative research.

5. The interviews in the five studies were all semi-structured. In semi-structured interviews, the researcher has a set of topics that he or she wants to learn about from the participants, but the interview format is not restricted to getting specific answers to those questions. The format encourages participants to offer comments, stories, and associations, as well as to initiate new topics.

6. In order to analyze participants' talk for meaning-making, the researchers *interpreted* what the participants said in the interviews. Interpretation goes beyond any simple compiling and sorting of phrases or sentences from interview transcripts. In Chapters 8–11, we take you through the different analytic strategies in interpretative research.

7. The details of the participants' talk were in focus for the analyses. In the different studies, the researchers were interested in different details, depending on their researchable questions. Details, however, were always given pride of place.

8. The researchers aimed to interpret each participant's accounts in the light of how that participant was situated in a particular context and what that participant's intentions might be. That context might be the interview situation or it might be a situation or setting that was talked about in the interview.

9. The researchers took care to situate those whom they studied, as well as their intentions, in the specific social, historical, and cultural contexts where they lived. The researchers used this knowledge to formulate and refine their researchable questions and to inform the analyses.

10. The researchers drew upon the participants' comments, reflections, and self-selected topics of conversation to refine the researchable questions. We discuss these processes of refining researchable questions in several chapters.

11. The conclusions that the researchers drew from their studies remained grounded in the specifics of the participants and the participants' contexts. The researchers did not extrapolate their findings to people in general, nor did they make general law-like predictions about human behavior or social life.

12. Although these studies were all interpretative (in traditional terminology, qualitative) studies, they all used quantities of some kind for their analyses. For instance, most studies referred to proportions of the participant group that shared a certain characteristic or experience. The researchers made different uses of those quantities, depending on their different knowledge interests.

The challenges and opportunities
in an inpatient environment.
staff experience ⟶

So ... got to say that its
worthwhile, beneficial, worth it ??
in background
— Both for pt and family ????

3 Planning and beginning an interpretative research project

In Chapter 2, we described some studies that used interpretative approaches. These descriptions gave you a taste of how the researchers went about their projects. They also pointed to some concrete steps involved in planning and doing interpretative research. In this chapter, we describe in closer detail what you need to think about and do during the initial stages of a project. In Chapter 2, we also introduced the terms "knowledge interest" and "researchable question." To recap, a knowledge interest is the general topic that a researcher sets out to learn about. As you learned, a knowledge interest is usually stated in general or abstract terms. It is usually not researchable in itself; researchers therefore need to devise one or more researchable questions. Developing researchable questions is a crucial first step in planning an interpretative research project. It demands a great deal of thought and effort.

Knowledge interests often have their origins in a researcher's everyday experiences, including his or her personal concerns and commitments. They may also originate from the concerns or experiences of a social group about which the researcher is knowledgeable, or from reading the research literature. The projects you read about in Chapter 2 originated in the researchers' general and overarching knowledge interests, which were based in different spheres of daily life and different spheres of society. Those descriptions, of course, show only a few of the possible knowledge interests that interpretative researchers might have and only a few of all possible settings where such interests can arise. When you read the research literature, you will see many more.

As you begin to map out a project, it is a good idea to clarify what your knowledge interests are, and the sphere of your life or of society from which they emerge. Make notes about your reflections and recollections. As we discuss in the next section, you should record such reflections in a research journal dedicated to the project. You will be able to use those reflections when you move from your knowledge interests to the detailed plan for your study.

This chapter is about laying out the plan of your project. After describing the research journal, we tell you about several ways to read the research literature in order to clarify your ideas about your study. We also suggest that you talk with knowledgeable people to further clarify your ideas. We then discuss the feasibility issues that are likely to crop up, and how to choose the most realistic courses of action for your project. Finally, we discuss how to develop questions that are researchable.

Keeping a research journal

The research journal is the researcher's log of a particular project. It is meant for the researcher's personal use; it is not a blog and not intended for public dissemination. The journal should be dedicated solely to the project and it should be kept for the duration of the project. It is difficult to know in advance exactly what will turn out to be important; therefore, the research journal should be a record of everything that *might* eventually be important. You should begin the journal at the beginning of your project preparation. Be generous in what you record. Enter notes about other studies you read, with the full citation details (including page numbers). You should also keep notes of discussions with others; these notes are especially important because they are the only record of such discussions. Your journal notes help you organize your thoughts while you are planning the project.

You will keep adding to the journal throughout the whole project. The notes that you make will be a good source of information when you write your report. You should be especially careful to keep detailed notes about the steps you take, and the choices you make, as you move through the project, and about why you did so. Such notes will provide a good basis for you when you arrive at the evaluation stage in the report writing and it is time to take stock of the adequacy of your work.

Reading as an interpretative researcher

As you plan your project, you need to read about what other researchers have done. This is how researchers get acquainted with a field and with the questions that have been studied and the issues that are being discussed and debated. In order for your reading to help you develop researchable questions, you need to read research reports with a number of different lenses, each focused on a different aspect of the report. We call this *reading as a researcher*. We describe the different types of reading below.

The first reading focuses on *findings*. You read the research literature to find out what is known about your general knowledge interest. You can begin by making notes about the findings that were reported in the studies. This will give you an overview of findings that are commonly accepted in a field and findings that are debated. After reading about the findings *per se*, you should note how the researchers discussed their findings. This is especially helpful if the topic is new to you, because it is in these discussions that authors write less technically and draw the most far-reaching conclusions. In these discussions, you will see how researchers connect their specific researchable questions to their general knowledge interests. This may give you ideas about how you could make such connections as your work proceeds.

Reading about findings will inform you about more than "findings" in the narrow sense. Interpretative researchers' researchable questions are firmly grounded in particulars, such as a specific historic time, geographic locale, and social context, as well as particular types of people. Therefore, when you read about research findings, you should make note of contextual details such as the local and larger settings where a study was done. You should also make note of who the participants were and the principle by which they were selected. This information will provide useful material as you formulate your own researchable questions. It will also be useful to you as you decide about how to select the participants for your own study.

The second type of *reading as a researcher* focuses on the *theoretical frameworks* of the studies you read. The value of this type of reading is often not apparent to beginning researchers. Why, you may ask, is this reading necessary? Is it not enough to gather information about the findings of previous studies? Our answer is no. Our reason is that the theoretical framework largely determines how researchers formulate their researchable questions. And these questions, in turn, determine how the topic will be studied, written about, and eventually understood. If researchers adopt disparate theoretical frameworks, even though they may seem to be studying similar questions, they in fact may be studying different things. This means that you should read the research literature with an eye to the theoretical framework of each study and ask how that framework shaped the study. Just as important, you should not limit your reading to studies carried out within a single theoretical framework. Try to read widely in order to capture as many points of view as possible.

The third type of *reading as a researcher* follows from the second reading and focuses on the ways that the researchers carried out their studies. This refers to details of the *methods* used to gather material and analyze it. Although research methods (especially detailed procedures) usually are not presented as "theoretical," methods are always developed within theoretical frameworks. In other words, research methods are not theory-neutral. Any method, whether it concerns selecting participants, gathering material, or analyzing that material, has built into its foundation certain assumptions based on theoretical and philosophical frameworks. You will find discussions about such theoretical aspects of methods in several places in this book.

The fourth type of reading focuses closely on the *researchable questions*. For instance, do the researcher's researchable questions specify locations and social categories of the participants or not? Do the researchable questions help the researcher to decide about which participants to invite into the study? As you read the research literature, you will see that different theoretical and methodological frameworks lead researchers to pose quite different researchable questions. As you move to formulate your own researchable questions, you should probably look especially closely at studies that speak most directly to your ways of thinking about your knowledge interest. The researchable questions of those studies may inspire your own formulations. However, you should also keep an eye on studies that come at your topic from angles that contrast with the one you have chosen. The contrasts may sharpen your thinking and perhaps also point to aspects that you have overlooked.

Learning from knowledgeable people

In parallel with reading the research literature, you should talk to people about your study. If you are a student, you will of course tell your supervisors about your ideas and discuss decisions about the study with them. But you will also benefit from talking to friends and listening to their reactions to your ideas. Your friends are probably not specialists in your field of interest, and therefore you will have to use ordinary language to tell them about your ideas. This will help you to keep your ideas grounded. In addition, you should seek out people who have specialized knowledge about the topics you want to pursue. You may, for instance, want to talk to scholars who are specialists in your field of interest or in fields close to it and ask them about their experiences in studying topics similar to yours. These conversations will give you more concrete and practical information about research in your field of interest than you can get from reading the literature.

Finally, you should talk to people who are personally familiar with the settings in which you want to locate your project, especially people who belong to the social groups in which you plan to find participants for your project. (Note, however, that you should avoid speaking to people who might become participants in your study.) In some cases, you might seek out people who are in the settings you want to study, but who have different roles and functions than your intended participants do. Ask these people for any views, opinions, and experiences that may connect with your knowledge interest. What they tell you can make you aware of specific and potentially researchable aspects of your knowledge interest. As with your reading of the literature, you should keep notes in your research journal about these conversations and your reflections on them.

Assessing feasibility

When you talk to knowledgeable people and read the research literature, you should be alert to what they can tell you about the *feasibility* of your project. Feasibility involves issues such as what questions you can realistically expect to study, what types of people you will be able to recruit, and whether such people can tell you useful things. Feasibility, as many experienced researchers have learned the hard way, is a key issue in research and should always be taken into account early in the planning process. Doing this minimizes the risk of later disappointment and misunderstandings. Some feasibility issues can be addressed, but others may prove to be insurmountable; in this case, you will need to modify your project.

You can benefit from others' advice about likely feasibility issues and about how to deal with them. For instance, you may have queries such as the following: Do others think it is possible to study the topic as you have formulated it or should it be modified? Do they think your ideas for researchable questions are practicable in the settings and with the people you propose to study? Can they advise you about which participants would best suit your study? Do they think the type of people you want to interview can be located? Do they think such people will be willing to talk to you? Do they think such people can tell you what you want to know? Do they think you can finish the project within your time frame? If people who are knowledgeable about the settings where you want to do your study, the people you want to interview, and the questions you are interested in give negative answers to any of these questions, then you need to step back and rethink your knowledge interest and the ways in which you have specified it and planned to study it.

It is crucial to ascertain whether you can locate the individuals you want to study. Some groups of individuals may be so small that you have little hope of finding a sufficient number of people to study. Some individuals may be hidden, either literally or figuratively. Some may not wish to disclose or discuss a stigmatizing condition, even anonymously. Gaining the trust of people who belong to communities with long experience of being exploited or misrepresented may require that you work in partnership with insiders in the community. Should you want to study people in institutional settings (such as school systems and medical clinics), you must be prepared to engage in lengthy bureaucratic procedures to secure entrée.

In planning research that aims to study people in their everyday surroundings, adjustments are inevitable. You may have to narrow your questions to make them more easily researchable. Furthermore, some researchable questions may not be acceptable to the people whom you want to interview. In other cases, you may have to consider using a method to gather your material other than the one you had planned to use. In yet other cases, you may have to find a group of people to study other than the one you had planned to study, or you may have to change the selection criteria for participants.

There are some situations that involve particularly difficult issues: What should you do if there are so few members of the group of people you want to interview that it is very expensive or difficult to find them? What should you do if most of the people you planned to interview do not want to talk to you about your researchable questions? And, in that case, what about the few persons who agree to participate? Can you consider them as being representative of the whole? Probably not. Such circumstances should lead you to rethink your project.

Should you do research about issues or problems with which you have personal experience? Researchers have different opinions about this. Some researchers have argued that those who are personally involved cannot step back from their own experiences sufficiently to study the issue dispassionately. For example, a person struggling with an eating problem or with clinical depression probably should not simultaneously do research on those problems. Others have argued that those who have had an experience have a special purchase on understanding it. For example, cancer survivors have contributed much to the study of social and psychological aspects of cancer and its treatment. We do not offer advice across the board on this matter, but we urge that researchers consider carefully the challenges that they will face if they undertake such a project. If you are a student, you need to discuss this matter forthrightly with your supervisor.

A different set of feasibility issues has to do with safety. You should assess whether your study as you have planned it could put participants at risk in any way. Researchers have an ethical duty to protect research participants from harm; "harm" encompasses psychological and social harm, as well as physical harm. You should also ask if carrying out the study puts you, the researcher, at risk of harm. For example, you should make sure to choose interview venues that are safe for you.

You should assess feasibility issues during the planning phase of a project, so that they do not trip you up in the course of the project. As we noted earlier, you can usually learn what you need to know about these issues and possible solutions by talking to knowledgeable people. Note that pilot testing may be necessary to settle many feasibility issues. We address pilot testing in Chapters 5 and 6.

Researchable questions in interpretative research

Researchable questions are specifications of the knowledge interest that a researcher brings to a project. The term "researchable questions" does not refer to the questions that the interviewer asks directly of the participants. Although there are no hard and fast rules for how the researchable questions in interpretative research should be constructed, the questions need to contain certain elements in order to be useful. These elements reflect interpretative researchers' interest in collecting and learning from people's own accounts of their experiences. The elements also reflect interpretative researchers' interest in interpreting those accounts in order to learn about people's meaning-making, as it is situated in cultural context. This means that in composing your researchable questions, you need to specify *what kind of people* to study, in *what settings* to study them, and what *specific aspects of the research topic are* in focus. To get a picture of what these requirements mean in practice, let us recollect some examples from Chapter 2.

Peggy Miller and her co-workers had a general interest in uncovering the ideologies or folk psychologies of child development in the USA and in Taiwan and in comparing the childrearing and disciplinary practices that flowed from those ideologies. In the study we reported, the researchers' specific knowledge interest was the concept of self-esteem. One of their researchable questions was: How do the concepts of self-esteem and self-respect figure in caregivers' ways of understanding children's development in the two countries?

Eva's general interest was the disjunction between ideology and practice in daily life, specifically the disparity between official gender equality ideology and everyday life in the Nordic countries. One specific knowledge interest was how heterosexual couples, and the men and women in each couple, made sense of the prevailing ideologies and cultural messages. One researchable question that Eva asked was: What are the cultural understandings that inform Nordic men's and women's accounts of themselves as mothers, fathers, spouses, and workers? Another researchable question was: How do couples vary in their ways of using those cultural understandings to negotiate the distribution of housework and childcare between the woman and the man?

Michelle Lafrance's general interest was Canadian women's experiences and understandings of depression and the cultural pressures surrounding women diagnosed with depression. Her specific knowledge interest was how biomedical explanations of depressive experiences are either maintained or contested as women attempt to understand their depressive experiences. One researchable question that Lafrance asked was: What are the societal discourses that the women drew on in their explanations of their depressive experiences?

You can see that these researchable questions were formulated in relation to specific contexts, specific categories of people, and specific aspects of daily life. Also, the questions were formulated within specific theoretical frameworks. Beyond these overarching similarities, researchable questions in interpretative research vary considerably.

Expect to modify your researchable questions

Interpretative researchers expect their researchable questions to shift over the course of a study. They are interested in gaining insight into their participants' ways of understanding the world and talking about it. Therefore, they are closely attuned to what the participants say and how they say it. As researchers learn from their participants, they alter their ideas and modify the researchable questions. Often this requires modifying some elements of the research procedure, such as expanding the number of participants or changing some of the interview questions. Allowing such changes may seem strange to researchers who are accustomed to hypothesis-testing research. For those researchers, changing one's hypothesis or altering one's procedures in the course of a study is seen as tantamount to fraud (and rightly so). However, interpretative research is not about hypothesis testing. In interpretative research, the purpose of one's researchable questions is not to aid in testing whether the researcher's preconceived ideas are empirically supported or not, but rather to help deepen and enrich those ideas. The knowledge interests of interpretative researchers involve learning about the participants' worldviews. The researchable questions are tools to help researchers do this.

Does expecting one's researchable questions to develop during the project mean that one can be vague during the first phase of defining them? Could one proceed with only a general knowledge interest and allow it to develop over time? No. It is only by being careful and thorough when developing your researchable questions that you will be able to know what you are modifying and why the modification is needed. We discourage researchers from embarking on designing interviews with nothing in mind except a wide and vague knowledge interest.

Once you are confident that you have a workable (though not immutable) set of researchable questions, you are ready to move forward to the next step of designing the project: making decisions regarding the research participants.

4 Making decisions about participants

This chapter takes up a number of questions concerning the participants in a research project. In the first part of the chapter, we address how to specify the group of participants that is best suited to your study. We emphasize that you need to keep your researchable questions in mind as you make decisions regarding those whom you will study. We also discuss the theoretical and practical issues that you have to take into account when you specify the group that you will study. In the next part, we discuss considerations about the appropriate number of participants to study. We then turn to the steps you take to locate potential participants, enlist their participation, and set up the time and the place for the interviews. We also present the ethical and practical concerns that you need to address in this process.

Specifying the group(s) of people to study

How do you decide who the best participants are for your study? And how do you decide how many individuals to interview? The answers to these questions are based on the choices that you made and the theoretical considerations you had when you developed your researchable questions. We described strategies for developing your researchable questions in Chapter 3. Here we offer guidelines for specifying the types of individuals whose participation will enable you to answer those questions.

When you set out to specify the group you will study, you must take into account the kind of knowledge you seek. Different types of research involve different types of knowledge, and therefore demand different principles for specifying the group to study. Each project's researchable questions form the basis for specifying its participants. We therefore take a moment to remind you of what we have said earlier about researchable questions in interpretative research.

The knowledge interests of interpretative researchers involve learning about the participants' worldviews as the participants themselves formulate them. The researchable questions are framed in terms of specific contexts, specific aspects of daily life, and specific experiences. Furthermore, and in special focus here, the researchable questions identify categories of people who are likely to have had those experiences. These categories could be, for example, people who experienced a particular situation or event, or people whose lives were affected by a particular circumstance, or people who are members of a particular social institution. Larry Davidson's project, which you read about in Chapter 2, offers an example. He and his colleagues wanted to understand how people with severe mental illnesses experienced repeated hospitalizations. The researchers identified certain background characteristics (such as a diagnosis of major psychosis) and certain experiences (such as frequent re-hospitalizations) to specify the group from which participants would be recruited.

Specifying groups to study is always purposive

The researchable questions that interpretative researchers ask concern close descriptions of people's experiences associated with some phenomenon. Researchers seek to learn about the many different experiences that people may have had. Researchers therefore select people for study who are likely to have had the experiences of interest. In doing so, they take care to include the full range of such experiences. Note that different types of experiences do not occur equally often. By definition, only a few people have atypical experiences. Therefore, the researcher needs to ensure that people with atypical, as well as typical, experiences are included in the group to study. If the group encompasses all the varieties of experiences, it is by definition representative of the larger group of which it is a part. This is true even though it does not tell you about the percentages of people in the larger group who have those experiences. Establishing such percentages is not part of the goal of interpretative research.

Sometimes researchers want to learn about experiences associated with a phenomenon such as a particular illness, a life-cycle event (such as first menstruation), or a historical event (such as a disaster). As in all research, the researcher needs a group with a range of experiences similar to that of the larger group. But how can a researcher know what that range of experiences is and which people have them? For the most part, researchers draw on the research literature for indications of both the range of experiences and the categories of people who might have had them.

Sometimes researchers want to compare the experiences of two or more groups with respect to a phenomenon. To facilitate comparison, the groups should be similar on relevant dimensions. Also, the groups should be more or less the same size. Eva's study of Nordic couples, which you read about in Chapter 2, offers an example. Based on her knowledge of earlier research, Eva took care to ensure that the groups of couples from the three countries were similar with regard to the range of educational backgrounds of the members of the couples, the ages of the men and women, and the ages of their children.

Sometimes researchers study a setting such as an organization or an institution and the social processes and experiences that take place within it. Examples of such settings are a workplace, a mental health clinic, and a school. Such settings have their own formal structures and informal hierarchies and relationships. As a general rule, members of an organization who hold different positions have different experiences and offer different perspectives on the organization. Taking this into account will help the researcher to specify a group that encompasses as closely as possible the full range of experiences among people in the setting. For example, Anne Galletta (2013), an educational researcher in the USA, wanted to understand how a large-scale long-term desegregation program had unfolded in a particular school district. Galletta interviewed school district officials, principals, teachers, parents, alumni, and students, both White and African-American.

Setting the number of participants for your study

How many participants should an interpretative research project have? This question evokes disagreement among researchers and often puzzles beginners. In order to try to clear up some of the puzzlement, we take a moment to look at the disagreements. To begin, it is common for researchers who do not do interpretative research to argue that interpretative research projects have too few participants. In response, interpretative researchers argue that for their types of research what is important is the quality and total amount of interview material that they gather, not the sheer number of participants. In some studies, a comparatively small number of participants is sufficient to generate a rich enough and large enough body of interview material; in other studies, a larger number is needed.

Interpretative researchers disagree among themselves about the optimal number of participants. If you were to ask several experienced interpretative researchers for advice about the appropriate number of participants, most of them would say that it is impossible to give such a number. (This is our position.) If you were then to press the researchers to suggest a general minimum number of participants, you would find that many would refuse to do so. (We would be among them.) Further, you would find that researchers who are prepared to give a general minimum number give very different numbers. Some say that a study needs a minimum of thirty participants, whereas others say that the minimum is six. Such a wide range of opinion suggests that you should regard any such "one-size-fits-all" prescription with skepticism.

To give a picture of how the number of participants in interpretative research projects varies, we look back at the studies we described in Chapters 1 and 2. Lisa Capps and Elinor Ochs interviewed one woman who suffered from severe agoraphobia. They did many interviews with her over a period of two and a half years. Ann Phoenix analyzed in detail the interviews of two women who were part of a larger study of adults who had experienced serial migration. Michelle Lafrance analyzed the interviews of eight women who, as participants in a larger study, had given biomedical explanations of their depressive episodes. Larry Davidson and his colleagues interviewed twelve patients suffering from schizophrenia who had had two or more hospitalizations within the previous year and who had taken part in an earlier program to prevent re-hospitalization. Dawn Currie and her colleagues interviewed eighteen young teenage girls who participated in leisure and sports activities that were atypical for girls in their setting. Peggy Miller and her colleagues interviewed sixteen caregivers in each of two countries, for a total of thirty-two participants. Andrea Dottolo and Abigail Stewart analyzed the interviews of sixteen African-American women and men and twenty-two Euro-American women and men, a total of thirty-eight participants. Jeanne and Chandanie Senadheera analyzed the interviews of twenty-two pairs of mothers and daughters, forty-four participants in total. They did two interviews with each participant. Eva analyzed interviews of thirty couples. Ten couples were selected in each of three countries, sixty participants in total.

As you can see, the number of participants varies widely among these studies. However, the number of participants tells us only a little. There are other quantities that we need to look at in order to get a meaningful picture of interpretative projects. One such quantity is how many times each participant was interviewed. Another is the amount of material that each interview provides, that is, its depth and detail. A third is the number and scope of the analyses that the researcher did in order to answer the researchable questions.

Capps and Ochs's study was unusual in studying only one participant. From previous studies (their own and others'), Capps and Ochs knew a good deal about anxiety disorders and agoraphobia. In this study, they wanted to get a detailed picture of what went on before, within, and after agoraphobic panic attacks. They decided that the best way to do this was to study one person's narratives in detail. Consequently, they did a large number of interviews of a single participant over two and a half years. In this way, they acquired a voluminous amount of material for their analyses. The participant told them many stories of her lifetime experiences of anxiety and panic, and about the resulting constriction of her freedom of movement. The collection of stories was the basis for a close examination of the grammatical forms and narrative structures by which the participant made sense of her agoraphobia. This project offers a striking illustration of how decisions about the right number of participants are inextricably intertwined with the researchable questions and the depth and detail of the interview material.

To conclude, there is no single fixed or ideal number of participants for interpretative studies. That is, the question about the right number of participants cannot be answered in the abstract. The answer always has to be: It depends! It depends above all on the researchable questions of the project. Different researchable questions point toward different choices about the number of interviews with each participant, the scope of each interview, and detail of the analyses to be done. Only when you have made these choices can you make the decision of how many participants to interview. If you interview each participant more than once, if you plan to do detailed and in-depth interviews, and if you plan detailed and exhaustive analyses of the interviews, a comparatively small number of participants will suffice.

Reaching out to potential participants

Once you have specified whom you want to study, the next task is to locate individuals who match your specifications. Broadly speaking, there are three ways that interpretative researchers usually use to locate participants. We first describe each one briefly and discuss how it is used. In the next subsection, we consider how these ways of locating participants can give you a group of participants that meets your specifications.

Advertising. Many researchers seek participants by posting notices that invite participation in the study. Such notices may appear in social media sites (such as chat rooms, Twitter, or websites), on public noticeboards or bulletin boards, in newsletters of relevant organizations, or in newspapers. Typically, such notices briefly describe the topic of the study, what will be required of participants, the payment (if any), and the contact details of the researcher.

Chain referral. Chain referral is also known by names such as snowball sampling or friendship pyramiding. A researcher who uses chain referrals seeks to gather a group to study by asking each participant to suggest the names of other potential participants. Typically, the interviewer ends an interview by asking the participant for names of other individuals who might be invited into the study. Of course, this is a request, not a demand; participants are free to decline. If names are given, the researcher then contacts those individuals and invites them into the study.

Chain referral is most useful when members of the group you have specified for study are difficult to find or reluctant to take part in a research project and when the researcher has reason to think that they might know one another. (Indeed, in some circumstances, a personalized referral or even an introduction might be needed.) For example, Becky Thompson (1994), a White sociologist working in the USA, wanted to interview African-American women who had experienced severe eating problems. Anticipating that such women might be reluctant to speak about their difficulties to a White woman, Thompson chose to draw on friendship networks in the local African-American community to locate participants. She asked her initial participants for introductions to other participants.

A common variant on chain referral involves identifying a single individual who is in a good position to recommend potential participants and enlisting his or her help. (That individual might or might not be a study participant.) An example is the procedure that Eric Stewart (2013) used for his study of women who had had serious brain injuries. As Stewart quickly learned, such individuals often wish to keep their medical histories, as well as their current disabilities and limitations, out of public view. Finding it difficult to locate potential participants, Stewart came to rely on the help of a woman who was a disability rights activist for introductions to possible participants.

Targeted nominations. A third way to locate potential participants is to enlist the help of individuals who are not participants in the study to nominate suitable individuals for study. This technique involves asking different individuals to name one potential participant who fits a particular set of characteristics. Eva used this method in her study of Nordic couples. Eva, as you have already read, had a detailed specification of the composition of her group – one that involved various countries of residence and differing demographic and family characteristics. She requested a set of individuals in each country to nominate couples to be invited to take part in the study. The requests were quite specific: each laid out a particular combination of demographic characteristics and family configuration. Each individual nominated only one couple. Compared to chain referrals, this way of reaching potential participants increases the diversity of the group of potential participants. Compared to advertising, it ensures that the set of potential participants will more closely match the researcher's specifications.

Caveat: be wary of using members of your personal networks as participants in your research projects. There is one final consideration about methods of locating participants for a study: Should you consider your personal acquaintances – friends, relatives, therapy clients, or close co-workers – as possible participants? Generally speaking, you should avoid this. When you interview people you already know well, you enter into a dual relationship, elements of which may conflict. First, personal acquaintances may feel obliged to take part in your study even if they do not want to. In that way, their freedom of choice is compromised. Second, the quality of the material you obtain from the interviews may be diminished. Friends and associates may refrain from disclosing certain experiences because they fear those revelations would jeopardize their friendship with you or because the revelations involve mutual acquaintances. They may avoid expressing certain points of view because they know that you disagree. In addition, as the interviewer, you might hold back on asking about issues that you know to be troubling or contentious or too personal. Third, as interviewees, personal acquaintances may feel obliged to disclose information that they would otherwise keep secret from you. Fourth, the information you learn during the interview becomes part of your knowledge of the individual and that will change your relationship to this person. Furthermore, you will obligated by the ethical rules of research to hold this information in confidence, and this may later become a burden.

Putting the recruitment techniques into use

We have described common ways of reaching out to potential participants. Now we turn to the question of how to use these recruitment techniques to obtain the group necessary to address your researchable questions. As you now know, this is not simply about enrolling a sufficient number of participants in a study; it is about composing a group of participants who, taken together, have a set of experiences that will enable you to answer your researchable questions. None of the ways of reaching out to participants that we described above offers a guarantee of yielding such a group.

Let us first take up chain referral. This technique is often appealing because it produces a string of potential participants without much effort on the researcher's part. But chain referral is not likely to yield a group with a range of experiences akin to the range in the broader population. The reason is that such referrals (as the term "friendship pyramiding" implies) are likely to yield a set of individuals who are quite similar to one another. For example, they are likely to be similar in age, social class, educational attainment, and other demographic characteristics. In addition, through their prior interactions with one another, they may also have come to share similar views. This severely limits the usefulness of chain referral. All told, chain referral is generally not advisable except in situations where you have no other means to reach the group of people that you wish to study.

Compared to chain referral, advertising for potential participants can yield a more heterogeneous group of potential participants, that is, a group that is likely to encompass a wider set of experiences. However, whether or not this is so depends on *where* the researcher chooses to advertise and, as we will discuss shortly, on how the advertisement is framed. If your advertising is targeted to a narrow segment of the population, then it stands to reason that the participants whom you enlist will be limited to that narrow segment. To take an obvious example, suppose you were embarking on a study concerned with heavy drinking. It might seem that an easy place to find people with histories of heavy drinking would be Alcoholics Anonymous (AA) meetings. However, people who attend AA meetings represent only a small and homogeneous segment of people with histories of heavy drinking. Put in technical terms, advertising to such a limited group severely restricts your access to the variation in the phenomenon under study. There are many other individuals with histories of heavy drinking who have different experiences.

We have observed that many inexperienced researchers think of support groups (e.g., for women struggling with eating problems; for individuals dealing with a suicide in their family; for breast cancer survivors) as a good source of potential participants. Whether or not this is appropriate depends on the researchable question. Support groups are, by definition, constituted of individuals who view themselves as needing the support of a community of others with similar experiences. Will members of a support group, taken together, provide the full range of experiences that you seek to study? If the answer is no, then you have two options. One is to advertise in a different venue where your advertising will reach a broader array of individuals. The other is to recruit from a support group but add a second recruitment technique, such as targeted nomination. In combination, the two could produce a group that meets your specifications. When you use such a two-phase recruitment technique, you must monitor the characteristics and experiences of the initial participants whom you interview, so that the addition of more participants gives you a group that meets the specifications of your study design.

Thus far, we have focused on the risk of obtaining an overly restricted group, that is, one that does not encompass the full range of variation in the phenomenon you wish to study. But now we shift the focus to another concern. If the procedure that you use to recruit participants is too open, the resulting group of participants will be a hodgepodge. Advertising, for example, may yield many potential participants, but there is no guarantee that they will fit your specifications. Put another way, advertising is usually far from purposive. You may have some control over who sees the ad, but you have no control over who responds. Therefore, what advertising yields is best thought of as a pool of potential participants. You will need to devise screening questions that enable you to select those who meet your study specifications and filter out those who do not. Some of the screening questions will concern the general criteria for participants that you had set at the outset. Other screening questions may screen for specific types of participants. The purpose of these latter questions is to ensure that the resulting set of participants provides the range of experiences and characteristics that you need to address your researchable questions. Note that as you interview more and more participants, the screening questions need to be more and more specific because there will be fewer and fewer types of people still needed to complete your group.

Composing the message to potential participants

Whether it is an advertisement, an e-mail, a letter, or a phone call, what you say to potential participants is crucial. You need to choose your words carefully because your language will shape the participants' image of your project. If your words appeal only to certain people, then your participants will not represent the full set of experiences that you want, but only a subset. Pantea Farvid, for example, found that when her advertisement identified her project as a study about "casual sex," the women who volunteered spoke enthusiastically about "hook-ups" and endorsed casual sex as "good" and "fun" (2010, p. 233). When Farvid advertised for a second study, she used a more neutral and open-ended description ("talk about sex"). This time, the women who volunteered for the study gave accounts of brief sexual encounters that encompassed a wider range of experiences, including both pleasures and difficulties.

Although there is no wording that is entirely neutral or bare of connotations, it is important to be sensitive to the possible meanings and connotations of the words you choose when you communicate to potential participants. This is equally true whether your first communication is an e-mail, a letter, a phone call, or an advertisement. It is helpful to consult with other researchers about possible wordings, as well as to pretest the wordings of your communications.

Contacting and enlisting participants

When you have names of potential participants, you need to contact them one by one. Whenever you contact participants, you must take care to protect their privacy. Such precautions may be unnecessary; however, you cannot know that in advance. It is good ethical practice to err on the side of caution. For example, if you are studying a sensitive topic, such as abortion decision-making, HIV status, or illegal drug use, participants may not want others to know that they are taking part in your study. If you leave messages by voice mail, they should be neutral; if you send postal mail, you should use an envelope without identifying information.

In your first interaction with a potential participant, you need to ask screening questions to see if the person is appropriate for your study. When people do not meet your criteria, you need to politely tell them so and thank them for their time. When people do meet your criteria, you move to explaining the study and trying to secure their agreement to participate. When possible, make this contact by telephone or in person, rather than by e-mail or letter. A live conversation enables potential participants to ask questions about what the project entails and to reassure themselves about what they can expect. This first conversation begins to establish the relationship between the interviewer and the participant. Therefore, if at all possible, the person who will carry out the interview should make this first contact.

The conversation with potential participants has four purposes: (1) to screen the people in the pool of potential participants to ascertain which ones fit in your study; (2) to provide information about the study to those who fit your selection criteria and to answer their questions about the study; (3) to encourage those individuals to participate;

and (4) to set the date and place for the interview. It is helpful to have a written script when you speak to potential participants, so that you are sure to cover everything. The following list covers the elements of such a script:

Box 4.1 Elements of the first conversation with potential participants

1. Your name and who you are (e.g., your position and the institution you work for)
2. The topic of the study, phrased in everyday language
3. How you got the person's name or why the person was selected
4. Screening questions that will enable you to screen in suitable participants

For those who are screened in, the conversation continues as follows:

5. What the main topics of the interview will be
6. How long the interview will take
7. Information regarding confidentiality and anonymity
8. Your need to audio-record the interview and why (e.g., "I want to be free to listen and talk with you without writing notes" or "I want to be able to review what we have talked about after we have finished")
9. Information regarding payments (if any) and reimbursement of expenses such as travel costs
10. Agreeing on a time and place for the interview

The way you describe the study (#2 in the table) and how you describe the topics of the interview (#5) will shape participants' expectations about the interview. That is, your choice of words will inevitably lead participants to anticipate what might be asked and to begin to gather memories and reflections accordingly. A striking example of this is the experience of Marjolein Morée, a Dutch sociologist. Morée invited women to take part in a study of mothers who had been engaged in paid work during the 1950s (Morée, 1992). She used the phrase "mothers working outside the home" (in Dutch, "*buitenshuis werkende moeders*") in communicating to potential participants. The phrase turned out to be an unfortunate reminder of the prejudices against employed mothers in the 1950s. Therefore, participants came to the interview prepared to defend themselves against charges that they had neglected their children. The lesson to be learned is that you should give careful thought to the script for your initial conversation with potential participants. You should try the script out in advance of using it.

If the person agrees to participate, you can then proceed to schedule the interview. You should set both the starting time and the ending time to ensure that the participant schedules enough time to complete the interview. Researchers often send a letter or an e-mail confirming the time and place of the interview, along with their contact information.

Sometimes a potential participant asks you to change the conditions of the interview. For example, he or she might ask to be interviewed by telephone or via e-mail. He or she might object to the interview being recorded. Except in extraordinary circumstances, you should politely decline such requests. Interviews carried out by phone or e-mail will produce material that diverges considerably from face-to-face interviews. Furthermore, all of the analyses that you will learn in Chapters 8–11 require full transcripts, not notes reconstructed *post hoc*.

Setting up the interview situation

Where should you conduct the interviews? Your decision should be guided by both practical considerations and considerations related to the goals of your project. The foremost practical consideration is that the interview location be safe for both the interviewer and the participant. The location should also be convenient, easy to find, and in a setting that is comfortable for the participant. For example, a university office might be a suitable place to interview students, but it is probably not the best place to interview working-class teenagers. Moreover, different considerations – convenience versus secrecy, for example – weigh differently for different participants. Therefore, you might propose some alternate locations to the participant and let the participant choose. It is not necessary to meet all participants in the same location. Your goal is to set optimal conditions for each participant.

Participants should not have to travel long distances or incur considerable difficulty or expense to get to the interview site. The more obstacles, such as unfamiliarity, inconvenience, and expense, that participants face, the fewer will agree to participate, the fewer will keep appointments, and the less likely it is that those who do show up will be comfortable. It is the interviewer, not the participant, who should bear the brunt of travel difficulties or expense.

In addition to safety and convenience, you should consider the possible connotations that a location might have for your participants. Choose a neutral location. For instance, it may seem convenient to interview employees at their worksite, but some employees may be uncomfortable being interviewed at their workplace. Note also that you should be wary of using a facility that is identified with a particular organization or political ideology. For example, if you were to use an office in a psychiatric clinic, your participants might infer that you were really interested in mental illness, no matter how you described the study. Further, participants may not wish others to know that they have participated in a research study. You should select an interview site that allows participants to take part in the interview in an unobtrusive way.

The interview room should afford privacy and freedom from interruptions. It should have comfortable chairs that face each other, with a table in between them on which you can place your recording equipment.

Compensating participants

Should you pay your research participants? Practices vary considerably. Paying participants is frowned upon in some settings; in others, it is the norm. When researchers offer payment as an incentive to participate, they typically mention the amount in the advertisements or letters of invitation. We suggest that you follow the usual practice in the setting where you are doing your study. However, if you do offer to pay participants, the amount should not be set so high that it becomes an irresistible inducement to participate. This would be a breach of ethics, because such high payments may contravene potential participants' freedom to consent.

Researchers who do not offer payment as an incentive to participate may give a small gift at the end of the interview as a token of appreciation. Such gifts, of course, are not mentioned ahead of time and therefore will not influence whether people participate in the study.

Reimbursing participants for their costs is another matter. Participants should always be reimbursed for out-of-pocket costs such as transportation costs, parking fees, or childcare costs. In addition, participants who forgo income in order to participate should be compensated.

Ethical regulations of research

Here, we briefly discuss formal ethical regulations that may govern how to recruit participants for research. Your project will be subject to a number of regulations – government regulations, regulations set by your university or research institute, and regulations in the setting where you hope to recruit participants. Ethical regulations vary between locales. You need to familiarize yourself with the regulations in the locale where your project is situated.

Ethical regulations usually require that each participant give informed consent at the beginning of the interview. Such regulations require that every participant be informed about the nature of the interview and the purpose of the study and about his or her rights as a research participant. Key among these rights are the right to decline to answer any questions, the right to end the interview at any point or not to enter the study at all, and the right to confidentiality and anonymity.

Regulations often require that researchers document informed consent in writing. To fulfill such regulations, you need to prepare a written document that describes the terms of the study. In addition to describing the nature of the interview and the purpose of the study, the document should enumerate the rights that participants have regarding the interview. You must give this document to the participant to read and sign before the interview begins. By signing the document, the participant signifies that she or he understands its contents and agrees to participate on the terms it sets. You should keep the signed documents on file. To safeguard the participants' anonymity, they should be kept separate from the interviews. For participants who have difficulty reading or in settings where signing a contractual document has negative connotations, it may be permissible to substitute oral consent. In this case, you can audio-record the conversation in which you read the consent document and obtain the participant's agreement.

Researchers who wish to study children or adolescents in research projects must pay attention to ethical regulations governing the participation of minors in research.

In most locales, parental consent is required for children and adolescents to take part in research. Researchers should also seek the minor's assent (i.e., agreement to participate). They should first assess the child's willingness to participate (even if this is not a legal requirement). Only if the child agrees to take part in the study and agrees to having his or her parent informed would the researcher seek the parent's consent. This procedure protects the privacy of the child and it gives the child the right to self-determination.

The regulations concerning informed consent vary from place to place. Note that there may be legal or other restrictions on your ability to keep interview material confidential, especially when interviewing children or minors. If there are such restrictions, you need to state these to your participants as part of the informed consent procedure. For specifics, you should consult the ethical regulations in your country or state, and at your university.

5 Designing the interview guide

This chapter shows you how to prepare a comprehensive interview guide. You need to prepare such a guide before you start interviewing. The interview guide serves many purposes. Most important, it is a memory aid to ensure that the interviewer covers every topic and obtains the necessary detail about the topic. For this reason, the interview guide should contain all the interview items in the order that you have decided. The exact wording of the items should be given, although the interviewer may sometimes depart from this wording. Interviews often contain some questions that are sensitive or potentially offensive. For such questions, it is vital to work out the best wording of the question ahead of time and to have it available in the interview.

To study people's meaning-making, researchers must create a situation that enables people to tell about their experiences and that also foregrounds each person's particular way of making sense of those experiences. Put another way, the interview situation must encourage participants to tell about their experiences in their own words and in their own way without being constrained by categories or classifications imposed by the interviewer. The type of interview that you will learn about here has a conversational and relaxed tone. However, the interview is far from extemporaneous. The interviewer works from the interview guide that has been carefully prepared ahead of time. It contains a detailed and specific list of items that concern topics that will shed light on the researchable questions.

Often researchers are in a hurry to get into the field and gather their material. It may seem obvious to them what questions to ask participants. Seasoned interviewers may feel ready to approach interviewing with nothing but a laundry list of topics. But it is always wise to move slowly at this point. Time spent designing and refining interview items – polishing the wording of the items, weighing language choices, considering the best sequence of topics, and then pretesting and revising the interview guide – will always pay off in producing better interviews. Moreover, it will also provide you with a deep knowledge of the elements of the interview and a clear idea of the intent behind each of the items. This can help you to keep the interviews on track.

To prepare a detailed interview guide, you have to think carefully about what the interview ought to cover and how it will help you address your researchable questions. This deliberation will help you compose and hone the interview items. It will also assist you in shaping the conversations that you have with your participants. In addition, devising the specific interview items forces you to foresee possible difficulties (such as possible misinterpretations of a question) and how you might handle them. Having thought in advance about these matters should help you to be more confident as an interviewer and to be able to focus your attention more fully on the participant's words.

In this chapter, we take you through the steps of designing interview items, arranging them into a sequence, and constructing the complete written interview guide. But before we begin, we describe the central elements of the type of interview that you will learn to do. This type of interview is semi-structured and has open-ended questions. It will generate what we call "rich talk," talk that is informal, free-flowing, and couched in words and expressions of the participant's choosing. You will also learn about the interviewer–participant relationship.

We recommend that you read this chapter in tandem with Chapter 6, "Doing the interview." Several of the issues that we talk about here will be taken up again in Chapter 6 when we describe how to carry out an interview.

Semi-structured interviews and open-ended questions

Interpretative researchers' interest in personal meaning-making lends their interviews a distinctive character. The interviews differ in a number of ways from interviews used in surveys, screening interviews, and other interviews focused on obtaining factual information.

To begin with, survey interviews often ask a series of questions that bear little relationship to one another. In a survey, we would not be surprised to be asked whether we drive a hybrid car and then, immediately afterward, whether or not we skip breakfast in the morning. However, the interview format that you will learn here is conversational, with special pains taken to put the participant at ease. The conversation ought to flow from one topic to another. Moreover, although the interviewer works from an interview guide with items listed in a specific order, the interviewer is not required to adhere strictly to that order for every participant. If the flow of the conversation suggests a different sequence of topics, the interviewer is free to adapt. This style of interviewing is called semi-structured.

In semi-structured interviews, the interviewer usually phrases his or her requests in a form that is open-ended. He or she invites the participant to tell stories about experiences, relate memories, and offer reflections and opinions. These invitations are rarely questions about specific facts or questions that merely call for agreement or disagreement (i.e., yes/no questions). In other words, the interview items do not have the form of the answer built into them. Such questions are usually called open-ended (as opposed to close-ended). They leave the participant free to respond in whatever way he or she chooses. As you will see from the examples below, such open-ended questions work well to elicit rich, full, and complex accounts from participants.

Rich talk in interviews

We use the term rich talk for the kinds of stories, opinions, recollections, and reflections that interpretative researchers seek out. It refers to the kind of things people say when they are encouraged to speak in their own ways and on their own terms. We avoid calling this "naturalistic" or "naturally occurring" talk because those terms are inexact. The talk that occurs in interviews is not naturally occurring. Unlike hotline phone conversations or talk overheard on a bus, for example, the talk in interviews is prompted by the interviewer's questions. To illustrate what we mean by rich talk in interviews, we provide some short extracts from different interview studies, which give a variety of examples.

1. INTERVIEWER: Has being a woman in your workplace changed over the years?
   PARTICIPANT: I have actually never suffered from being a woman. Why that is, I don't know, but I have never felt that. Of course the management is different now from before, and I mean, if you take older – maybe even very much older male colleagues – well, I mean, they were like, well like what you can expect from men of their age. It has something to do with how old you are, too, but not very much; but a little, that's how it is. So – but there have always been [women on the lowest rungs of the career ladder], but I was the first to [get a higher position], and that was really odd. There were only men then, and then there was me, you know, for several years. But then maybe one had to push a little to show that one existed, otherwise one might be forgotten at meetings and such things – that was part of it [taken from Magnusson, 1996].

2. INTERVIEWER: Are you one of those "conscientious housewives"?
   PARTICIPANT: Yes! I mangle our clothes – I don't clean house a lot. I mangle and iron everything except underwear! [laughs] And some people have stopped doing all such things. But it – I do it for my own pleasure, because I want it that way! [..] Yes, I think it's great! I have a mania for tidying things up – but not for cleaning. Well, I don't have a dirty house, you know, but I – it doesn't matter if some dust rolls about, no. The kitchen has to be a kitchen, and that's the way it should be! And I have taught all the others that one should pick up one's clothes and put them away. But you know, it – and since I pick up things, the place is never untidy. But a mania for tidying up, that's quick. And then you yourself are satisfied, because they can come to visit whenever they want to, the house isn't messy. And I think that would be harder for myself. But I can be terribly lazy sometimes … [taken from Magnusson, 1998].

3. INTERVIEWER: Please tell me about the worst time an argument with your partner became physical.
   PARTICIPANT: We were battering each other at that point, and that's when she was in the bathroom. This is – it's like forty-five minutes into this whole argument now. She's in the bathroom, messing with my [gun]. And I had no idea. So I kicked the door in – in the bathroom, and she's sitting there trying to load this thing, trying to get this clip in, and luckily she couldn't figure it out. Why, I don't – you know, well, because she was drunk.

So, luckily she didn't. The situation could have been a whole lot worse, you know, it could have been a whole lot worse than it was. I thank God that she didn't figure it out. When I think about it, you know, she was lucky to come out of it with just a cut on her head. You know, she could have blown her brains out or done something really stupid [taken from Anderson & Umberson, 2001].

4. INTERVIEWER: How have your ideas about feminist therapy changed over time?
   PARTICIPANT: I've gotten better in my ability to use that [feminism] in my therapy. I think early on in therapy, I was probably much more blatantly confrontative. You know, I just wanted to shake it out of these guys, kind of thing. "What the matter with you? Don't you get it?" Over the years, I've learned how to get the message across in ways that are more effective. I don't take them on so directly . . . and I think the end result is, is better. Cause I'm not modeling the very things that I'm trying to teach them not to do [taken from Marecek & Kravetz, 1998].

5. INTERVIEWER: Does managed care ever affect the approach you take right in the moment when you are in a session with a client?
   PARTICIPANT: No. No, it doesn't. But again, that's because of where I am in this particular practice. When I was in in-patient psych, it absolutely did, because you couldn't do psychoanalytic treatment. I'll tell you a funny story: We had a psychiatrist and he was a psychoanalyst, and he was in the wrong job, he should not have been in this job. He had a metaphor that he used with every single client, which I think was poor practice, because you had people coming from the inner city, and he'd say "OK, if you were Atlas and you were holding the world up, you know, what would it say, or how would it feel," and then he'd ask some very intricate psychoanalytical question. Half the therapists didn't know what he was talking about. And the parent or kid would have already developed a rapport with me, would look at me and say "XXX, what the hell is he talking about?" You know, what was I supposed to say? [taken from Cohen, Marecek, & Gillham, 2006].

In these examples of rich talk, you can see a wide variety of speaking styles, opinions, and ways of communicating. You may also notice that people often seem to contradict themselves. That is, as their thoughts develop, ideas that they originally expressed may change. Their ideas may become more complex and more qualified, or perhaps an idea may even be repudiated. An interview format that encourages rich talk allows people to speak at length and develop their thoughts as they wish. This format also enables researchers to glimpse the process by which people work out a response and "think aloud" while doing so.

The interviewer–participant relationship

We have said that semi-structured interviews have a conversational tone. By this, we mean that they should be relaxed encounters, with the interviewer making efforts to put the participant at ease. The interviewer should use accessible and informal language. The interviewer's style should invite participants to tell full stories, without fear of contradiction or criticism or disapproval. Interruptions should be kept to a minimum.

Establishing a conversational tone, however, is not the same thing as having a conversation. Interviews differ from ordinary conversations in several crucial ways. First, the interviewer has the task of guiding the interview and constraining the content of the talk. With the aid of the interview guide, he or she keeps the conversation on track by shaping the overall process and asking appropriate follow-up questions. Second, the conversation and the relationship are asymmetrical: the participant is there to share experiences and information; the interviewer, by contrast, is there to listen and to facilitate the participant's responses. Participants may disclose quite a bit about themselves and their lives. Interviewers ought to disclose very little. And participants offer (and are asked to offer) judgments and opinions, but interviewers ought to refrain from offering their points of view. Moreover, interviewers should be cautious about either concurring with or taking exception to the views of a participant.

Having described the key elements of interviews, we now describe how you go about constructing an interview guide. The process begins, not surprisingly, with reviewing the researchable questions that you want to address.

Researchable questions are not interview questions

The stories, reflections, and accounts that participants provide during their interviews form the material that you will analyze to shed light on your researchable question. Let us emphasize the difference between the researchable questions (i.e., the questions that you set out to answer in your project) and the interview questions (i.e., the questions that you will ask the participants). Researchable questions are the researcher's formulations about what he or she wants to know. Such questions are framed within a theory. They are general in the sense that they do not concern a particular person's experiences. Interview questions, in contrast, are particular. They pertain to an individual participant's experiences; they should invite stories about concrete and local experiences. In other words, the interview questions are invitations to participants to tell about experiences and events from their own lives and to offer personal reflections about them.

Researchers who are new to interpretative research often overlook the distinction between researchable questions and interview questions and mistakenly ask their participants to answer the researchable questions. For example, one of our students proposed to ask ten-year-old girls the following: "How does your body image affect your identity?" This was, as you might guess, the researchable question that the student wanted to answer. It is a valid researchable question. But it is not a plausible interview question. Words such as "body image," "affect," and "identity" are the wrong words to use in a conversation with young children. But more important, this would not be a useful question to ask *any* participant, no matter his or her age. "Body image" and "identity" are abstract terms taken from psychological theories. When presented with such abstract terms, participants are likely to flounder around, searching in vain for a hook on which to hang an answer. If they are able to respond at all, they may answer in terms that are so abstract and general that what they say is uninformative.

What would be a better way to gain material pertinent to the researchable question "How does body image affect young girls' identity?"? An interpretative researcher would want to collect stories from girls about their experiences regarding body size and shape. Possible interview questions could ask about participants' ideas about desirable body shapes and sizes for girls; efforts that they and other girls (or female members of their families) have made to change their bodies; whether kids tease one another about being the "wrong" size or shape; ideas about pop stars' bodies; and so on. Instead of theoretical concepts (e.g., body image and identity), the researcher could ask the girls about their everyday lives, seeking stories about experiences and relationships, as well as beliefs and opinions. The analysis of the themes and patterns that occur in these stories would provide evidence for how these girls' body image and identity might be linked.

Now we turn to a discussion of how to develop interview content that will help you to address your researchable questions.

Developing the interview content

To select interview topics, the first step is to consider again your general researchable questions. Now your goal is to "unpack" the researchable questions into several specific topics. These topics may relate to particular aspects or elements of the researchable questions or they may concern specific incidents. With these topics in mind, you are in a position to think about ways to ask for relevant stories and experiences. Box 5.1 gives a brief description from one of our studies.

How do you develop interview topics? First, you should review your research journal for ideas from the literature and ideas from your conversations with knowledgeable people. You might also draw upon your own experience. In the example in Box 5.1, for instance, Eva brought to her study the knowledge she had gleaned as a consultant for the

---

Box 5.1 Developing interview questions from research questions

As part of a larger project, Eva wanted to learn about women's experiences of gender inequality in their daily lives as office workers. This was her researchable question. One of the topics she developed from the research question was whether women in different hierarchical positions in the same workplace experienced different amounts and kinds of discrimination and other kinds of gender inequality.

To gather material about that topic, Eva decided to ask her participants about problematic events in their daily working lives. In the course of hearing such problem stories, she developed a sense of which stories to follow up. The follow-up questions asked for more detail about who did what and when; how the participant had reacted; how others had reacted; and so on. Once she had a large number of such detailed accounts, Eva was able to discern the gendered patterns of office life, and to see how those gendered patterns were affected by the participants' hierarchical position in the organization.

organization. Another example is a project carried out by Anne Galletta (2013), an educational psychologist. Galletta, working in a large city in the USA, was interested in the city's efforts to end racial segregation in its schools. Prior to taking decisions about the interview topics, Galletta conducted extensive archival research, studying the minutes of school board meetings, newspaper reports and editorials, and so on.

What should you keep in mind as you decide about the topics for your interview guide? First and most important, the topics should be ones that the participants are able to talk about. We earlier gave the example of a novice researcher who intended to ask ten-year-olds to discuss their "body image" and "identity" – terms they were unlikely to know. But even if a topic is couched in simple language, it may be one that participants are unable to speak about. Consider another example posed by a novice researcher.

The researcher's topic was as follows: Do parents think about their child as a boy or a girl, or simply as a "kid"? The words are simple enough. But could participants (in this case, parents of elementary school children) formulate a response to an interview item of this nature? One stumbling block is that the topic is so general that parents would find it difficult to relate it to their own experiences. But there is a larger problem: In the USA (where this study was to be carried out), children's names, toys, clothes, hairstyles, and many other things are gender-coded; many children's activities and interests are quite gender-typed and children are often segregated by sex. Thinking of a child as "simply a kid" seems nearly impossible. What might be a better way to get at the question of whether (or when) a child's sex category is salient for parents? Here are some suggestions of interview topics: Ask what toys and games the child enjoys; ask who the child's favorite playmates are and what activities they do together; ask about whether the child has requested toys associated with the other sex and how the participant dealt with such requests; ask about any occasions when the child has wanted to wear clothing, jewelry, or hairstyles that are not typical for his or her sex and how the participant handled that; ask whether the child has wanted to engage in activities that are strongly associated with one sex or the other and how the participant thought about that. These suggestions do not exhaust the possibilities. As you can see, however, all ask participants to describe actual, concrete experiences they have had with their child.

Composing interview questions about your topics

Good interview questions have two crucial characteristics. First, they elicit full, rich, and personalized stories from participants, and encourage them to volunteer their reflections on their experiences. Interviewers make requests for stories, opinions, and reflections and ask open-ended questions. Such requests and questions serve to open a conversation about a topic. We use the general term *interview item* to signify that interviews usually include a mix of requests and questions. The second characteristic of good interview items is that they provide material directly related to the interview topics. Box 5.2 illustrates the logical flow from a researchable question to two relevant interview topics to several specific interview items in a study about first-time fatherhood.

Box 5.2 Interview items in a study of first-time fathers

Researchable question: When fatherhood has turned out to be more difficult than a man anticipated, what are his experiences, recollections, and reflections?

One topic: How did men who have found fatherhood difficult experience the transition to fatherhood?
Some interview items designed to gather accounts about this topic:

* I would like you to tell me about how it was for you to become a father. For instance, what were your thoughts when you learned that your partner was pregnant?
* What were things like for you during your partner's pregnancy?

Follow-up question: Were there things you enjoyed and things you did not enjoy?

Another topic: How did fatherhood change men's lifestyles and activities?
Some interview items designed to gather accounts about this topic:

* I would like to know about your everyday activities now that you have a child.

Follow-up questions:

* Have your activities changed from before you had the child? If there were changes, which activities have changed? What made them change?
* Are there things you no longer do? Are there new things you now do?
* Do you and your partner do more things together now or fewer things together?

[taken from Stefan Björk, in progress]

The example in Box 5.2 illustrates some of the general principles for composing good interview items. First, as you can see, all the interview items are directly relevant to the topics. Second, several of the interview items are requests for a story. Third, some of the items are followed up by items in the form of open-ended questions. Fourth, each interview item concerns only one aspect of a topic. Let us offer some general rules:

– Interview items should be clear and easy to understand. They should not contain convoluted grammar, difficult words, foreign language, or jargon.
– Interview items should relate directly to the interview topics.
– Interview items should ask only one question at a time. Items that have many parts can confuse participants. Furthermore, participants are likely to overlook some parts of the item in attempting to respond. The interviewer too runs the risk of overlooking parts of the question that were not answered.
– If at all possible, the interview items should be phrased as open-ended invitations. Such invitations give the participants latitude to develop what they might want to say. They also enable participants to answer in their own words. Seasoned interviewers seldom pose yes/no questions; such questions elicit short answers and close down conversations.

- When you compose interview items, avoid assuming that you know what the participants think. This can be difficult when you are interviewing people who seem very much
like you. Include pertinent questions in the interview guide even if you feel sure that you
know what the participants will say. At least some of the time, you will be surprised.
- Any question or request that an interviewer poses inevitably constrains participants'
answers to some degree. You should avoid leading questions – questions that "give away"
the answer that the interviewer expects or prefers. ("You wouldn't do that, would you?")
Interview items that have an obvious socially desirable answer are equivalent to leading
questions. As a general rule, there should be no such questions in your interview guide.
- Take care to learn what words and terms are acceptable among members of the
community that you will be studying and to use them in your conversation. The
other side of the coin is that you should take equal care to avoid expressions that are
objectionable to your participants or that might be taken to criticize or disparage them
or the communities they are part of.

Box 5.3 lists some common ways of framing open-ended questions and requests.

Box 5.3 Ways of framing open-ended questions and requests

Can you tell me about a time when . . .?
Could you tell me what happened when . . .?
Can you give me a specific example of . . .?
I'd like you to tell me about what you did yesterday.
I wonder if you have ever experienced X.
What was your experience of X like?
How do you think X came about?
I'd like you to tell me about how X happened.
I'd like to know what you think about X.

Follow-up questions

Interviewers use follow-up questions to help participants to fill out their stories. You saw
some examples of follow-up questions in Box 5.2. You need to use both general and
specific follow-up questions during your interviews, and therefore your guide should
include them. Below we discuss two types of follow-up questions: general follow-ups
and focused follow-ups.

General follow-up questions encourage the participant to expand upon the subject
matter. In fact, such questions are sometimes called "expansion questions." Such questions
are useful, for instance, if the participant gives a brief and uninformative account. They are
also useful if a participant's response seems to point to something that is beyond the topics
in the interview guide and could offer important input to your researchable question.

Focused follow-up questions are more directed. In some cases, you might simply want
more concrete details – who, how, when, where, etc. In other cases, focused follow-up
questions serve to redirect the participant's attention toward matters that are specifically
of interest to the interviewer.

Box 5.4 Examples of general and focused follow-up questions

General follow-up questions
I would like you to tell me more about that.
What did that make you think about?
What did you do then?
I would like to hear if you know of more examples of that.
Could you walk me through that?

Focused follow-up questions
What did that mean to you?
How did you feel about that?
What did you think was going on?
Were you a student when that happened?

Box 5.4 gives some examples of general and focused follow-up questions.

You need to have at hand another kind of follow-up question for situations in which a participant offers statements that contradict one another or gives an account that you do not understand. For example, consider the statement, "No. No, it doesn't. But again, that's because of where I am in this particular practice. When I was in in-patient psych, it absolutely did, because you couldn't do psychoanalytic treatment" (taken from the excerpt drawn from an interview with a psychotherapist, cited earlier in this chapter). Responses like these are common in open-ended interviews, just as they are common in everyday conversation. When you need to follow up on contradictory or confusing answers, you should avoid seeming critical or accusatory. Put the onus for the confusion on yourself, not on the participant: "I'm not sure if I understood you right" or "Would you mind explaining that to me again so I can make sure I understand?"

Putting the items in sequence

After you have composed the interview items, you need to decide about the order in which they will be presented. The main considerations are what will make the participants feel most at ease and what will best aid their recall and reflections. The best order may not be the order that seems most logical. In what follows, we break the interview into a series of steps, beginning prior to the interview proper. Chapter 6 describes much the same sequence of steps, but from the standpoint of an interviewer actually conducting an interview; it augments the material here.

The first segment of the interview guide

In this first part of the interview, the goals are to establish the terms of the interview, to set a conversational tone, and to begin to build a relationship between yourself and the participant. You should begin the interview by introducing yourself and the project. You also need to attend to preliminary ethical requirements, such as obtaining informed consent. You may have already communicated the ground rules for your research to your participants when you invited them to participate. Nonetheless, you need to reiterate those ground rules before the interview proper begins. We have described these ground rules in detail in Chapter 4.

Once you have taken care of these requirements, you can turn to the interview proper. Often, the interview guide begins with questions that gather demographic information, such as age, occupation, and educational background. (Note, however, that researchers sometimes choose to place questions about demographic information at the end of the interview guide. The latter strategy is preferable if being asked for such information may offend or worry some participants.)

You might want to include in the interview guide a few warm-up questions – questions that are intended to build the relationship between yourself and the participant and to put the participant at ease. These questions may be only loosely related to your research project or not related at all. A warm-up conversation may be especially helpful if the topic of the interview is a difficult one or likely to be embarrassing or painful for the participant. For example, when Jeanne composed the guide for interviewing Sri Lankan teenagers who were in the hospital following a suicidal episode, she did not want to turn attention immediately to the episode. So the interview guide began with a warm-up question that focused attention away from the participant's behavior: "How have the doctors and nurses treated you while you've been here in the hospital?"

The main body of the interview guide

Here the focus turns to designing items to gather stories, experiences, and reflections from the participants. It is a good idea to open this section of the interview guide with items that are easy to answer. What do we mean by "easy to answer"? We mean two things. First, the items should not be cognitively demanding; participants should not have to stretch for an answer or admit that they have no answer. Second, the items should not concern sensitive or emotionally distressing topics. Beginning with "easy" items assures the participant that he or she is capable of taking part in the interview and able to provide the interviewer with what is needed. Moreover, easy questions give the participant and the interviewer a chance to feel their way gradually into a relationship. General orienting questions, which establish a foundation of information, are good for beginning the main body of the interview guide.

You should organize the items in the main body of the interview guide in such a way that they cluster into sections. Make sure that items that relate to a certain topic are kept in one cluster and not sprinkled at random through the interview guide. This will enable you to work through a topic fully and then move to another topic. You should consider how the items within a section are related to one another and then order them so conversation can flow from one to the next as naturally as possible.

Generally speaking, it is wise to place sensitive topics late in the interview guide. This gives the participant time to become comfortable with the interviewer and the interview situation before engaging with difficult material. However, it is wise not to place such topics at the very end. If you end the interview with a sensitive or difficult discussion, you run the risk that the difficult discussion will be the participant's most salient memory of the interview.

Ending the interview guide

The final portion of the interview guide is devoted to closing the interview. Sometimes researchers put requests for demographic information at the end of the interview. As we said before, if you think that the demographic information is sensitive, this is a good idea. That way, any embarrassment or ill will that these questions might generate will not negatively affect the interview. Some examples of sensitive information might be age, income, level of education, and sexual orientation.

There should be items in the closing segment that give participants an opportunity to reflect on what they have said and to add to it. For example, the guide might include questions such as "Is there anything that you would like to add?" or "Is there anything that I have left out?" or "Are there other things that you expected me to ask you about?"

The interview guide should conclude with a question that offers the participant the option of asking the interviewer about the study ("Is there anything that you would like to ask me about this study?") and by an item that reminds the interviewer to thank the participant.

Pretests and pilot tests

Preparing a set of interview items that comprise an interview guide is an iterative process. It takes several drafts to produce a set of items that elicit the kind of responses you want. It also takes several drafts to arrive at wording that your participants can understand, that sets the right context, and that does not unintentionally cause offense. It may also take several adjustments to arrive at the sequence of items that produces an easy flow of conversation.

As we said at the beginning the chapter, the care that you put into the preparation of the interview guide will ultimately pay off in the quality of the interview material. If you are a student, ask your research supervisor to work with you on revising or fine-tuning the interview guide. When you have a complete draft, you need to carry out two sets of trial interviews. These constitute the pretest and the pilot test. Pretesting the interview involves mock interviews with a few friends or colleagues who role-play an imaginary participant. The pretest interviews should conclude with a reverse debriefing session. That is, you need to ask your pseudo-participants to give you extensive feedback about the items in the interview and the interview process. The pilot test is a small set of interviews with people who are akin to your intended participants. Chapter 6 includes a discussion of how to carry out pretests and pilot tests.

6 Doing the interview

Research interviews are not ordinary conversations. The interviewer is there to learn something from the participant; therefore, the focus is on the participant, and the participant does most of the talking. The questions in the interview guide govern the content of the interview. The interviewer asks those questions and also manages the interaction throughout the conversation. The interviewer is responsible for ensuring that the conversation flows smoothly and that the participant feels comfortable.

In this chapter, you will learn the principles and practices for conducting face-to-face interviews. The chapter focuses on the interviewing craft: what experienced interviewers do in typical interview situations and what they can do when problems arise. We begin the chapter with an overview of the sequence of an interview. Then we describe techniques for guiding an interview and maintaining its structure. This is followed by a section about complicated situations that sometimes occur during interviews and how the interviewer can resolve them. We then discuss what it is like to be an interviewer in a research interview. We also discuss the relationship between interviewer and participant. Finally, we give advice on how to conduct pretests and pilot tests of your interview guide.

An overview of the research interview

This section is an overview of the interviewer's main activities during the successive phases of a research interview. The purpose is to give an overall sense of the flow of an interview; we will describe complications later.

The preliminaries

Most of the preliminary decisions will be made before you enter the interview situation. You will have made the decisions regarding the participants, which we described in Chapter 4 – for example, whom to interview, how to reach and recruit participants, and where to hold the interviews. You will also have composed the interview guide, as we described in Chapter 5.

There are a few more choices to make before you enter the interview situation. You need to consider how your appearance and demeanor – dress, makeup, hairstyle, and manner – will be "read" by the participants. Such things influence how participants think about you as the interviewer and about the interview questions. It is good practice to present a neutral appearance, that is, an appearance that does not lead participants to prejudge you in unwanted ways. It goes without saying that you should take care to present an appearance that is unlikely to be offensive to participants. Participants will differ, of course; therefore, no single type of appearance will always be the ideal. Your appearance should be low-key enough not to draw attention and interest away from the topics of the interview.

Even before the interview, participants always make inferences about who the interviewer is, what he or she already knows, what he or she might want to hear or expect to hear, and whether he or she can be trusted with certain kinds of information. This is inevitable, and it means that you will have to earn the confidence of each participant as you begin each interview.

Another important preliminary step is to make sure that the recording equipment is in working order. You should check this before each interview. You should also be sure that you have thorough knowledge of how to use the recording device.

Opening the interview

At the beginning of the interview, your task as the interviewer is to put the participant at ease and to create a good working relationship with him or her. In order to facilitate this, interviewers pay attention to the participant's language style and, if possible, adjust their language to that style. When the interviewer is seated with the participant, a number of things need to happen. The interviewer welcomes the participant and introduces herself or himself briefly. The interviewer asks the participant how he or she would like to be addressed in the interview. The interviewer then describes the project in enough detail that the participant can see the point of participating.

Then the interviewer informs the participant about the rules regarding privacy and anonymity, as well as about the right to withdraw from the study and to refrain from answering questions. Many interviewers prefer to read these rules and rights from a script, so that they can be sure that nothing is left out. The interviewer then presents the written informed consent form for the participant to read and sign. The interviewer keeps the signed copy. In some cases, the participant also gets a copy. In some locales, the interviewer is required to give the participant a written form listing these rules and rights, along with the contact information of the interviewer. Some institutions further require that researchers provide participants with information about how to lodge a formal complaint if they believe that their rights have been violated. The rules about these matters vary from place to place and time to time. You need to check the guidelines specific to your setting.

The interviewer then reminds the participant that the interview is to be recorded and turns on the recording equipment. In order to ensure that the interview will not be interrupted, both the interviewer and the participant should turn off their phones. The interview proper then begins with the interviewer giving a brief overview of the topics of the interview and the type of information the interviewer wants to learn from the participant. From here on, the interviewer follows the interview guide.

The main body of the interview

The "main body" of the interview refers to the main part, in which the interviewer collects practically all the relevant information and narratives. During this part of the interview, the interviewer is focused both on collecting information, narratives, and reflections and on keeping the interview conversation going smoothly. The latter includes keeping the participant engaged and at ease while responding to the requests and questions. Interviewers need to keep track of time and the movement through the interview guide, because it is their responsibility to ensure that the interview finishes on time. The main phase takes up most of the time in the interview. Most detailed advice for beginning interviewers deals with this phase. This book follows the same pattern: the advice sections of this chapter are devoted to learning how to carry out the main body of the interview.

Closing the interview

After having gone through all the interview items, the interviewer's task is to achieve a good conclusion to the interview. The conclusion should ideally feel as natural and unhurried as possible. However, because participants – and therefore interviews – are different, all interviews do not end in the same way. Often, interviews come to a natural conclusion: the conversation seems to be winding down and there is a joint sense of closure, of having achieved a common goal. In some cases this is not so, and then the interviewer has the responsibility to end the interview when the allotted time is up. This is why monitoring progress is important. At the end of the allotted time, ideally all the topics in the interview guide should have been covered.

Interviewers may want to hear the participant's thoughts about matters that the interview guide did not bring up. Therefore, it is common to end by saying something like "These are all the questions I have. Is there anything else you would like to tell me?" or "Is there something I have forgotten?" This will sometimes yield interesting information. On another tack, some interviewers will also be interested in the participant's reactions to being interviewed and will therefore ask "What was it like to be interviewed?" or "Did the interview turn out as you expected?"

Finally, the interviewer thanks the participant. At this point, participants may ask questions about anonymity and confidentiality or about who will have access to the interview material or how it will be used. The interviewer should be prepared to answer these questions.

As soon as possible after the interview has ended, the interviewer should make notes about what transpired – for instance, about noteworthy features of the content; about striking aspects of the interview relationship; about the participant's degree of engagement or expression of emotions; or about hesitations on certain issues. In the ideal case, the interviewer should transcribe the interview within a short time after the interview and finish each transcription before the next interview. Transcribing right away makes it easier to recall body language and nonverbal cues.

Practical techniques: typical situations

In this section we give practical advice on how to handle common situations in an interview. Sometimes more complicated situations arise, and we deal with those in the next section.

How to establish and maintain a conversational tone and atmosphere

An essential part of the craft of interviewing is the ability to adjust the interview to suit each participant. For example, interviewers must be able to adjust the conversational tone (for instance by using a more or less formal address). They must also be able to adjust the wording of items and questions. This is one point where there is a distinct difference between survey interviews and interviews in interpretative research. In surveys, the interviewer's task is to read the questions from a form so that they are phrased identically for all informants. In interpretative research, the interviewer instead aims to create equally good conditions for all participants to tell their stories and give their reflections. The interviewer needs to do this in order to achieve comparability of the interview material across participants. Because participants are different, this task will sometimes require the interviewer to phrase questions and requests differently for different participants.

Differences that you may need to take into account are participants' interest in or experience with a topic, their educational background, age, social class, language background, and speaking style. As the interviewer, you also need to consider your own characteristics. How similar to or different from a particular participant are you? Should these differences or similarities lead you to alter the conversational tone and phrasing of requests? When the interviewer shares some significant characteristic with a participant, this often makes conversation more relaxed. However, you cannot assume this will happen automatically; it is an open issue for each participant. As a general rule, the more similar you and a participant are with regard to salient characteristics, the more likely it is that your everyday language will be appropriate for the interview. When there are distinct discrepancies on salient social characteristics, you should try to adjust your language and approach to be congruent with the participant's experiences and habits of speaking.

To be able to adjust your language and speaking style to the participant's, you need to be familiar with the category of people you are studying. Therefore, you need to gain some preinterview experience of speaking to people in the group to be interviewed. Pilot interviews with people from this group are indispensable, for they enable you to learn how questions and requests "work." We discuss this in some detail in the section about pilot testing.

How to provide structure for the interview conversation

Interviews in interpretative research consist of one person – the interviewer – asking a second person – the participant – to tell about personal experiences and to reflect on those experiences. Because it is the interviewer who has set up the interview in order to learn certain things from the participant, the responsibility for providing a working structure for the conversation lies with the interviewer. The main responsibility is to complete the interview within the agreed-upon time frame. The participants have agreed to set aside a certain amount of time for the interview, and you should respect this agreement. This means that you need to keep track of time while the conversation is ongoing to make sure that there is time for all items. This need to time the interview appropriately is one of the reasons why pilot interviewing is indispensable: pilot testing gives you an opportunity to see which parts of the interview are likely to require the most time and to see whether the interview guide is too long. It also gives an indication of how long the interviews are likely to last. This in turn enables you to be realistic when setting times with participants.

Interviews in interpretative research are usually described as semi-structured. What this means in practice may become clear by comparing semi-structured interviews with fully structured interviews. In the latter type of interview, the questions have to be asked and answered in a preset order, and no deviations from this order are tolerated. In a semi-structured interview, the topics of the interview are similarly preset, and the interviewer is equally concerned to get answers to all questions and requests. But in a semi-structured interview, neither the questions nor the answers need to appear in the order that they are set out in the interview guide. When participants are allowed to talk freely and in their own words, their answers often expand beyond the specific questions that they were asked. Participants then often give answers to questions that appear later in the interview guide. In such instances, you should allow participants to complete their thoughts. You should make a note that later items in the interview guide have been dealt with and should be omitted. This leads us to the next subsection.

How to guide the content of the conversation

In interviews that allow participants to speak in their own words and to associate freely, the interviewer has to keep track of which parts of the interview guide have or have not been covered. If participants stay within the bounds of each interview item, keeping track of content is not difficult; the content of their narratives follows the interview guide. And often it will be obvious when the participant has exhausted a particular question. He or she may pause or ask the interviewer what comes next, showing that he or she is ready to go on. Then you can simply carry on with the next item in the guide. Novice interviewers sometimes worry that their movement from item to item will seem unnatural and stilted. In practice this is seldom a problem. The participant knows that the interview is not a "normal" conversation and expects the interviewer to steer the conversation. As long as the interviewer has begun the interview with a reasonably clear exposition of what the topics are to be and the participants are therefore not subjected to major surprises, the interviewer does not have to master the art of conversational smoothness.

If a participant's stories and associations stray to topics that fall far outside the interview guide, you need to guide the conversation back to the content of the interview guide. (Note that this is a different situation from the one we described in the previous subsection. In that case, a participant had answered a question that appeared later in the interview guide.)

How does one know when a participant's stories and associations have moved outside the scope of the interview? This is not always possible to determine with certainty while the interview is ongoing. It is, after all, part of interpretative research to expect new angles and perspectives on the original researchable questions and to expect such new angles to emerge from the participants' stories. This is a main reason why interpretative researchers encourage associations and reflections about the question under consideration.

Usually a participant will eventually show – by pausing or by asking about what is next on the agenda – that he or she has no more to say about a topic. Then you can go on to the next item in the guide. However, sometimes, for instance if time is running out, you may have to direct the participant back to the interview topic. You need to do this without implying that the excursion was outside of bounds. The reason for this is that many participants worry about "saying the wrong thing." You can turn attention back to the interview guide by saying something on the order: "This is a really interesting issue, and I'm sorry that we don't have time to talk about it now." Interview participants are as a rule keenly aware that they have agreed to provide the interviewer with experiences and stories related to the interviewer's interests; therefore, gentle directives will seldom be felt amiss.

How to be an active listener

Different participants require different degrees of direction on the part of the interviewer. Some participants only need a short description of an interview topic. However, most participants require more. We have already mentioned some ways that interviewers encourage participants to speak: adjusting their speaking style and language use to each participant, maintaining the structure of the interview, and guiding the content of the interview. In this section, we focus on the task of maintaining a conversation about a particular topic.

There are many things that experienced interviewers do and say to enable a participant to explore a topic thoroughly and with confidence. We use the term "active listening" for these things.

Active listening means being prepared to help participants explore a topic. This includes providing clarifications about the topic if necessary; asking the participant for clarifications when an account they have given is unclear or unfinished; and providing prompts when a participant hesitates. This kind of active listening is similar to what people are used to doing with one another in everyday conversations. Therefore, active listening usually comes fairly easily to new interviewers. You should remember, though, that interviews are one-sided: the interviewer has the full responsibility for determining when extra active listening is needed and for providing it.

An extra effort at active listening will be needed, for example, if a participant appears insecure when talking about a topic and uncertain whether what he or she has to tell is worth hearing. In our experience, this situation is less likely to occur when you have taken care to compose clear and easily comprehended interview questions. Further, this situation is less likely to occur if interviewers have adjusted their language style and choice of words. However, what if these measures are not sufficient and you are faced with a participant who expresses great uncertainty about his or her ability to contribute? You should take this uncertainty seriously and deal with it in a forthright manner. One strategy is to describe the topic again, taking special care to use words that are as close as possible to the participant's language style.

Extra efforts at active listening are also needed when the interviewer and the participant belong to subcultures or language communities that have little in common. In such cases, the interviewer is clearly an outsider with respect to matters that are relevant to the study. As we mentioned above, you should work hard before you start doing the interviews to prevent differences from creating difficulties. Learning about the subculture of the participants by talking to other members of the subculture is one way to minimize difficulties.

Being an active listener in an interview means taking a position of ignorance, in the sense of acknowledging that the participant is the expert on what he or she has to tell. The interviewer is by definition an outsider to the world of the participant. This is true, no matter how well informed the interviewer is and how similar the interviewer and the participant are.

Practical techniques: complicated situations

This section contains further explorations of the practicalities of interviewing, now with a focus on what to do when things do not go according to plan.

When a participant seems reluctant

Interview participants are of many different kinds, and they are not equally eager to take part in interviews or equally adept at being interviewed. Some people may not be "interview-conscious." That is, the idea of "being interviewed" may not be familiar to them. There are such people even though, in Western, high-income countries especially, many people have some experience of being interviewed. People who are not interview-conscious may have little idea what to expect in an interview. This is likely to be true for children, who will therefore need more introduction to an interview situation than adults. Others may have experience with interviews, but their experiences were bad ones. Yet other people may have idiosyncratic reasons for being reluctant to take part in an interview or even be generally skeptical of the value of research.

Any participant may become reluctant during the course of an interview if it deviates too much from what he or she had been led to expect. This is one reason why it is essential to give a clear presentation of the study, both at the time that you make initial contact with a potential participant and at the start of the interview. These presentations constitute an informal agreement between you and the participant about what kinds of topics will be broached in the interview. The interviewer should not go beyond what was mentioned. For instance, if personal topics, such as questions about sexual intimacy, have not been mentioned in the initial presentation, the interviewer should not bring them into the interview. If a participant is reluctant to continue with the interview, you might try to explain again the purpose of the study and the topics remaining to be discussed.

Sometimes a person who has seemed happy to cooperate chooses not to answer a particular question or questions. In such cases, the interviewer must not put undue pressure on the participant, regardless of the reason for the refusal. Often, such reluctance is driven by a fear that the information will not be kept confidential. In such cases, it may reassure the participant if you repeat the institutional rules under which the study is being done. If not, you can ask the participant to anonymize his or her stories while telling them, so that no real names are disclosed.

In rare cases, a participant may come to feel during the interview that he or she does not belong to the proper category of persons, or does not have enough knowledge of some specialized kind, to be taking part in the study. If this happens, it is wise to double-check the participant's background and other selection criteria: the participant may be right! If so, you should politely bring the interview to a close. However, if the participant does belong in the study, you will want to keep him or her in the study. It is then necessary to set aside the interview items for a while and put effort into encouraging the participant to carry on. It may be helpful to return to the introductory description of the study and elaborate on the portions that underscore why this person's participation is important to the study. In our experience, such efforts to encourage a reluctant participant will be aided by the interviewer's knowledge about and familiarity with the group that is being studied.

When a participant is taciturn and takes few initiatives to speak

Semi-structured interviewing rests on the assumption that people want to speak freely and fully. Many people do, but not all. Some people give short answers and seldom spontaneously enlarge on what is being talked about. Such speaking habits can make the interviewer feel like a failure or even become irritated with the participant. Note that this difficulty differs from the ones described just above. Now we are not talking primarily about reluctance or skepticism, but about variations in people's speaking habits and self-confidence in social situations.

With taciturn participants, you have to provide extra structure such as detailed questions and extra prompts for the interview to move forward. It will also help if you give extra encouragement. Such encouragement could take the form of acknowledgments like "I'm really interested in that" or "That connects to something I wanted to talk with you about." This is one of the interview situations where it pays off to have prepared yourself thoroughly so that you have at your fingertips a set of strategies for prompting and following up.

Interviews with uncommunicative participants should not be seen as failures, even though they take another form than most. They are usually characterized by shorter answers by the participant and more directive activities by the interviewer than the typical interview. However, the material they provide may be just as rich and illuminating as that from a self-propelled participant.

When a topic or question does not "work"

All interviewers have sometimes found themselves getting bland or noncommittal answers to a particular question or set of questions. The reasons for this can vary, and, therefore, what to do will also vary. It may be that the phrasing of a question is too general and therefore does not evoke the memories and associations that the researcher hopes to hear. Ideally, such problems should have been caught and resolved during the pilot stage. If they remain, you need to revise the interview guide.

If a question does not "work" for one particular participant, even though it has worked for the others, you should not drop the topic entirely. You should try rephrasing the question in several ways.

One reason why a topic or question might not "work" is that it concerns experiences that the participants you selected have not had. This situation is quite unusual. But it may happen if the researcher was mistaken about some aspect of the category from which participants were selected. In such a situation, you have two choices. First, you can drop the topic from the interview guide. Second, if the topic is central to your study, you need to recruit participants who are more suited to your study.

Another unusual reason why a question might not "work" is that the interviewer and the participant are unable to find common ground in relation to a topic. That is, the ways that they think about a particular topic are so divergent that they give incompatible meanings to the words they use. The best way to prevent such stalemates is to develop the topics in the interview guide into specific requests for concrete experiences and reflections. The discussion in Chapter 5 about composing interview questions will help you. Sometimes, however, the lack of common ground goes deeper than word choices. It may be that you and the participant have such different experiences that no common ground exists. That is, the topic – at least as you have conceived it – is not part of your participant's experience. In this case, you have to let go of a topic.

Uncomfortable or painful feelings in interviews

It is not unusual for participants to react emotionally to some interview questions. This is not surprising because many research projects deal with complicated or troubling issues. Usually the feelings are mild enough to allow the interview to continue. However, in rare cases a participant may become very distressed. What should you do then? This is a signal that the situation should – at least temporarily – no longer be seen as an interview. You should immediately stop recording and allow the participant space and time to recover. Some participants may want to spend time alone. Others may want to talk about what is troubling them. In that case, the conversation should not be considered part of the interview and should not be recorded or reported. If the participant in such a situation continues to find it difficult to continue the interview, you must be prepared to stop at once. Indeed, you should state clearly to the participant that he or she is always free to end the conversation. You may also offer to continue the interview at a later occasion.

You should remember that research interviews should not be turned into therapy-like sessions, not even briefly. To be prepared for the possibility that a research participant may signal the need or desire for professional counseling, interviewers often have on hand flyers or brochures about services or organizations that the participant can contact for help.

The interviewer in the interview

What is it *like* to be the interviewer in the kind of interviews we have described here? How does it feel? Is there an ideal interviewer persona that one should strive for? And does one have to act in ways that are very different from one's usual ways? We take a moment here to share some of our own and other researchers' reflections on these issues.

What it feels like to be the interviewer will vary because so many aspects of the interviewing situation can vary: how experienced the interviewer is, how interested the participant is, how different or similar the interviewer and the participant are on salient characteristics. More mundane aspects also come into play, such as whether the interviewer or the participant is tired or feeling ill, and what type of interview one is doing. Naturally, the interviewer's degree of experience has a great impact on how it feels to be in the interviewer role. As seasoned interviewers, we can testify to how different it felt to be doing our first interviews compared to our fiftieth. All interviewers remember their anxiety before and during their first interviews. And all of them made blunders in their early interviews (and even seasoned interviewers do not claim to be immune from blunders). But you can learn from mistakes by reflecting back after each interview and writing notes in your research journal, by inspecting the transcripts of your interviews, and by talking with supervisors or colleagues. As we hope to convey, interviewing is a craft, and like any craft, it requires time and work for interviewers to become proficient. Inevitably, the beginning steps feel wobbly and uncertain.

One aspect of interviewing in interpretative research that may feel particularly unsettling for the beginner is the fact that the interviewer gives the participants free rein to enlarge upon and associate to requests and to suggest topics. This, of course, means that the interviewer does not have total control over what topics are covered during the interview. Surprises happen! In our experience, though, after some initial worry over loss of control, beginners are able to relax. They come to view themselves as engaged with the participant as a partner in producing knowledge, not as the interrogator questioning a subject.

Because participants are different, there is no single interviewer persona that is always best. However, there are some attributes that should always be present:The interviewer keeps a mind-set that is as open and "not knowing" as possible.

Participants are the experts on their experiences, views, and practices, and the interviewer is there to listen to them. Interviewers are experts only in that they know about the research topic as a whole. If a participant asks the interviewer for an expert opinion on a topic, a wise interviewer remembers the purpose of the interview and avoids being drawn into giving advice. Moreover, as we discussed above, the interviewer does not step into the role of therapist.

Although the interviewer strives for a friendly tone, he or she does not strive to become a friend of the participants. Therefore, the interviewer does not make personal disclosures. If the participant asks a personal question, the interviewer will give a brief answer if the question is reasonably neutral (e.g., "What subjects do you teach?"). When faced with a charged personal question (e.g., "Did you and your husband disagree about whether or not to have children?"), the interviewer should politely remind the participant that the purpose of the interview is to discuss his or her experiences, not the experiences of the interviewer. A similar response is called for if the interviewer is asked for an opinion about a controversial issue. This should be done politely, that is, in a way that does not shame the participant for asking. The interviewer then steers the conversation back to the interview, for instance, by associating from what the person had just asked about.

A mark of interpretative interviews is that they are open and sometimes almost chatty. A good interviewer, however, keeps the focus of the interview on the material necessary to answer the researchable questions. And no more. Digging up as many sensational details as possible, dragging a secret out of a participant, or provoking extremes of emotion is not what good research interviewing is about.

The relationship between interviewer and participant in the interview

Is it possible to map out *one* ideal interviewer–participant relationship? No, of course not; people are too different for that. Even so, there are some significant characteristics of the relationship to keep in mind. We have described many of them in the preceding pages of this chapter; here we present some central ones in condensed form.

The interviewer has a good deal of power over what transpires in an interview: what topics are broached, what issues are followed up, and the general tone of the conversation. This power must be used in a responsible and beneficent way. On the other hand, participants also have power: they can answer questions in whatever way they want, they can refuse to answer a question, they can terminate the interview, and they can retract part or all of their answers. At the beginning of each interview, the interviewer makes sure that the participant knows that he or she has this power. However, the interviewer needs to consider how far to go to accommodate a demanding interviewee. This may be especially germane in interviews where there is a status differential between the interviewer and the participant. For instance, a young student interviewing a professional who is twenty or thirty years older may feel at a disadvantage because of the status difference. In our experience, most participants will not deliberately use their status to diminish or intimidate an interviewer. But some will. It behooves supervisors to help beginners prepare for such eventualities.

In interpretative research, the interviewer sees the relationship with the participant as a partnership for producing knowledge. This means that the interviewer does not regard the participant as a container of information from which to extract the right information. Rather, the interviewer and the participant are engaged together in exploring the participant's experiences and reflections. Though it is certainly true that the interviewer has decided what the interview is about, the idea of the interview as a partnership means being open to ideas and suggestions from the participant.

In one sense, the relationship between interviewer and participant begins even before the interview has begun. Participants will have thoughts about how the interviewer will behave, what the interviewer already knows, and what he or she might want to hear or expect to hear. The interviewer's appearance and demeanor during the first part of the interview can go a long way toward dispelling skepticism and, perhaps, confirming positive expectations.

The relationship in an interpretative interview requires the interviewer to avoid criticizing a participant who reveals actions and opinions that are less than honorable or distasteful to the interviewer. However, this does not stretch to expressing agreement with everything that is said. This distinction may be most easy to see if you envision interviewing a person whose political opinions were diametrically opposed to your own. However, it is necessary to avoid interjecting your own opinions in other situations as well. For example, participants often express strong opinions about people who are not present. If the interviewer affirms such opinions, this may make it difficult for the participant to revise such categorical statements later in the interview.

People often contradict themselves when being interviewed. They may express one opinion about an issue or a person in one part of the interview and another – perhaps opposite – opinion in another part. This should not be seen as wrong. Indeed, as you will see later, expressing contradictory or inconsistent points of view is exceedingly common in everyday conversations as well as interviews. Above all, the interviewer should not take a participant to task for expressing contradictions or inconsistencies. Instead, you should put the onus on yourself, by saying, for example, that you had missed something of what was said and that you want the participant to elaborate.

Interviewers need not be afraid of silences. Sometimes silences ensue because a participant needs time to reflect after being asked a question. Or, having given an answer or told a story, a participant may want to reflect further and needs some time to formulate his or her thoughts. Inexperienced interviewers often worry about not filling all interview time with talk and therefore risk rushing in too fast to clarify or elaborate or pose the next question. In doing so, they may miss opportunities for significant reflections by their participants.

Pilot-testing the interview guide and practicing the interview

When you have constructed a preliminary interview guide for your project and you have finished reading this chapter, you are ready to pilot-test your interview guide. Pilot testing accomplishes two goals, both crucial. First, it is a means to help you refine your interview guide or revise your researchable questions. Second, pilot testing gives you some experience in carrying out the interviews for your project. This experience enables you to become a more adept and more confident interviewer. In this section, we devote space to both these objectives.

Why should you pilot-test the interview guide?

There are several reasons for pilot testing. The main reason is to check the wording of your interview questions, the order of the questions, and the scope of the contents of the interview guide, and then to make changes as necessary.

You need to check the wording to make sure that your participants understand the questions in the way that you intend. Otherwise, the answers you get to your questions might not be relevant to your researchable questions. You should also check the wording to make sure that the language you have chosen is easily understandable. And you should check the wording to ensure that your choice of words does not inadvertently cause offense. What if you find that it is impossible to find a formulation that leads your pilot participants to give the kind of responses that you hoped? Perhaps this is a sign that something is amiss in your researchable questions, not in your interview question. You may need to revise or adjust them.

You also need to check whether the order of the items works, to make sure that there is a good flow from one topic to another during the interview. Also you need to check what is covered by the interview guide to make sure that the guide yields all the material you are interested in. You also should check that the items do not consistently lead participants into areas that are outside your research interest. And you also need to check that the guide does not contain too many questions for the time you have allotted for each interview.

Another reason to pilot-test interviews is more important for beginning interviewers than for those with long experience. Doing pilot interviews is a means of getting used to doing interviews; they afford a chance to get comfortable with responding to a variety of answers from participants, many of which will take an unexpected turn. However, both beginners and those who have long experience need to familiarize themselves with asking the particular questions and follow-ups that are specific to a project.

How to pretest, pilot-test, and revise the interview guide

There are two stages of testing the interview guide. The first stage is a pretest, which involves interviewing friends or colleagues who can give comments on which questions work and which ones do not work. The second stage is a pilot test, which uses the revised interview guide to interview "real" participants. We first consider pretests and then we turn to pilot tests.

For your pretest, you recruit a few friends or colleagues and ask them to role-play a participant in your study. You should carry out an interview with each of them, using the guide exactly as you expect to do with your real participants. Afterward, you and the pretest participant need to work through the interview guide together, question by question. For each question, you should ask the pretest participant to tell you what he and she thought the question meant, if the meaning of the question was unambiguous, and if it was possible to give an answer to it. For questions that posed problems, you and the pretest participant should explore what the problem seemed to be. Was the language too difficult to understand, or was the meaning ambiguous? Was the question itself too abstract or too general? Or did the question contain several questions that need to be separated?

After you have finished the pretest interviews, you should make whatever revisions of the interview guide seem necessary. The section in Chapter 5 on composing interview questions may help you with this.

You are then ready to pilot-test your revised interview guide with a small set of people drawn from the group of potential participants. The pilot interviews are real interviews in the sense that you should go through the entire process of selecting, recruiting, and contacting participants, as well as informing them about ethical rules and consent, as we have described it in Chapter 4 and in this chapter. You should record the pilot interviews so that you can review them afterward. You may find that there are problematic wordings and questions that come to light with real participants, but did not surface during the pretests with your friends. Furthermore, pilot interviews with real participants may lead you to realize that you failed to include certain important topics. If this happens, you need to make further revisions. If you find that your revised interview guide has worked well with the pilot participants, you can include their interviews in your study material.

How to use pretesting to develop your interviewing skills

An interview guide is an indispensable tool in research. Even the best guide, however, does not guarantee a good interview. As we have emphasized throughout this chapter, interviewing is a skill that one acquires through experience. Pretesting and pilot-testing your interview guide provide experiences that can help you develop your skills as an interviewer. While you are pretesting the interview guide, you should take a moment at the end of each interview to ask the pretest participant how she or he reacted to your way of asking questions and to your ways of following up questions and prompting for further answers. Note that this discussion is about *how* you asked and how the participant experienced your manner or style; it is not about the wording of your questions and items. By reflecting with your pretest participants on how you asked questions, you have the chance to get insights about yourself as an interviewer that you could not obtain without their feedback. Sometimes you may also get valuable suggestions for alternative ways of approaching a topic.

Another way to develop your skill as an interviewer is to observe yourself. One opportunity for such observation occurs when you take a moment at the end of an interview to contemplate what happened during that interview. Make notes of what worked and what did not work. Listening to the recordings of pilot interviews gives you another opportunity to observe your style and manner. Listening to interviews enables you to scrutinize your ways of asking and prompting, your pace, the volume of your voice and the rapidity of your speech, and so on during the interview. Things to observe include whether the tone of your talk seems conducive to a relaxed interview situation, whether you tend to put undue pressure on the participant, whether you fill in silences too quickly, and whether you tend to move forward too quickly after certain questions. You should also note whether you have a tendency to agree or commiserate overtly with a participant; this practice, though it may seem like an easy way to build rapport, cuts off chances for the participant to express other feelings or develop her own thoughts.

This kind of post-interview reflection on and scrutiny of your interviewing skills should not be restricted to pilot interviews, nor is it useful exclusively for beginners. In fact, all interviewers, regardless of their experience and skill, can benefit from this kind of reflexivity.

7 Preparing for analysis

Up to this point in the research process, the researcher's main tasks have been to plan the project, construct researchable questions, keep notes in the research journal, and do interviews. We now move toward the next phase: doing the analyses. Before you enter the analysis phase, there are several steps you need to take. You need to transcribe your interview material. You also need to consider what to do in order to ensure that your project will meet high standards of quality. You also need to orient yourself to the possible frameworks and procedures for analysis of interview material. We discuss these things in this chapter, turning first to transcription.

Transcribing your interviews

The analyses in interpretative research involve close work with people's words. To do this work, neither listening to an interview recording nor working from notes is sufficient. You must work with a written transcription that is a verbatim (i.e., word-for-word) record of what was said. Transcribing interviews is arduous and time-consuming. You listen to a small segment of talk (often just a phrase or two or a part of a sentence), then stop the playback device, and type what you have heard. You should keep the segments that you play short, otherwise you will either miss words or inadvertently add your own words to what you have heard. Because people often do not speak clearly, you are likely to have to listen to some segments more than once in order to be sure that you have heard and recorded correctly. Transcribing semi-structured interviews is a slow process. It may take between three and five hours to transcribe an hour of talk; depending on the level of detail that you want to capture in the transcription, it may take even longer. You need to plan your time accordingly.

When to transcribe

If at all possible, you should transcribe each interview right after you complete it. At that point, you will still remember what happened in the interview and may be able to complement the spoken words with notes about body language, tone of voice, and so on, as well as with your own reflections during the interview. Furthermore, if you transcribe an interview soon after you have conducted it, you may find it easier to recontact a participant if you find that some critical element is missing or is unclear.

What to transcribe

In a semi-structured interview, what the interviewer says is as much a part of the interview process as what the participant says. Consequently, an interview transcript should include both the words of the participant and the words of the interviewer. Further, a transcript for interpretative analysis should not be merely a reproduction of the bare words that were spoken. It should be a comprehensive record of the interview conversation: that is, it should include indicators of meaning such as punctuation marks and indications of pauses, interruptions, and so forth in the conversation. You should take equal care to punctuate the transcript to accord with what you hear on the recording as you take to get the words right. Indeed, getting the words right and getting the punctuation right serve the same purpose: to capture as exactly as possible the talk of the participant and the interviewer.

Because there are no punctuation marks in people's talk, some researchers have argued that punctuating interview text as one transcribes it distorts the "real" flow of talk. Some even argue that adding punctuation during transcription imposes the transcriber's meaning-making onto the participant's talk. These arguments are both problematic. First, they assume that a transcriber could produce a transcript that does *not* impose something of the transcriber's interpretation of what went on in the interview. This assumption is false. Any method of transcribing involves interpretation in one way or another (Ochs, 1979). Second, a transcription that is written completely without punctuation will be very difficult for a reader to interpret. In some instances, it may even be impossible to read passages in which commas or periods have been omitted. It is, after all, not unusual that moving a comma or a period from one word to another may change the meaning of a statement. Therefore, punctuation is crucial when representing spoken talk in written form. And the only way to gain any sense of where punctuation marks should be entered into a transcript is to listen to the recording of the interview.

Apart from punctuation, the transcript should also record such elements as hesitations, interruptions, laughter, and other nonverbal elements such as "hemming and hawing." A notation system for recording these elements on a transcript is appended to this chapter. Notation systems like that one are common in interpretative research. However, several systems for notating transcripts exist, some of them capturing more fine-grained detail than the system in the appendix, and some capturing less. (See Howitt, 2010, pp. 139–161, and Taylor, 2001, pp. 29–38, for discussions about levels of detail. See Jefferson, 2004, for a highly detailed system.)

How much detail to note down on the transcript depends on the analytical procedures the researcher intends to use. Even the least detailed transcribing is time-consuming, and the most detailed transcribing systems are many times more time-consuming. Therefore, researchers should not expend effort to include more details in their transcriptions than they need for their analyses. Transcriptions that use the notation system in the appendix are sufficient to carry out most of the analyses described in Chapters 8–11. Sometimes you may benefit from listening again to a segment of an interview as you are doing the analysis. That also gives you the opportunity to add more details to the transcription of that segment.

There are some instances when one might not transcribe everything that is said during an interview. For example, were someone else to intrude into the interview conversation, it likely would not be necessary to record that conversation. Also, occasionally, a participant may stray so far from the topic that you can be certain that what is said is not relevant to the analysis. In addition, a participant may ask you to omit certain statements from the record. Whenever you omit material from the transcript, you should note on the transcript the point at which material has been omitted.

Completing the transcription

When you have finished each transcript, you need to create a backup copy of the transcript file. You should store the original and the copy in different places. The file names should not reveal the identity of the participants.

You should also make sure to preserve the audio-recordings of all interviews. They should not be erased. You may need to consult the audio-recording in order to clarify a segment of the transcript or you may wish to re-listen to a particular portion of an interview. Moreover, if you decide to pursue analyses such as those described in Chapters 10 and 11, you may find it helpful to augment your reading of the transcript by listening to the audio-recording. Note that you need to protect the anonymity and the confidentiality of the audio-recordings. The labels on the audio-recordings should not indicate the participants' names.

Ethical issues in transcribing

Participants' anonymity and confidentiality must always be safeguarded in research. First, you have to make it impossible for others to connect the interview material with a specific individual or group of individuals. Therefore, participants' names must never appear in an interview transcript. Moreover, the transcript must not be labeled with the participant's name. Most researchers use pseudonyms or numbers in lieu of names. In addition to removing participants' names, all names of people or places that are mentioned in the interview must be removed and replaced either with pseudonyms or with bracketed descriptions such as [father], [boyfriend], [hometown], or [college]. This will protect the identity of other individuals who are mentioned in the interview. (The exception is references to public figures, such as politicians, TV or film stars, and so on.) Second, you must guard the transcripts from unauthorized access. Third, you must not disclose to others what you hear in interviews.

Sometimes protecting participants' privacy and anonymity requires more than removing or disguising their names. In some cases, an unusual combination of identifiers (e.g., an unusual occupation, the specific locale studied, and the individual's sexual orientation) may make a participant readily identifiable to some people. Overly detailed descriptions of participants' appearance or demeanor may jeopardize the participant's anonymity. Even though they serve to vivify your report text, such descriptors should be limited to those that are in some way pertinent to the research topic. If you are unsure about whether you have adequately safeguarded anonymity, check this with a knowledgeable member of the participant's community.

Storing the interviews and transcripts. You should store both the audio-recordings and the transcripts in a safe place. In many locales, ethical regulations governing confidentiality prohibit researchers from storing transcriptions or audio files in online data storage utilities (such as Dropbox). There are also different rules in different countries about the length of time researchers are obliged to store their material. To be sure to handle these issues correctly, you need to check your local regulations.

Original language in transcripts and publishing language

It is not unusual for researchers to use one language to do their interviews and use another language when they publish articles or reports about the analyses of those interviews. If at all possible, the analyses of the interviews should be made using transcripts in the original language. After the analyses are finished, the excerpts to be used in publications in another language can be translated into that language. Some journals offer the possibility of including the original-language excerpts as supplemental material on the journal's website.

Our use of transcripts in this book

In the next four chapters you will see several pieces of interview text that we use to illustrate analytic procedures. These pieces are not "raw" transcriptions of the sort produced by the procedures we have described here and in the appendix. Instead, the pieces of talk that we present in these chapters are in the form they had when the studies were published. This means that many of the details of the original transcripts have been removed in order to make it easier for readers to follow. We have chosen this form of presentation because reading raw transcripts is often difficult for beginners, and we did not want such difficulties to draw attention from the analytical procedures. In the excerpts that appear in the following chapters, we use pseudonyms for all participants.

Ensuring that your project meets a high standard

Before you move into the analysis phase, you should take time to consider how your research will be evaluated and how you can ensure that your project meets a high standard. Evaluation of research is an issue that has been much discussed among scholars. There are many diverging opinions about what are the appropriate criteria to apply when assessing the merits and shortcomings of a project. There are no universal criteria and no assessment procedures that are adequate for judging all types of research.

The purpose of evaluating research is to assess how well a study can answer the researchable question(s) that the researcher set out to address. This is what should be evaluated. Research that is done within different theoretical and epistemological frameworks inevitably addresses different types of researchable questions. These differences make it impossible to transpose evaluative criteria from one framework to another without doing violence to important qualities of the project that is being evaluated. For instance, you may have learned in a methods course in your discipline how to evaluate research that uses quantitative methods. There you encountered concepts such as reliability, validity, and replicability. These concepts, and the principles behind them, were developed within theoretical and epistemological frameworks that differ substantially from those of interpretative research. The concepts and the procedures connected with them are therefore not adequate for evaluating interpretative research. It stands to reason that each type of research should be evaluated by criteria and procedures that are consonant with its theoretical and epistemological framework.

Because there are different theoretical frameworks for different types of interpretative research, interpretative researchers have diverging ideas about what the most important criteria and procedures are for evaluating research. Consequently, many procedures and criteria have been proposed for evaluating interpretative research. To decide which criteria and procedures for evaluation you should apply to a specific project, you need to take into account both the epistemological commitments of the researcher and the purposes of the project. Furthermore, while you are first learning about interpretative research, it makes good sense to adopt the most commonly used and accepted practices for evaluating interpretative research in the setting where you are doing your research. They are likely to serve you as good initial guides.

On the most general level, the criterion for judging a study as adequate or not is whether or not the study can answer the researchable question(s). This general criterion is of course too nonspecific to be put to practical use. It can, however, be broken into a number of specific criteria that pertain to different phases of the research process. We have reviewed a large number of such criteria for different types of interpretative research, together with procedures that are commonly used to assess projects on these criteria. We then "translated" the assessment procedures into a list of actions. Taking these actions while you are carrying out your project can ensure that it will be of a high standard. Note that this list does not cover every assessment procedure that has been proposed by interpretative researchers. However, the list is likely to be acceptable to most interpretative researchers.

The list is as follows:

> The researcher needs to document the specific elements of the method and design and describe the reasons for choosing one procedure rather than another. Notes on these matters should be written in such detail that you can draw on them to

demonstrate the adequacy of your work when you write the report of your study. The research journal, which we described in Chapter 3, is the place where these actions and steps should be documented in detail.

The researcher needs to keep a set of notes that document the steps and details of each analysis, along with a summary or overview of the results of that analysis. As you will see in the chapters that follow, we recommend that you write separate documents pertaining to the analyses for each researchable question.

In composing reports about interpretative research projects, the researcher should do the following:

The researcher should clearly describe the knowledge interests and researchable questions in the project. The researcher should also describe what kind of knowledge was sought. For instance: Was the research aimed to produce specific or general knowledge?

The researcher should carefully locate the study with respect to the relevant research literature, including empirical studies of the topic and theoretical works relating to the topic.

The researcher should adequately document the reasons for choosing the methods for selecting participants, collecting material, and analyzing the material.

The researcher should thoroughly document the research process. The report should describe the steps in the process of the project in as much detail as necessary for the readers to understand what has been done.

The researcher should describe the setting of the study and the group(s) of participants in detail. This detail should be sufficient to allow readers to draw conclusions about how the results of the study might be applicable beyond its specific context.

The researcher should present results and substantiate conclusions with examples or illustrations taken from the research material.

The researcher should clearly demonstrate how the conclusions that are drawn during the analysis are tied to the interview material. The analyses must offer interpretations of the interview material, not just paraphrases.

The presentation of the study's results should be coherent. That is, results should not be presented as unrelated items, but rather as integrated parts of a larger narrative. This narrative should also synthesize the results of the present study with previous theory and findings.

Turning to analysis

In the chapters that follow, we offer a number of analytical frameworks and analytical procedures typical of interpretative research. An analytical framework directs a researcher's gaze to particular aspects of people's talk. The analytical procedures associated with that framework are structured procedures for examining those aspects of people's talk. In the chapters that follow, we describe frameworks and procedures alongside each other. In our experience, this is the best way to learn about how to analyze people's talk. Because of the intimate connection between frameworks and analytical procedures, the analysis chapters have a double mission. They invite readers into a specific framework for thinking about people's talk and they instruct readers in analytical procedures that are congruent with that framework.

The analytical frameworks that we describe in the next four chapters are all commensurate with the general theoretical framework that we have presented in this book. That is, they hold people to be actively engaged in making meaning of the events in their lives, they see people as always located in social context, and they hold that the sociocultural context sets the frame for personal meaning-making.

Although the analytical frameworks we describe all are nested within the larger theoretical framework, they nonetheless differ from one another. As you will see, they involve different analytical procedures. In addition, they orient researchers toward thinking about people's talk in different ways. This latter difference is fundamental, and researchers need to pay close attention to it when they decide about which analytical frameworks and procedures to adopt.

Before researchers commit to one framework, it is important that they learn about several other frameworks. Above all, they need to have knowledge of the variety of ways of thinking about people's talk that different analytical frameworks offer. These different ways of thinking about people's talk inevitably direct a researcher's gaze toward different aspects of the talk, leading the researcher to ask different types of questions about the interview material. In order to make informed choices about the analysis, researchers need to know not only about each framework, but also about procedures that each framework entails.

We chose the analytical frameworks and procedures presented in this book because they satisfied four criteria. First, the analytical frameworks are compatible with the overall theoretical framework for the book. Second, the analytical procedures can be made transparent enough that someone outside a research project can follow the researcher's inferences and conclusions. Third, both the analytical procedures and the findings of the analyses can be communicated in comprehensible and persuasive ways to a readership without specialized training in interpretative methods. Fourth, because this is a book for readers who are not seasoned interpretative researchers, the analytical procedures had to be clear and specific enough that a beginner would be able to use them.

Overview of the analysis chapters

When we present the analytical frameworks and procedures in the chapters that follow, our aim is to provide readers with sufficient knowledge to do their own analyses. To achieve this aim, we give step-by-step descriptions of analytical procedures, coupled with illustrations of analyses from studies we know well. We hope this will allow readers to experience what it is like to do analysis. To keep the descriptions reasonably easy to follow, we do not describe the many variants of the procedures that have been devised. Let us now turn to a brief overview of the four types of analysis.

Chapter 8: Finding meanings in people's talk

In daily life, people continually make sense of their activities, experiences, and relationships: that is, they imbue them with meaning. In this chapter, we describe analyses that address how people make sense of the events or experiences that are your focus of study. The analyses answer questions such as "What is the picture of the world that the participants have communicated to the interviewer?" The analyses enable you to examine the range of experiences that your participants have had that are germane to the phenomenon and how those experiences shape their thinking about it. The analytical procedures in Chapter 8 focus mainly on what it is participants have elected to talk about in response to the interviewer's queries. This includes recollections, reflections, and points of view that participants brought forward. The analyses focus on discerning typical patterns of meanings as well as variations in meaning among the participants in your study. The chapter also describes analytic procedures that enable researchers to draw contrasts between groups of people. Using these procedures can help researchers learn about the different pictures of the world and patterned meanings that differently situated people, such as people in different social locations or from different cultural backgrounds, might have.

Chapter 9: Analyzing stories in interviews

Like conversations in everyday life, interviews are replete with stories. People tell their life experiences as stories. They also use stories to illustrate a point or strengthen an argument. Interviewers ask participants for stories in order to concretize abstractions. Stories embed participants' inferences about cause and effect. They also embed evaluative perspectives: they reveal the moral visions and ethical sense of the teller. Directly or indirectly, stories lay blame on some parties and exonerate others. Chapter 9 introduces an analytical framework drawn from theories of narrative analysis. It also introduces a set of procedures that enables researchers to select out and examine a small set of elements of stories. Participants tell their own stories in their own ways, but, nonetheless, they must rely on the store of meanings in their interpretive communities. Therefore, the analyses can help you address researchable questions about elements of meaning-making that are shared within the interpretive communities of which the participants are members.

Chapter 10: Analyzing talk-as-action

Research interviews are occasions for gathering material pertinent to your researchable questions. But they are also occasions when people interact. That is, when people talk to each other, whether in interviews or in other conversations, they always do more with their talk than asking questions and giving answers. Their talk also works to persuade, dissuade, or impress their listeners; speakers are in turn affected by their listeners' responses. Chapter 10 introduces an analytical framework for studying the kinds of interaction work that a piece of talk may do in a conversation. The framework combines a focus on the details of talk with attention both to the immediate interpersonal context and to the larger societal conditions. The chapter describes a number of conversational features that often appear when there are important issues at stake in a conversation. Studying these features in the flow of conversation can often add important dimensions to a researcher's answers to a researchable question.

Chapter 11: Analyzing for implicit cultural meanings

When people make sense of their activities, experiences, and relationships, they always do so in the light of a culturally shared background of meanings. Chapter 11 is devoted to analytical frameworks and procedures that attend particularly closely to such culturally shared backgrounds. The chapter introduces an analytical framework that centers on *implicit cultural meanings*. This term denotes the meanings that are shared within an interpretive community and that serve to enable or constrain the possibilities for individual meaning-making. To analyze for implicit cultural meanings, researchers consider the interview conversations they study in the light of the larger sociocultural context. The chapter presents two analytical procedures, one for analysis of material from a set of interviews and one for analysis of individual narratives.

Appendix: Notation system for transcribing interview talk

Speakers: use consistent terms for the interviewer and the participant (e.g., **I:** for interviewer; **P:** or the pseudonym for participant).

Turns: begin each new conversational turn (i.e., change of speaker) on a new line.

Pauses: if there is a noticeable pause in the flow of speech, note this in the text with square brackets, that is, [pause]. If you want to include more detail concerning such pauses, use [.] for a short pause and [..] for a long pause.

Laughing, coughing, etc.: note when a person laughs or coughs by inserting [laughter] or [coughing]. If both persons laugh, use separate lines to note this for each of them.

Nonverbal sounds such as supportive "hemming and hawing" by the listener/interviewer that do not interrupt the speaker's utterance: note such supportive nonverbal sounds inside the text of the speaker, by inserting, for instance, [hm].

Inaudible speech: use [inaudible] to mark places where you cannot hear what a speaker is saying. If you think you can guess what they were saying, put your guess in parentheses in the text.

Loudly spoken words: write loudly spoken words in capitals.

Especially quietly spoken words: put degree symbols around very quietly spoken words: °—°.

Unfinished words: if a speaker does not finish a word, mark this by adding a dash at the end of the word fragment. For example, morn-.

Extra information offered by the transcribing researcher: enter within double brackets ((...)) any information about tone of voice, body language, etc., that may add to what is being said.

Reported speech: speakers sometimes quote other persons, in what sounds like a verbatim account of what the other person said. Mark such reported speech by single quotes: 'words'.

Overlaps/interruptions: if the speakers speak simultaneously, note this at the start of the overlap by [overlap]. If one speaker clearly overrides another speaker, note this by [interrupts].

If you leave out a portion of the interview, for instance, in a research report, mark this with a forward slash: /.

8 Finding meanings in people's talk

In semi-structured interviews, participants talk about various topics, stories, and reflections that are pertinent to the researchable questions that a researcher has. Such interviews yield a substantial amount of loosely structured material, much of which pertains in some way or another to the researchable questions. In this chapter, we take up analyses that address questions such as: What sense do people make in regard to the phenomenon that you are studying? What are the experiences that shape those meanings? These questions flow directly from the general theoretical framework of this book. The analyses we describe are based in a view of people as actively engaged in making meaning of the events in their lives and as located in social contexts that set the frames for personal meaning-making.

The analyses that you will learn in this chapter enable you to examine the patterns of shared meanings and variations that typify the group of people whom you interviewed. You could say that these analyses concern the "what" (or rather the "whats") of people's talk. In other words, what reflections, points of view, experiences, and emotions do people typically bring forward to give meaning to their experiences? Larry Davidson, for example, whose work you read about in Chapter 2, studied the ways that people with severe mental illnesses understood their experiences of frequent re-hospitalization. Sometimes meanings are explicit and directly stated. In such cases, they are fairly easy to identify. But people also make meaning in less explicit ways. You may therefore have to attend to oblique references, to participants' use of "loaded" words or phrases, and perhaps to asides or tangential remarks made during the interview. You may also need to consider what goes unspoken – that is, what is simply not part of the local talk about an issue.

This chapter explains analytical procedures for getting at people's meanings. The procedures involve interpretation: that is, they go beyond a mechanical search for specific words or phrases. They require you to exercise your judgment about the meaning of what participants say. They also require you to draw on your expertise regarding the cultural background of your participants.

We begin at the point when you have completed transcribing your interviews. We work through systematic procedures for identifying shared meanings and end with a discussion of how to synthesize the shared meanings. As with every systematic analysis of rich talk, the analysis begins with narrowing your focus of attention. There are two steps involved in doing this. The first is to formulate a set of sub-questions that amplify and specify your researchable questions. The second step is to select the portions of the interview material that pertain to each of the sub-questions. This process of narrowing your focus enables you to do systematic and close analyses of the interview material. We now turn to these two steps.

Formulating sub-questions for analysis

The researchable questions that a researcher formulates at the beginning of a project are usually quite broad. You saw some examples of researchable questions in Chapter 2. To move forward with your analysis, you have to "unpack" such broad questions. In other words, you need to compile a set of specific sub-questions that can shed light on the researchable questions. Having such a set of sub-questions enables you to work systematically with the interview transcripts. Together, the questions and sub-questions provide a plan for the analysis. In what follows, we describe three steps that will help you to devise sub-questions.

A first step is to review the notes you made in your research journal. Reading these notes may yield ideas about possible sub-questions to explore. The second is to review the interview guide. When you designed the interview guide, you composed interview items that would help participants to talk about experiences, issues, and ideas that were germane to your researchable questions. You are likely to find that some of the items can be used directly as sub-questions to organize the analysis. Other items may point the way to formulating sub-questions. The third step is to read and reread the interview material. You need to read with an eye to the portions of the material that are relevant to your researchable questions. In the process of reading, you will begin to see that the relevant material is relevant *in different ways* to a researchable question and *to different aspects* of it. As you come to recognize these differences, you will see possible sub-questions and issues to explore in the entire corpus of interview material. Furthermore, as you reread the interviews, you are likely to see passages in which participants expressed perspectives, experiences, and ways of thinking that you did not foresee. These passages can point the way to additional sub-questions. What you learn from the interview material may even lead you to rethink your researchable questions: you might revise a question or add a new question.

We give two examples below. The first one is from a project carried out by Karin Sannetorp (2012). Reading the interview material led Karin to formulate an additional sub-question for analysis. The second example is taken from a project carried out by Matthew Oransky (Oransky and Marecek [2009]). Matt's reading of his interview material led him to expand the focus of his original knowledge interest and thence to develop an additional researchable question.

Karin's project

Karin's general knowledge interest centered on how nonheterosexual persons (specifically, gay men and lesbians) in Sweden experienced being "out" or closeted in their workplaces. One of the researchable questions that Karin had formulated was:

In what situations and settings and in what ways is nonheterosexuality made salient in the workplace?

Using the procedures that we outlined above, Karin devised sub-questions and issues that were pertinent to this researchable question. Initially she identified four sub-questions, which she named as follows. (Incidentally, you may note that some of the sub-questions are not literally questions, but rather issues and areas to investigate. This is very common.)

Should nonheterosexuals see themselves as an information resource in the workplace?
Heterosexual people's ignorance
The disappearance of homo jokes
Negative encounters

As Karin contemplated the interview material in its totality, she realized that many of the participants spoke at length about aspects of their appearance (such as their style of clothing, their hairstyles, their body build, and their gait). They described how others repeatedly "read" (or failed to read) these aspects as gay or lesbian or straight. The matter of appearance and dress styles had not been included in Karin's original researchable questions. Nor was it something that she had queried participants about in her interviews. However, participants' talk about these matters was certainly relevant to her general interest in being out or being closeted at work. Moreover, these matters were frequent topics of conversation in the interviews. Therefore, Karin added *Clothing and appearance* to her list of sub-questions. As Karin did, if you see that many of your participants spoke about a topic, and if that topic is relevant to your researchable question, you should add it to your list of sub-questions.

Matt's project

Matt's general knowledge interest concerned middle-class American boys in early adolescence and their ideas about and practices of masculinity. In this project, Matt initially had two researchable questions:

What are boys' ideas about proper masculinity?
What are boys' ideas about and experiences of caring, emotional support, and intimacy in close friendships with other boys?

Matt's initial list of sub-questions and issues contained the following:

When can boys disclose hurt feelings and vulnerabilities to other boys?
Activities and practices in boy–boy friendships and male peer groups
How do boys respond to a (male) friend's distress?
What are boys' ideas about "manly" self-presentations?
The continual presence of homophobic and sexist insults in boys' interactions

As Matt carried out the interviews, he saw that many boys described themselves as habitually engaged in "mocking," "teasing," and "making fun" of others, and some described themselves and other boys as "pushing around," "shoving," and "picking on" boys who seemed weak and vulnerable. The boys said that the intention behind such actions was "toughening up" a boy who was "weak" or preventing a boy from "breaking down" in public, crying in public, or otherwise "going down the tubes." This unexpected aspect of boys' emotional lives was certainly germane to Matt's general knowledge interest, though it was not incorporated in any of his researchable questions. Therefore he formulated an additional researchable question: *What is entailed in the mutual upkeep of masculinity?*

As with Matt and Karin, you may sometimes find that participants introduce a new perspective regarding your general knowledge interest. This is neither uncommon nor surprising. When you listen closely to people's talk about their experiences, you inevitably encounter stories about a topic and ways of thinking that you did not expect. As a meaning-centered researcher, your goal is to capture how your participants make sense of a phenomenon, whether in ways that you anticipated or in ways that you did not. Therefore, you need to be open to – and take note of – *all* the meanings in the interviews that are relevant to your knowledge interest. If the participants' accounts veer in directions that you had not foreseen, you should adjust the researchable questions or the sub-questions to accommodate those accounts.

How many sub-questions should you formulate? There is no single correct number. Karin initially identified four sub-questions. She added one as she gained familiarity with the interview material, giving her a total of five. Matt had developed four sub-questions from his first researchable question and added others. As you will see below, carrying out the analysis of each sub-question adequately requires a considerable amount of work. Therefore, having more than eight sub-questions is likely to prove unworkable.

Selecting excerpts and assembling a file for each sub-question

The next step is to prepare the interview material for analysis. You need to reduce this material to a manageable amount by selecting the portions of each interview that pertain to each sub-question. Taking the sub-questions one at a time, you need to reread the interviews in order to select the segments that pertain to each sub-question. You should excerpt these segments and place them into files, with a separate file for each sub-question. These files are called the sub-question files.

To assemble sub-question files, consider each sub-question in turn, and create a separate word processor file for each. To compile a sub-question file, read each interview with that sub-question in mind. Copy every segment that seems relevant to the sub-question and paste it into the file. Some segments of an interview may seem relevant to more than one sub-question. When that is so, you should copy the segment into every sub-question file for which it is relevant. Note as well that substantial segments of an interview may not be relevant to any of the sub-questions; these segments will not be entered in any of the sub-question files.

You should continue to work on the sub-question files until you have completed the entire set.

How much material should be included in an excerpt?

An excerpt cannot be just a single word; in fact, most will be longer than a single sentence. The amount of material in an excerpt should be ample enough to retain important parts of the context within which it was spoken. That is, it should give a sense of what was going on in the interview interaction and how the participant understood the topic that was being discussed. Most often, the excerpt should include the interviewer's question or comment immediately prior to the segment of the participant's talk. This additional material is needed in order for you to make an accurate judgment about the meaning that the participant intended. You also need to include information that identifies the participant as well as the location in the interview from which the excerpt was drawn. In the examples below, this identifying information is in the lower right-hand corner.

Examples of excerpts

Example 1

KARIN: How do you usually tell someone that you are a lesbian?
LISA: It isn't that I introduce myself and then tell them what my sexual orientation is, it's more that you have a conversation, just this everyday thing, like 'My girlfriend Linnea and I are going away to do this or that.' It sort of comes naturally.

[Lisa, pg. 8, lines 9–13]

Example 2

MATT: Can you think of the type of thing that someone might do to get called a fag?
BRIAN: Actually, personality has a lot to do with it. And interest, like if you have a particular – I don't know – athletic sport – or you swim – that's one that people get called fag for. It normally has to do with just personal preferences of activity [.] swimming, um, let's see – tennis. For some kids, it's not – If you're good in any sport, almost never. But then there's also, umm, it depends on some [.] um, certain types of [.] like photography. Kids who are in photography class. What else? Art. Drama is another one. You know, if you are really into drama. There was a kid last year named Martin who [.] was an amazing composer – like a really natural genius on the piano and people made fun of him, called him a fag.

[Brian, page 6, lines 20–28]

Deciding if an interview segment is relevant to a sub-question

Selecting pieces of talk for the sub-question files requires interpretation. It is not a matter of mechanically searching for particular words or phrases. When you decide to select a piece of talk for a particular sub-question file, you make a judgment about whether or not the *meaning* of what was said pertains in some way to the sub-question. How much interpretation is involved in such a judgment varies. In some instances, the talk clearly bears on the sub-question, and hence it requires little interpretative effort to connect the excerpt to the sub-question. In other instances, the connection may be indirect, and therefore it may be more difficult to decide whether or not the piece of talk is relevant to the sub-question.

Let us first consider instances in which it is easy to judge whether or not a piece of talk is relevant to a sub-question. One such instance is the situation in which the interviewer's question is directly related to the sub-question and the participant gives a direct reply. Consider this example from Karin's research:

KARIN: Can you give me an example of a time at work when you were made especially conscious of your sexual orientation?

LISA: [after saying that IVF is a frequent topic of conversation over coffee in her work place] Because of the IVF debate ["The IVF debate" refers to the public debate about lesbians' rights to assisted fertilization, which was ongoing at the time] and all the problems that can arise for men and women, this has been a theme in many conversations. And then, of course, I am always the answer book [laughs]. [a short piece of talk left out] And I have a colleague who came to me and said that she had thought a lot about me now that that question had been brought to her notice. So she came to me because I am homosexual, and she had questions about it. [a short piece of talk left out] And she thinks it's unfair and was upset, though I wasn't. [a short piece of talk left out] Then I explained how I think about it.

This excerpt clearly is pertinent to the sub-question *Should non-heterosexuals see themselves as an information resource in the workplace?* Similarly, it is easy to judge that a spontaneous statement (i.e., one that is not a direct response to a question about a topic) pertains to a sub-question if the participant uses words that are explicitly related to the sub-question. The following example from Karin's study is such an instance. Per, a gay man, commented as follows:

PER: I think there are many heterosexuals who do not realize that as a gay man, one always has to think about – for instance, if you are traveling as a couple – where you travel to. You can't travel to just any country. But you have to sort of check which hotels you can stay in and such things, so that you can stay there without being harassed. That there are those things that you have to check on all the time. And they probably don't think about that, because, I mean – why should they?

Per's comment is directly pertinent to the sub-question *Heterosexual people's ignorance*. In many instances, however, it may require more judgment (i.e., interpretation) to see the connection between a piece of talk in an interview and a sub-question. Participants often say things that are relevant to a sub-question without using the expressions or terms that the researcher uses or expects. In some cases, participants may say something that is obliquely or tangentially related to the sub-question even though they are speaking about a different topic. It may not be apparent that the talk is relevant to the sub-question on the first reading. Sometimes, it may become apparent only after reading further in the interview. Or the relevance of a piece of talk may become apparent only as you read other interviews and encounter similar examples. For example, one of the boys whom Matt interviewed gave this description in response to Matt's question *"What are the kinds of things you and your friends talk about?"*

GEORGE: Um, we talk about either how, like, fat our [female] teachers are or how, like, stupid they were in class today. "Oh, I don't want to go to English class today because all they do is moan about, like, Native Americans, not, like yeah, whatever." And then, we either talk about stuff like that or we talk, like, uh, in a way that, like, will be accepted. We translate "How was your day?" [said in a singsong voice] to, like, "Oh yeah, how was your day with your English teacher?" [said in a sneering, sarcastic tone of voice] or something like that. We always complain about how stupid [the daily community meeting] was.

Although George was answering Matt's question about what he and his friends talked about, George's answer also introduced many other ideas. He placed himself and his male friends in clear opposition to girls and women. His choice of words gratuitously disparaged women and girls ("fat," "stupid," "moan about," his singsong imitation). Further, George took pains to distance himself from (and make fun of) concerns for social justice, everyday courtesy, and community-building activities – practices that he identified as feminine. Ultimately, Matt included this excerpt in two sub-question files: *Activities and practices in male friendships and peer groups* and *What are boys' ideas about "manly" self-presentation?*

We close with some general guidelines for selecting excerpts for the sub-question files. First and most important, you should not select excerpts for the sub-question files on the basis of haphazard hunches or vague feelings. The interpretations you make are not matters of intuition. They are judgments that are grounded in your knowledge of the sub-questions, the theoretical background you have accumulated through your reading of the research literature, and the practical knowledge you have gained through carrying out the interviews and through your close reading of those interviews.

Second, if you are in doubt about whether a piece of talk is relevant to a sub-question, you should include it in the sub-question file. In other words, it is better to err on the side of over-inclusion when you are entering excerpts into files. If an excerpt does not actually pertain to the sub-question, this will become apparent in the later phases of the analysis and you can set it aside. If you omit it, however, it is likely that it will be overlooked.

Third, double-check your work! After you have read through all the interviews, you will have a sharper eye for relevant material than you had when you began. In particular, you will have a greater appreciation of the variety of ways that people talk about a sub-question. Therefore, when you have finished your first reading and excerpting, you should read the interviews again, this time to pick up material that you might have missed. In this second reading, it is likely that you will add more excerpts to your files.

Annotating the excerpts

At this stage, you have a set of sub-question files, each containing a number of excerpts from the interviews. The next task is to write brief notes about each excerpt. You can write the notes either in the margin next to the excerpt or just below the excerpt. These notes serve as thumbnail sketches of the contents of excerpts, which will enable you to do a rough sorting of the excerpts into clusters of repeating ideas.

To compose the notes, you should work with one sub-question file at a time. Begin by reading the whole file from beginning to end. Think about the meanings of what you are reading as you read the file. This reading will give you a first impression of the variety of meanings in the interviews and perhaps a sense of which meanings occur frequently. Write your impressions and reflections in your research journal. At this point your ideas can be speculative. It is useful to check them against the literature, which may contain additional ideas. After this preparatory phase, you are ready to make notes about the excerpts.

In the excerpting phase, your task was to decide whether or not a piece of talk had anything to do with a sub-question. When composing the notes for each excerpt, your task is to judge *how* that piece of talk relates to the sub-question. The notes you make are succinct records of these judgments. There is nothing mysterious about such judgments; people make similar judgments (i.e., interpretations) repeatedly in daily life. That is, people often judge *in what way* something is relevant to something else.

Each note should describe in brief how the excerpt relates to the sub-question. You may have several things to note about this. You might briefly describe the substance of the excerpt or comment on how the material in the excerpt relates to the sub-question. You might also jot down a telling turn of phrase or word. There are no hard and fast rules about what to say. The more thoroughly you have thought about your researchable questions as you were developing the sub-questions, the easier it will be to decide what to note about an excerpt. The notes you make are meant for your eyes only, and therefore you can use any shorthand and abbreviations that are efficient. Below, we give several examples of notes about excerpts.

Examples of notes about excerpts

The first two excerpts are taken from Eva's study of Nordic heterosexual couples sharing housework and childcare, which you read about in Chapter 2. Eva's researchable question was *How do couples go about distributing housework between themselves?*

Excerpt 1: This excerpt relates to the sub-question concerning how the couples think their distribution works.

INTERVIEWER: Do you think that your distribution of housework works well as it is now?
MALIN: Yes, I think it works.
MATTIAS: Yes, it works. It would be sort of difficult to do it in a different way, too.
MALIN: Yes, if you have to begin shopping and cooking, we may get dinner at six, perhaps. Then they [the children] – they would have to go to their activities without food – it's the most practical to do it this way, yes.

Notes to Excerpt 1
- (i) they say that their distribution works well
- (ii) they say that it would be impossible to change it
- (iii) they say that it is the most practical distribution; thus it is a compromise

Excerpt 2: The excerpt relates to the sub-question of whether the partners have similar or different standards of cleanliness.

INTERVIEWER: If you compare your situation with that of your female friends and their husbands . . .

MALIN: There are sort of friends who have had less luck and more luck perhaps. I don't know. Of course one could sometimes wish that one got a little more help at home, and things like that, but it's – because Mattias works so much more, it has to be this way. And because I – my threshold is lower than his for what needs to be done [in the household] and such things – so I guess I have myself to blame if I think I get too little help.

Notes to Excerpt 2
- (i) she wants to get him to "help" her more [presumably meaning it is her household]
- (ii) she has a "lower threshold" for when cleaning is needed than he has
- (iii) it's her own fault if he helps her too little in the household
- (iv) demands of the husband's work mean that it must be this way

Excerpt 3: This excerpt is from Karin's study about gay men and lesbians being out or closeted in the workplace. The excerpt relates to the sub-question *Should non-heterosexuals see themselves as an information resource in the workplace?*

KARIN: Can you give me an example of a time at work when you were made especially conscious of your sexual orientation?

LISA: Because of the IVF debate and all the problems that can arise for men and women, this has been a theme in many conversations. And then, of course, I am always the answer book [laughs]. [a short piece of talk left out] And I have a colleague who came to me and said that she had thought a lot about me now that that question had been brought to her notice. So she came to me because I am homosexual, and had questions about it. [a short piece of talk left out] And she thinks it's unfair and was upset though I wasn't. [a short piece of talk left out] Then I explained how I think about it.

Notes to Excerpt 3
- (i) this excerpt relates to recent legal changes in Sweden that were much debated at the time
- (ii) Lisa has become the "homosexuality expert" in her workplace. Is she happy about this or not?
- (iii) Lisa gives an instance of educating her colleagues about lesbians' experiences

Excerpt 4: This is the excerpt from Matt's study of boys' everyday practices of masculinity. The notes pertain to the sub-question *What are boys' requirements for "manly" self-presentations?*

MATT: What kinds of things do you and your friends talk about?

GEORGE: Um, we talk about either how, like, fat our [female] teachers are or how, like, stupid they were in class today. "Oh, I don't want to go to English class today because all they do is moan about, like, Native Americans, not, like yeah, whatever." And then, we either talk about stuff like that or we talk, like, uh, in a way that, like, will be accepted. We translate "How was your day?" [said in a singsong voice] to, like, "Oh yeah, how was your day with your English teacher?" [said in a negative, sarcastic tone of voice] or something like that. We always complain about how stupid [the daily community meeting] was.

Notes to Excerpt 4
 (i) boys' talk among themselves is chronically sarcastic, hostile, and hypercritical
 (ii) the actions of girls and women are targeted for complaint, criticism, and mockery in boys' talk
(iii) "translating" ordinary talk to trash-talk is something a boy must do to be "accepted" by other boys

As you can see from these examples, notes can capture several types of information. Some notes are summaries of what participants say. Some notes record a condensed version of a story about the participant's experience (e.g., note iii about Lisa's statement). A note might also record what the participant gives as a cause or a reason for his or her action or for someone else's action (e.g., note iii for Excerpt 4, regarding George's statement about "translating" ordinary talk in order to be "accepted"). A note might also point to what strikes you as a revealing word choice or phrase. For example, note i for Excerpt 2 flags Malin's use of the word "help" to describe her husband's contribution to housework. That note also includes the researcher's tentative inference about this choice of words.

You need not worry about making too many notes about an excerpt. When you search across the excerpts for similarities, the more notes you have made about each excerpt, the more likely you are to spot common elements.

As you work through a file of excerpts, you will probably notice that some elements (whether points of view, arguments, causal statements, word choices, or implications) occur many times. For example, Matt found that quite a few boys said that hostile talk, crude language, and a tough demeanor were ways of acting that garnered acceptance by other boys. Similarly, Eva found several instances in which the language that a couple used clearly implied that the responsibility for household work belonged to the wife. You should take careful note of such similarities. Use the same terms or phrases every time you make note of them.

Note that your goal is to identify similar ideas in the set of excerpts. The goal is *not* to "divide up" all the material in the interviews into clumps. The goal is to collect the portions of the interviews that are relevant to your sub-questions. You should expect that a sizeable portion of every interview will not be relevant to any sub-question and therefore not excerpted.

Composing notes is easier if you are familiar with what other researchers have reported. Reviewing earlier work may provide you with some preliminary ideas about what is important in the interviews. Reading the literature may also provide you with some terms and expressions for your notes. However, using the work of other researchers for inspiration is only a first step. Do not stop there! If you did, it is likely that you would merely be reiterating what is already known. Furthermore, you would almost certainly overlook important, and perhaps unexpected, aspects of your participants' meanings. You should be open to, and take note of, *all* meanings that your participants expressed, not just the meanings that have already been described by other researchers.

Being open to the unexpected is not easy. When participants have said something that is outside your frame of reference, you are in fact at a loss for words, that is, at a loss for terms and categories needed to grasp the meaning of what was said. The participant has used a frame of reference different from yours and another set of words. Your task is to apprehend the participant's frame of reference. To accomplish this, you must try to understand what your participants said without relying on terms that are familiar to you.

In urging you to be open to the unexpected, we do not imply that it is possible to approach a piece of talk in a way that is completely free of your own ideas, experiences, and social location. Such a "view from nowhere" is impossible to attain. Nonetheless, we believe that researchers can become at least somewhat aware of the preconceptions that constrain their understanding. Such awareness may enable them to sidestep those preconceptions, and by doing so become open to alternative meanings.

How might you be able to sidestep your preconceptions? You could begin by making notes about "odd" sentences or "out of place" expressions in an excerpt. Noticing, and then making a note about what you noticed, may be what is needed for an "undescribable" piece of talk to become describable. The note could say something like "This piece of talk doesn't fit with the rest of what is said." Then you can think carefully about *what* it is that does not fit. Perhaps you will find that it is the substance of what is said that does not fit. Or perhaps you will find that the speaker's angle of vision is different from yours. You can then try to describe what it is that seems to make the excerpt relevant to the sub-question or issue. Another possibility is simply to make a note that quotes or paraphrases the participant's words. You can then think carefully about what the participant might have been using those words to mean at that point in the interview. As you continue to work through the excerpts, your increasing familiarity with the material may make statements that had once seemed mystifying intelligible to you.

Finding repeating ideas and composing integrative summaries and labels

When your notes for all the sub-question files are complete, you are ready to look for commonalities among the excerpts. The commonalities of interest are those that pertain to the sub-question. These commonalities, or repeating ideas, can be discerned in the excerpts either because the participant has stated the idea outright or because the idea is alluded to in the talk. Identifying the repeating ideas in the excerpt file involves systematically comparing the excerpts in each sub-question file and making groups of those that are similar.

To begin with, you make a rough set of groups, using the notes you have just written. The notes serve as an index of the excerpted material. Like an index, the totality of the notes comprises a type of description of what you have decided that the excerpts tell about the sub-questions. However, as you can imagine, a statement in this form is difficult to comprehend. The statement needs to be condensed into a summary that can be readily understood. To create such a summary, you need to search through the notes for repeating ideas among the excerpts in a sub-question file. This involves system-atically comparing the notes to one another. As you begin to find notes that are similar, you should copy the notes and the excerpts that they pertain to into another file, with a different file for each repeating idea. There will likely be some excerpts that do not go into any repeating idea file. Set them aside.

When you have two or three excerpts in a repeating idea file, write a brief *integrative summary* that captures the repeating idea that unifies those excerpts. We give some examples below. Writing this summary gives you a record of your thinking, but that is not all this writing does. It also compels you to clarify your thoughts. As you continue to add more excerpts to a repeating idea file, you will revise and refine the integrative summary.

Once you have read through the notes for all the sub-question files, sorted the excerpts into the repeating idea files, and written integrative descriptions for the files, you are ready for the second step: verifying your work. This requires that you turn from your notes to the full excerpts. Read each excerpt against the integrative summary with two questions in mind:

> *Does this piece of talk truly fit in the file in which I thought it did?*
> *Does the integrative summary adequately capture the meaning of this excerpt?*

You are likely to find some instances in which the answer to one or both of these questions is "No." The most common reason for this is that the note did not capture the full or exact meaning of the excerpt. When you scrutinize the excerpt in full, you will be able to see what adjustments you need to make. We next describe some of these adjustments.

One possibility is that on close reading and with hindsight, you see that an excerpt does not belong in the file in which you had placed it. In this case, you simply need to remove it. Another possibility is that an excerpt differs from the other excerpts in the file but contains an idea or meaning that you see as important to the repeating idea. If you want to keep it in the repeating idea file, you need to devise a more complex integrative summary, one that captures the heterogeneity you now are able to see. A third possibility is that upon reading the full set of excerpts in a file, you see many "misfits." In that case you probably need to divide up the items in the file. How do you decide whether to expand and reformulate the integrative summary or to split the file into two smaller files? The decision to expand or split the file rests on your judgment as to whether the distinction you identified among the excerpts sheds light on your researchable question.

You should also decide upon a tentative *descriptive label* for each repeating idea file. This label (which some writers call a "theme") should point to what unifies the excerpts in the file. The descriptive labels will come into use later when you start to synthesize the pieces of analysis. The descriptive labels ought to be full statements or short sentences; a single word or phrase is rarely sufficiently informative.

Below, we provide several examples of collections of excerpts that speak to a repeating idea, along with integrative summaries of the excerpts and tentative descriptive labels.

Example 1

Karin's research concerned being "out" or closeted as a nonheterosexual person in the workplace. One of Karin's sub-questions was *What is it like to come out in the work place?* As she read the notes for the excerpts in the sub-question file, she sorted four of the excerpts into a repeating idea file:

> *Excerpt 1*: It [coming out] becomes pretty natural – such that they ask what you do and, yes, who you live with.
>
> *Excerpt 2*: It isn't that I introduce myself and then tell them what my sexual orientation is, it's more that you have a conversation, just this everyday thing, like "My girlfriend Linnea and I are going away to do this or that." It sort of comes naturally.
>
> *Excerpt 3*: I guess it was usually the case that I talked about him [his partner] in some way: "Peter and I are going away for the weekend."
>
> *Excerpt 4*: You get into it in a pretty natural way. If you're in a relationship, and especially if you live with someone, then in everyday conversations . . .
>
> *Integrative summary*: For many of the participants, coming out to their workplace colleagues was most readily accomplished as part of a conversation in which they could "naturally" insert the information that they were in a steady relationship with a partner of the same sex.
>
> *Descriptive label*: Mentioning your partner in everyday conversation is a natural way to reveal that you are gay or lesbian.

Example 2

One of the researchable questions in Eva's study about heterosexual couples (which you read about in Chapter 2) concerned how wives and husbands shared housework and childcare. The following excerpts show some participants' talk about the way they decided upon the distribution of family responsibilities.

Excerpt 1

INTERVIEWER: What is it that makes Bengt a good person to live with and have a family with?

BRITTA: [..]

INTERVIEWER: Yes, these are difficult questions.

BRITTA: Well, but it is as I say, that I think we complement each other. We sort of flow so well one into the other that [.] Bengt is good at being with the kids at their sports activities but I take care of the rest. And also he has been very tolerant about my working hours and such things. You know, it's me who has been trying to get us to have as few childcare hours as possible. So, really, I just have to ask him. He has never objected. He is docile, you could say. [.] We *never* have any conflicts, as a matter of fact.

Excerpt 2

INTERVIEWER: If you compare your situation with that of your female friends and their husbands . . .

MALIN: There are, sort of, friends who have had less luck and more luck, perhaps. I don't know. Of course one could sometimes wish that one got a little more help at home, and things like that, but it's – because Mattias works so much more it has to be this way.

Excerpt 3

MALIN: And because I [.] my threshold is lower than his for what needs to be done [in the household] and such things [.] so I guess I have myself to blame if I think I get too little help.

Integrative summary: The words these women use to characterize their husband's contribution to household work imply that housework and childcare are the wife's responsibility. In these women's eyes, their husband's contribution seems to be a matter of his choosing. Further, the women imply that there is no current negotiation about tasks. And if a woman's standards of cleanliness are higher than her husband's, the extra work falls on her.

Descriptive label: Housework and childcare are the wife's responsibility and the husband's contributions are contingent on the demands of his workplace or his desires.

Example 3

Matt's researchable question centered on boys' friendships and on how boys' practices of masculinity shaped their relationships with one another. One of his sub-questions concerned boys' disclosure of hurt feelings and vulnerabilities to other boys. In the interviews, Matt asked boys directly what they had said (or would say) to a friend who was upset or who was facing a problem. Some of the responses to this question were as follows:

Excerpt 1: Well, I wouldn't really put my hand on his shoulder and say "It's all right." I would just say, like, "C'mon let's go eat a pizza or something" or "C'mon, let's go play a video game." And I always let him choose what he wants to do.

Excerpt 2: [I would say] "Why would you cry about that?" You know, "It's no big deal."

Excerpt 3: Basically, I haven't had anybody come to me with something *really* wrong. They just have a problem and then we end up just joking about it or something. And it seems like they just forget about it or something like that.

Excerpt 4: Um, you know, like, "Just get over it." Like, "It's over with." Like,"'Just take it like a man." "Move on."

Integrative summary: Boys often reported downplaying or minimizing a (male) friend's problems. This could be done directly. It could also be done indirectly by joking about a problem or making light of a friend's fears or distracting an upset friend with pizza or a video game. Urging a boy to "take it like a man," or "suck it up" implies that the manly way to deal with difficulties is to ignore the problems and not allow distress to be visible.

Descriptive label: "Just take it like a man": Boys urge one another to disregard distressing problems and events.

Things to keep in mind while you select excerpts and make summaries

1. *Focus on repeating ideas that are analytically useful.* As you read through the interviews, you may see many repeating ideas in the interview material. Which are the ones that are important? A first principle is to keep the sub-question and the researchable question in mind. Does a particular repeating idea tell you something about the sub-question? Does it shed light on the researchable question? If it does not, then you should set it aside, at least provisionally.

2. *Keep the participants' talk at the center of attention.* In interpretative research, the goal is to learn about the ways that participants make sense of the phenomenon you are studying. The purpose of identifying repeating ideas is to capture the shared ways that participants see the world. The integrative summaries and labels should describe the meanings that the participants' spoken accounts share. The summaries and labels should not put forward your guesses about unconscious motives or other causes of participants' talk.

   An example of what to avoid might clarify this point. It comes from a project about the experiences of women in clandestine relationships with married men. Instead of identifying the repeating ideas in the participants' own talk, the researcher put forward a number of speculations about the unconscious motivations behind such relationships and their possible origin in early childhood experiences. These explanations did not capture the *participants' meanings* or ways of understanding their experiences. No participant spoke of her childhood and, of course, no participant talked about her unconscious motives.

3. *Do not use* a priori *constructs to sort your excerpts.* Taking constructs from the literature to serve as repeating ideas is contrary to the goal of interpretative research, as well as to the principle of keeping participants' talk at the center of attention. An example of such mistaken borrowing comes from a novice researcher who studied high school students who had experienced serious athletic injuries. Before the researcher began to sort the interview material, he had settled on the construct "emotion-focused coping," which was drawn from the psychological literature on stress and coping. He then combed the interviews for examples of what seemed to be "emotion-focused coping." Not surprisingly, he found many such examples. But, also

not surprisingly, this construct was too global and too generic to capture the specific ideas and experiences of the participants. As a result, this strategy produced little knowledge that was new and useful.

4. *Avoid repeating ideas with more than one meaning.* When you decide whether a repeating idea is specific enough to be meaningful, you should begin by making sure that the repeating idea has only a single meaning. Again, an example of what to avoid may be helpful. The example comes from a project concerned with the experiences of late adolescent men who were engaged in commercial sex. In the interviews, the young men described aspects of their lifestyle, which the researcher subsequently grouped into repeating idea files. One repeating idea file was labeled "Independence." That file included excerpts that contained ideas such as the following: selling sex is a way to get money for living expenses; the earnings from sex work can be used for luxury items, like expensive watches and jewelry; customers often provided the worker with recreational drugs or alcohol; it is OK to steal customers' money and valuables. The researcher viewed all these as indications of the interviewees' independence. In our view, these diverse statements are too diverse to be unified into a single repeating idea. The four statements refer to at least two ideas that are quite different. One idea pertains to economic self-sufficiency. The other concerns the willful flouting of laws and societal norms.

5. *Be prepared to move back and forth among the different stages of analysis.* For instance, you can expect to read through, and perhaps also reinterpret, the excerpted material several times. As you think more deeply about what the participants have said, you are likely to refine the sub-questions, the repeating ideas, the integrative summaries, and the descriptive labels for each repeating idea. The participants' talk should always be at the center of your thinking and writing, for your task is to learn about the ways the participants give meaning to the phenomenon you are studying.

Exploring differences between people

Your participants were purposively chosen to embody key similarities. Perhaps these similarities involved a combination of demographic characteristics such as age, sex category, sexual orientation, and nationality. Or you may have purposively selected participants who shared a specific life experience, such as an illness condition, an unintended out-of-wedlock pregnancy, or forced migration. But although you found some commonalities among the participants, it is likely that these ideas were not universal in the group. Often there will be one repeating idea that is brought forward by several participants, and others that are brought forward by one or more smaller sub-groups.

It could be that the different repeating ideas are based in some important variations among the participants. You might therefore consider whether there are any characteristics or experiences that are common to a subgroup of participants who have offered the same repeating idea. For example, in his project, Matt found three boys who were highly critical of the masculinity standards put forward by the majority of boys. Exploring these three boys' backgrounds and interests enabled Matt to identify certain experiences that they had in common. The point was not to make causal claims. Instead, this examination provided a fuller picture of the range of available meanings and of the way that individual meaning-making may be tied to social identities, relational contexts, or cultural locations.

Researchers often have researchable questions that involve comparing different groups of people. For example, they ask whether people from different cultural groups or social backgrounds "make sense" of particular phenomena in similar or different ways. Recall the research examples you read about in Chapters 1 and 2. In Chapter 1, you read about the project by Andrea Dottolo and Abigail Stewart; they compared the recollections of Black Americans and White Americans regarding experiences during which racial identity and race relations were made salient. In Chapter 2, you read about research by Peggy Miller and her colleagues that drew comparisons between mothers in the USA and mothers (or grandmothers) in Taiwan regarding their ideas about raising young children.

Another kind of difference between people focuses on different experiences. Sharon Gold-Steinberg (1994), for example, interviewed women in the USA about their recollections of having an abortion. Gold-Steinberg gathered interviews with women who had had an abortion during the time when abortion was being legalized (a process that took place unevenly across the fifty states of the USA). Even though all the abortions had been carried out within a very narrow time frame, some women's abortions were legal and carried out in *bona fide* medical settings, but other women's abortions were illegal and clandestine. In her analysis, Gold-Steinberg contrasted the stories, memories, and emotions of the two groups of women.

To compare different groups of people, you need to make separate excerpt files for each group and then analyze them separately. This enables you to see how the two groups differ, as well as what is similar among participants in each category.

A word of warning. Comparing participants who are members of categories that you have selected *a priori* might distract your attention from other ways of grouping participants that may be relevant to your researchable questions. *A priori* categories may also focus your analytic attention on differences between people in the different categories, and unduly focus it away from possible (perhaps unexpected) similarities among those different categories. Eva's study of Nordic couples affords an example. The research literature claimed that couples from middle-class and professional backgrounds would share housework and childcare more equally than working-class couples. Such findings have been long established in family research. However, when Eva divided the couples in her study into groups based on socioeconomic status, she found no differences between these groups in their sharing of housework. This led Eva to ask whether some other differences might be implicated in patterns of housework sharing. She went on to explore such questions in later parts of her study.

Drawing your analyses together

When you have completed the integrative summaries for all your excerpt files, it is time to draw together what you have learned and organize it into a coherent whole. This calls for a synthesis of the integrative summaries you have assembled, one that orders them and examines the interrelationships among them. There is no single formula for how to do this. We give some suggestions below.

When you begin to synthesize, you can use your integrative summaries as your material and the researchable questions and sub-questions as the anchors. That is, the sub-questions can serve as an initial organizing framework for your synthesis. For each sub-question, look at each integrative summary that has been associated with it and ask: "Does this integrative summary help me address this particular sub-question?" If you conclude that it does, you should write a description of the way (or ways) it speaks to the sub-question. After scrutinizing all the integrative summaries in this way, you may see similarities and differences between them that will help you to further synthesize your findings.

The initial organizing framework that your sub-questions provide is likely to take into account most of the integrative summaries. However, there will probably be some that do not fit into that initial framework. Such summaries should be set to the side temporarily. Do not discard them! What should you do with them? First, you should see them as indications that your initial framework may not in fact have "caught" everything of importance that your participants were telling you about your knowledge interest. Second, you should see these "leftover" summaries as potential pointers to unexpected patterns in your material. Remember that one of the strengths of interpretative research is that you can take the participants' words and meanings as the starting point of the analysis.

In order to synthesize your findings further, you should also search for ways that the integrative summaries link with one another. Is there a bridging idea or unifying construct that ties some of them together? Matt's project offers an example. Matt saw a thread running through three summaries. The summaries concerned (1) boys' concerns about appearing weak or vulnerable; (2) boys' reports of urging one another to "suck it up and take it like a man"; and (3) boys' fears that "breaking down" would earn them jeers like "pussy" or "fag." All of them, Matt saw, were linked by the bridging idea that masculinity is a joint project that demands continual upkeep. Karin's project offers another example. She drew a link between these integrative summaries: (1) nonheterosexual people shoulder the task of furnishing information about gay and lesbian life to their co-workers; and (2) nonheterosexual people strive to "come out" in ways that do not disturb their co-workers' equanimity. Karin conceived a bridging idea that united these two summaries: the idea that in the workplace, nonheterosexual people assume the responsibility for smoothing relations with their heterosexual colleagues and for maintaining their comfort.

As you are drawing your analyses together, it is a good idea to focus your attention on the aspects of your work that speak to current issues in the research literature. Further, it is especially useful to attend to the findings that amend or take issue with existing research findings or conventional wisdom. The purpose of research is to add new knowledge, not to reiterate what is already known or self-evident.

The work of synthesizing and integrating your results continues as you begin to formulate the written report of your work. Therefore, Chapter 12 picks up the further steps of synthesizing the results. There we address not only relating sets of results to one another, but, more importantly, tying the results to the researchable questions.

9 Analyzing stories in interviews

Stories are a means by which people impose order on their experiences. They are, therefore, a key element of how people make sense of themselves and their worlds. The narrative theorist David Herman (2009) offered a succinct definition of "story": "stories are accounts of what happened to particular people and of what it was like for them to experience what happened – in particular circumstances and with specific consequences. Narrative, in other words, is a basic human strategy for coming to terms with time, process, and change" (p. 2).

By looking closely at the way that people make stories out of their experiences, researchers can glimpse the worldviews and understandings that are the building blocks of their stories. Although people's stories about their experiences are personal, their meanings are put in place through joint action, that is, in transactions with others. Meanings are both local (i.e., negotiated within local interpretive communities such as family and friends) and cultural (i.e., shared by broader interpretive communities). As people tell their stories, they may make many kinds of meanings. For example, they may attribute motives to themselves and others, they may ascribe or imply causality, and they may convey, directly or indirectly, their evaluative perspective regarding the events in the story.

The analyses we describe in this chapter have goals similar to the goals of the analyses you learned about in Chapter 8. As in Chapter 8, the analyses aim to identify regularities or shared features in a set of interviews. Such analyses can help you answer researchable questions about your participants' meaning-making in relation to the interpretive communities of which they are part. Although different persons do not tell the "same" story, people who are members of the same interpretive community build their personal stories from similar building blocks of meaning.

How can analyzing stories told by your research participants help you address your researchable questions? It is unlikely that your initial researchable questions would be "What stories about the phenomenon did the participants tell in the interviews?" However, it is likely that a close look at the stories that participants tell in interviews will tell you things that would be difficult to find out in other ways. For example, stories open a window onto people's evaluative perspectives. What you learn by analyzing stories can add to the body of knowledge that you are accumulating about the researchable questions.

The analyses that you will learn about in this chapter are part of the field of narrative study. This is a broad and multidisciplinary field, which engages sociolinguists, linguistic anthropologists, literary critics, oral historians, and psychologists. As you might expect, researchers in these different fields ask different questions about stories, storytelling, and storytellers. For example, some researchers are interested in how children develop the capacity to tell stories and to understand the stories of others. Other researchers study the role of narratives in forming personal identities. Others may be interested in the aesthetic qualities of literary narratives. Others study everyday stories for their rhetorical qualities. Life history researchers may gather stories to gain a deep understanding of a particular individual, perhaps a notable figure. Oral historians may gather a collection of personal stories for an in-depth study of a historical period or a particular event. The stories we are concerned with here are stories that are about personal experiences and that are told in interviews.

In what follows, we first present a brief overview of our assumptions concerning the nature of personal stories and we give some brief definitions of four broad dimensions on which you can analyze stories. Then we describe a set of procedures that enable you to examine those dimensions.

Analytical framework

The analytical framework that we present does not presume an extensive theoretical background. Its main theoretical premise is that the stories that a person tells are always shaped by that person's context; at the same time, those stories shape what tellers and listeners take as reality. We begin with a brief overview of the main assumptions of the analytical framework.

One assumption is that people tell stories to give order to the flow of events in their lives (Bruner, 1986). By telling stories, people create plots from unordered experiences. Such plots give reality "a unity that neither nature nor the past possesses so clearly" (Cronon, 1992, p. 1349). Tellers make stories by pruning away what does not make sense to them from the totality of what could be said. Further, stories link events to antecedent conditions and to consequences. Stories usually impute reasons, intentions, motives, and feelings to the actors, including the teller. In making stories, tellers are also making what they take to be reality.

A second assumption is that stories are re-presentations. They are not (and cannot be) copies of reality. Rather, they are "edited versions" of reality. When stories concern past events, tellers rely on memories, which are inevitably colored by the tellers' present understanding of those events. Such understandings change as time passes and as new events and experiences lead the teller to adopt new perspectives. Stories are embedded in language, and the language of the teller alters the meanings in the story. Furthermore, stories are told with an audience and a purpose in mind.

A third assumption is that storytelling is always selective. This is true whether one is composing an autobiography, writing history, gossiping, recounting one's life to a therapist, or responding to a query from an interviewer. That is, only some elements of the total are included in the story; other elements are excluded. To a great extent, the meanings of the story are determined by what is included in its telling and what is not.

These meanings include, for example, the putative explanation for the events that take place, the locus of responsibility for those events, the teller's evaluation of those events, and the moral that the teller draws from the story.

The fourth assumption is that stories are cultural products. Stories are situated in a time and place. Tellers draw on existing meanings, assumptions, and formulations that are specific to their time and place when they make stories about their experiences. If they did not, their stories would be neither plausible nor persuasive to their listeners. Tellers also make use of the reigning conventions of storytelling; otherwise, their stories would not make sense (i.e., they would not get the point across) to listeners. The store of available meanings and conventions could be thought of as a communal tool kit (Bruner, 1990). It is a product not only of the culture at large, but also of the smaller groups of which people are members – families, peer groups, workmates, religious congregations, political organizations, and so on.

The analytical framework we give below is based mainly on the ideas of two central theorists of narrative and storytelling: the narrative psychologist Jerome Bruner (Bruner, 1990, 1991) and the linguistic anthropologist Elinor Ochs (Capps & Ochs, 1995a, 1995b; Ochs, 2005). This framework focuses on two broad and overlapping aspects of stories: *what is told* and *how it is told*.

What is told includes the depiction of events. For instance, tellers convey their view of what caused what by imposing a sequential organization or temporal ordering on the events. Moreover, the depiction of events is always selective; the events that a teller leaves out of a story are made irrelevant or even invisible. In addition, stories convey an evaluative perspective; stories are shot through with indications of the teller's evaluations of events and actions, as well as of the actors who people the story.

How a story is told concerns the teller's use of language. Tellers have available a wide variety of lexical, grammatical, and paralinguistic means of expressing themselves. They insert into their stories maxims, similes, bromides, and allusions, which evoke images, associations, and memories. *What* and *how* – that is, content and form – are not as neatly separable as we have just implied. We distinguish between them mainly to underscore that *how* a story is told carries as much import as *what* is told.

We have selected four dimensions of stories and storytelling from among the many dimensions that narrative researchers have studied. We give a brief overview of each of these dimensions of analysis and, in a later section, we demonstrate procedures for studying each of them.

Dimensions of stories

"Trouble": the instigation to make a story

"Trouble" is the term that Jerome Bruner (1990) uses in describing what motivates people to make stories. People engage in making stories, Bruner says, when they experience a breach in their routine or a departure from the expected. That is, people do not make stories about the seemingly automatic flow of their everyday lives. A story in which "nothing happened" would not seem like a story at all. It is when something out of the ordinary happens (or when people are in a situation in which they are called on to "explain" themselves) that they are prompted to formulate a story that accounts for what has occurred. "Trouble" in Bruner's sense need not be a troublesome or negative event. Indeed, unexpected happiness or unwarranted good fortune constitute Trouble just as much as a setback. Trouble is something that must be reckoned with or accounted for. Trouble, in other words, demands an explanation; it calls forth a story.

The analysis of the Trouble that sets the story in motion is a good starting point for analyzing stories told in interviews. You may wonder what can be gleaned from an analysis of Trouble in cases in which the interviewer has already directed participants to tell a story about a specific topic or incident. Hasn't the interviewer already specified what the Trouble is? Analyzing stories to ascertain Trouble *from the participant's point of view*, however, often uncovers significant departures from what the interviewer had in mind. That is, participants often respond to the interviewer's query in ways that take the query in unforeseen directions, as you will see in the two research examples given below.

The teller's "Theory of the Event"

In telling a story, the teller puts forward at least one "Theory of the Event." As Capps and Ochs (1995b, pp. 15–16) put it, "a theory of the event is the author's attempt to provide an explanation of what happened." A teller's Theory of the Event involves a plot, that is, a sequential organization of events and circumstances. To make a collection of events into a story, tellers impose an order in which some events are antecedent to other events; some events precipitate other events, some events are consequences, and so on. In telling a story, the teller includes only certain elements; a multitude of other events, circumstances, and responses are left out. This selective telling shapes the meaning of the story in a particular way. In telling stories about events, tellers intertwine content and form to convey a Theory of the Event and make it credible.

A study carried out by Kristen Anderson and Debra Umberson (2001), two American sociologists, provides an illustration. They interviewed men who had been court-mandated to participate in a domestic violence educational program. In the interviews, each man was asked to tell about a time when "an argument with your partner became physical." Men's stories in response to that request often omitted or minimized their own violent acts. In short, the way men told their stories diverted fault and blame from themselves. Anderson and Umberson also contrasted expressive details in men's descriptions of their own violence versus their female partner's violence. Many men belittled and even ridiculed their partner's violence and described themselves as unafraid of it. Some portrayed their own violent acts as rational steps undertaken in order to control a woman who had become irrational and "hysterical."

The teller's evaluative perspective

Stories also tell about the moral stance of the teller. Stories convey judgments about the goodness of the events they depict (and perhaps raise questions about the moral status of the events). Stories may confer opprobrium on certain actors in the story or absolve others. When the teller is the protagonist in a story, it is likely (though not certain) that the protagonist will be granted the moral high ground. In addition, a story may include an explicit didactic component, such as a "take-home" message or a "moral of the story." (Think of the morals that conclude each of Aesop's Fables, for instance.) Whether or not a story has such a pointed moral message, both the *what* and the *how* of the story convey information about the evaluative perspective of the teller.

Canonical narratives

Canonical narratives are socially accepted, common, and routine accounts of an occurrence. They are cultural templates that furnish established understandings of sequence and consequence (Bruner, 1991). Some theorists have used the term "master narrative" to capture the idea that certain narratives have a hegemonic status in a cultural setting. An example is the assertion that a so-called chemical imbalance in the brain is the cause of clinical depression. This claim has recently acquired that status of a canonical narrative in the USA, owing to vigorous pharmaceutical advertising campaigns.

Canonical narratives serve as templates for understanding people's own experiences and as guides for their actions. If you recall the work of Peggy Miller and her colleagues, which you read about in Chapter 2, you will remember that US mothers gave pride of place to high self-esteem as a condition necessary for their child's future happiness, achievement, social success, and well-being. In the US context, this could be seen as a canonical narrative, at least among middle-class parents. Among the US mothers whom Miller and her colleagues studied, bolstering their child's self-esteem was a prominent aspect of their childrearing practices. Canonical narratives also serve as templates for surmising causes and reasons behind events. When a couple splits up, for example, we wonder, "Which one is having an affair?" When someone is diagnosed with lung cancer, we automatically think "He (or she) must have been a smoker."

How to interpret stories: reading content and form together

In telling stories, tellers intermingle content and form to make meaning. As you analyze stories for the dimensions we have just described, you need to keep your focus attuned to both. Stories give information about occurrences, temporal settings, actions, and the like, as well as about the people involved. This information is what we have called the "what." But how people tell stories – that is, the elements of style and language – also gives information. Poets, fiction writers, and essayists consciously choose elements of language to vivify what they say and add emotional resonance. Debaters deliberately choose styles of speech and structured sequences to underscore a certain point. Orators and political leaders deliberately choose certain registers of speech and styles of delivery that convey authority and trustworthiness.

In everyday talk also, speakers use elements of style and language to project layers of meanings, emotional resonance, and moral stance. In the case of professional writers and speakers, these elements are deliberately and painstakingly chosen. In the case of ordinary speakers and everyday talk, such features are not chosen with so much care. However, whether the choices of style and language are wholly deliberate, wholly spontaneous, or somewhere in between, elements of style and language are key to the meanings that are conveyed.

Note that in everyday conversations, people often do not tell stories in a logical or chronological sequence. They may begin with the conclusion or the "moral of the story" or anywhere else in the sequence of events and reactions. Much of the time, you will find that you cannot "tick off" antecedents and consequences in a single reading of a story; oral storytelling in particular often involves convoluted sequences of events.

When you are analyzing stories, you need to attend both to *what* a participant tells you and to *how* a participant tells it. You are probably quite used to attending to *what* is being said; in everyday life, that is the usual focus of attention. Therefore, let us consider some aspects of the *how*. The *how* of talk includes lexical features such as word choices; grammatical features such as the use of transitive versus intransitive verbs or active versus passive voice; paralinguistic features like laughter, a falsetto voice, or an emphatic tone of voice; and stylistic features, such as repetitions. In talk, such features may, for instance, intensify the meaning of what was said or indicate the speaker's evaluative stance. They may also obfuscate questions of responsibility. Consider, for example, the grammatical form of sentences like "There will be firings" or "Rapes happen" or "It was thought that . . ." Statements that take this form linguistically eliminate the doer of the action. Or consider a word choice like "glory-hogging jerks" (see below), which conveys an unmistakable evaluative judgment. It is easy to see that *how* a speaker says what he or she has to say builds up certain meanings. To interpret the meanings in a specific story, you must rely on your competence as a speaker of the language in which the story was told, as well as on multiple readings of the story. In Chapter 10, we discuss further aspects of speakers' style and rhetoric and describe other ways to analyze such features of talk.

Analytical procedures

For ease of presentation, we have chosen as examples stories that are brief, that were clearly demarcated as stories, and that could be readily identified in the stream of talk. Interview participants often tell brief stories spontaneously. In other instances, interviewers elicit them directly. For example, in Chapters 5 and 6, you learned to ask follow-up questions in order to obtain specific instances of a generalization or to direct an interview participant to elaborate on a reference to an incident by telling a story about it.

Creating a file of excerpts

To begin your work, you need to create a file that contains the excerpts that you will work with. For the type of analysis we describe here, that file will contain stories that you have identified in your transcripts. The stories will be ones that pertain in some way to a specific topic in the interview or to one of your researchable questions. As in all the interpretative approaches that you learn in this book, the purpose of creating a file of excerpts is to enable you to focus on those particular excerpts so that you can examine them in close detail.

If you have asked specific questions in the interview that invited storytelling, it is usually quite straightforward to select stories to excerpt. Some examples of such prompts or questions are as follows:

> "Can you give me a specific example of that?"
> "Can you tell me about a time when [a particular thing happened]?"
> "Tell me about the last time this happened."
> "Can you walk me through that?"

Sometimes participants spontaneously tell stories that are relevant to the topic or your researchable question. You should add such stories to your excerpt file.

Becoming familiar with the contents of the file

Once you have a file of stories that pertain to a topic or to a researchable question, the next step is to familiarize yourself thoroughly with the contents of the file. As you read and reread the stories, you should make notes in your research journal about stories that particularly capture your attention, about distinctive expressions or uses of language, or about what might be similarities across the stories. At this point, the notes you take are just meant as signposts pointing toward things you might later explore; they can therefore be broad-ranging and fairly informal. Your notes might concern commonalities in the content of the stories or in the plot sequences or a record of clichés or maxims that are frequently repeated. The notes could also concern variations among the stories, for instance, differing ascriptions of causality, as well as your sense of how blame and opprobrium are distributed. Not all the notes will ultimately serve as seeds for your analysis, but some will. At this point, it is better to make too many notes than to omit observations because they seem tangential.

Selecting dimensions of stories for analysis

In Chapter 8, you learned to compose sub-questions by reading and rereading the interview material, with an eye to your researchable questions. The process that you use here is parallel, though it is not identical.

To begin with, it is unlikely that your original researchable questions pertain directly to the dimensions of stories that we described earlier. Therefore, you need to read the file of stories once again, this time keeping in mind both the set of possible dimensions to analyze and the researchable questions. That is, as you read the stories that your participants told, consider whether a particular dimension of analysis (such as Trouble or Theory of the Event) might bear on the researchable questions. Would considering that dimension of the story tell you something important about your researchable question? Would considering that dimension corroborate or add to the results of other analyses of the interview material? If the tentative answer to questions like these is yes, then you should proceed to carry out a systematic analysis of that dimension.

We illustrate the selection of the dimensions for analysis by describing one of our research projects. The project, which was carried out by Jeanne and Jessica Salvatore, concerned young women's experiences in the gyms and fitness centers at their universities. In the USA, federal legislation specifically prohibits educational institutions from discriminating against individuals on the basis of their sex category. Among other things, this legislation requires colleges and universities to provide for equal access to athletic and recreational facilities. Yet, as gym users, Jeanne and Jessica were well aware that campus fitness facilities retained distinct (though not formally designated or enforced) "men's" and "women's" sections and that many female students carefully avoided the gym at certain times of the day.

The main participants in the study were young women in college. They were asked several questions about their gym use and athletic participation, and so on. One item was designed specifically to elicit a story about a specific incident in a gym:

Have you ever felt uncomfortable at [the college fitness center] or at your high school gym?
 If you have, can you describe the situation – what happened, who was involved, who else was there, and how the situation was resolved.

Jeanne took responsibility for analyzing the stories that the participants recounted in response to this question. Her initial *researchable questions* were as follows:

1. What did participants report about their experiences in gyms/fitness centers? Did participants experience barriers to using the facilities?
2. Did the participants perceive gyms (or parts of gyms) to be male preserves? If so, what experiences brought about and sustained that perception?
3. What did participants say about their negative experiences? What/whom did they hold accountable for those experiences?

Jeanne placed the stories into an excerpt file. She read and reread the stories in the excerpt file and on the basis of that reading decided on a subset of the dimensions of the stories that seemed to bear on her researchable questions:

1. Trouble as construed by the participant;
2. The participant's "Theory of the Event," with particular attention to the following:
   a. The events or circumstances that led to the Trouble;
   b. Complicating factors and additional events;
   c. The participant's report of her feelings and thoughts in relation to (a) and (b);
   d. Ascriptions of causation, responsibility, and blame for the problematic events;
   e. The outcome of the incident;
3. The participant's evaluative perspective and moral stance.

Making notes about participants' stories

In Chapter 8, you learned to compose brief notes about the material that is pertinent to your research questions. Those notes provided you with a way to scan across the excerpts in search of similarities and differences. Here, you need to compose notes about the stories in the file, which you can use the same way. As in Chapter 8, these notes are not the product of a mechanical search through the stories for particular words or phrases. The notes are interpretations that draw on your background knowledge about the phenomenon you are studying and your competence and experience as a speaker of the language that you and the participant share. Further, the notes are based on your judgment of how what the participant said is related to the researchable questions.

To write the notes, you need to read each story in the file of stories that you have created. Write down your notes alongside the story. These notes should contain your observations about both the content (the "what") and the form (the "how") of what the participant has said. In addition, you should make sure to include specific information about what the participant has said about each dimension. For instance, note down what the story seems to indicate as Trouble. The notes might also include questions to yourself about possible larger patterns of meaning that you might explore.

To illustrate what a set of notes might look like, we present accounts told by four participants and the notes Jeanne made about each account.

Example 1: Katie

I always feel out of place at athletic activities. Back in elementary school I'd miss simple catches in kickball or tray and shoot a basket and have the ball bounce back and slam into my face. Middle school was much worse. I was always among the slowest, clumsiest people in class. In high school I thankfully only had to take PE [Physical Education] once. When I displayed my utter clumsiness and poor shape, people would fall silent for a minute, then say something like "Good try!" What they meant was "I sure am glad I'm not that idiotic! Poor Katie; it must be hard being an evolutionary mistake." My friends tried to be helpful, but there really isn't a solution. Then there's swimming, a sport worse than basketball. The shame of going to pool parties and showing my ugly thighs and fear of water to the world is equaled only by the bother of 8:30 am Aquatics 1 [a mandatory class for students who cannot swim] this semester. At least that's over, but I'll always be clumsy and slow and bitter.

Notes
* Katie moves immediately from speaking about a "situation in a gym" to recounting a life history of lack of ability and athletic failure.
* She uses reported speech to denigrate herself.
* Katie runs together athletic incompetence, being in poor shape, and having an "ugly" body as if they were one thing.
* Her description of her shortcomings is full of hyperbole. Does this exaggeration excuse others for ridiculing and shaming her?
* Her reference to evolution and the repetition of the word "always" imply that her condition is unchangeable.

Trouble: She always feels out of place at athletic activities.

Theory of the Event: As a child, she was athletically incompetent.

As a preteen, she was clumsy, slow, and out of shape.

As a teenager, she had ugly thighs and a fear of water.

Showing her body at pool parties led to shame.

[Therefore] she will always be "clumsy and slow and bitter."

Example 2: Jennifer

When it is about 4:00 and all the sports players arrive – I am not an athlete [i.e., a member of an athletic team] –, it can be very uncomfortable to begin with. They talk loudly to each other, sometimes about the way that girls look. On one day, a friend of mine and I were getting a drink of water from the back of [the fitness center, an area dominated by male users] and a guy talked about how flabby a girl's legs were at the exercise bike. She didn't seem so flabby to me. It's hard to already feel uncomfortable, like it isn't your place to use. That is, only the athletes can. And also to know that people criticize the bodies of people in there when they are so vulnerable.

Notes

* What is signaled by Jennifer's expression "it's not your place to use"?
* Jennifer makes no direct statements that condemn the men's practice of evaluating women, though she says three times that she finds it distressing. Does Jennifer regard men's behavior as out of line or not? Does she regard it as something men are entitled to do?
* Jennifer often uses pronouns and nouns that are not gender-specific, even though her story is clearly about "men" and "women." Does this work to suspend a moral judgment of men?
* The girl whom the men judged to be "flabby" didn't seem "so flabby" to Jennifer. Does this suggest that Jennifer feels that men could judge *any* girl negatively? Or could it suggest that (in Jennifer's eyes) it is OK for men to criticize girls' bodies as long as their bodies *are* flabby?
* The story ends with no indication that change is possible and no mention of a strategy for change.

Trouble: It can be very uncomfortable to begin with.

It feels like it isn't your place to use.

It's hard to know that people criticize people's bodies.

Girls are already so vulnerable in the gym.

Theory of the Event: Men's sports teams arrive in the gym *en masse* and talk loudly to one another.

They sometimes talk about how girls look and criticize their bodies.

This makes her feel out of place, as if the gym were only for [male] athletes.

Knowing that men criticize women's bodies makes her feel vulnerable.

Evaluative perspective: The men's practices make Jennifer feel bad.

However, she does not overtly register a moral judgment of the men who engage in them.

Example 3: Lucy

I don't really go into gyms very often – it's not really one of my interests. I don't want to put on lots of muscle and I don't like treadmills. However, on the very rare occasion that I do enter a gym, I feel slightly less than comfortable, merely because it's sweaty and gross. Germs don't seem to be the only contagion present. Most guys who spend a lot of time in gyms tend to act like glory-hogging jerks. I can't really remember any specific incidents of uncomfortableness, however, it's sometimes awkward when a large group of people, especially the lacrosse team, commandeers the gym for themselves. I'm not a huge fan of meathead culture and these large teams generally produce quite a bit of that.

Notes
* Lucy's words to describe gyms are visceral and very negative: sweaty, gross, and germ-ridden.
* Her words for male gym-users are intensely negative: glory-hogging jerks, meathead culture.
* The verb "commandeer" implies that the men's behavior is out of line.
* The germs/contagion simile for the meathead culture of men's athletic teams suggests that that culture is akin to a disease.

Trouble: She is slightly less than comfortable.
It is sometimes awkward.
Theory of the Event: Gyms are sweaty and gross and unsanitary.
Guys who are regular gym-goers are glory-hogging jerks.
Men's teams "commandeer" the gym for themselves.
Men's athletic teams generate quite a bit of meathead culture.
Outcome: She really doesn't go to gyms very often. It is not her interest.
Evaluative perspective: Lucy offers a clear and strong criticism of male gym users and especially men's athletic teams.

Example 4: Maribeth

I only feel uncomfortable when I start to notice how much I'm sweating in comparison to other people working out. Sweating does not feel attractive, especially when you can tell that others notice you sweating. I also get a bit uncomfortable when I look at what I'm wearing in comparison to other girls at the gym. I wear baggy clothing sometimes that isn't that flattering, so combine that with a really sweaty appearance, and I become very self-conscious. Mostly because I don't feel that the guys think I'm attractive, especially when compared to the other girls who are hardly sweating and are wearing form-fitting clothing.

Notes
* Most of what Maribeth says is couched in terms of what *she* notices, judges and believes about herself.
* She compares her appearance to other girls, and the comparisons are always negative.
* The comparisons center on attractiveness (or not) to guys.

* She uses her beliefs about what guys think about her to exacerbate her negative views of herself.
* She makes many references to excessive sweating and she views excessive sweating as peculiar to herself.

Trouble: She feels uncomfortable because she feels unattractive (to guys).
She becomes very self-conscious.
Theory of the Event: Compared to other girls, she sweats a lot.
She sees that others notice that she is sweating and that makes her feel unattractive.
She compares her baggy clothes to what other girls are wearing and feels uncomfortable.
Her unflattering clothing choices and sweaty appearance make her very self-conscious.
Guys find her unattractive compared to girls who don't sweat and wear tight clothes.
She does not include any solution or resolution.

Finding similar meanings and composing integrative summaries of them

When you have completed notes for all the stories in the file, what is the next step? Now you need to examine the meanings that your participants brought forward in relation to each dimension of the story. To do this, consider one dimension at a time, looking for similar meanings in the notes about your participants' stories. You therefore need to read the notes you made for each story, focusing especially on the notes pertaining to the dimension under consideration. Compare the notes about one story to the notes about the other stories. When you find similarities between notes about two or more stories, copy the excerpt along with the notes into a new file.

When you have finished making these comparisons for a dimension, you will have a number of files related to that dimension, each of which contains stories that offer a similar idea (i.e., a meaning) related to that dimension. Give each file a label that summarizes what the stories have in common. Set aside stories that do not fit into any of the files.

The next step is to write an *integrative summary* that states what the stories in the file have in common. Below we give an example of a portion of an analysis from Jeanne's project, including the integrative summary. (To save space, we do not include the notes Jeanne had written about each story.) The dimension of the stories that was under consideration was the Theory of the Event. Following the procedures described above, Jeanne had placed four stories together into a file because they put forward similar meanings related to the dimension Theory of the Event.

Stories in the file Theory of the Event

(a) In my high school gym, I used to feel quite uncomfortable. In a fitness class, a certain gym teacher would consistently require us to do a pretty intense ab [that is, abdominal] workout, some portions of which my friend and I couldn't do. We tended to laugh about it, but in reality I always felt fat, uncoordinated and stupid for not being athletic enough to complete the workout. As a result, unless I had to be there for a class, I never went to the gym on my own time. I have never felt *that* out of place at [the college gym], though I do sometimes feel overly conscious of my weight and lack of stamina.

(b) I have only been in the fitness center when required by classes. As one of the overweight, awkward, un-athletic girls, *everything* made me uncomfortable, but especially being there with people in much better shape than me, as some of my classmates invariably were. I was intimidated by their skill and embarrassed by the knowledge that they could be watching me or see how bad I am. This situation probably has something to do with the reason I don't go to the gym. I hate feeling fat and awkward.

(c) I can't think of a particular situation but often times I feel very fat at the gym and I hate how my face gets really red from working out. I also don't like how sweaty I get but then I think "Whatever. At least I'm getting a good work-out."

(d) I always feel out of place at athletic activities. Back in elementary school I'd miss simple catches in kickball or tray and shoot a basket and have the ball bounce back and slam into my face. Middle school was much worse. I was always among the slowest, clumsiest people in class. In high school I thankfully only had to take PE [Physical Education] once. When I displayed my utter clumsiness and poor shape, people would fall silent for a minute, then say something like "Good try!" What they meant was "I sure am glad I'm not that idiotic! Poor Katie; it must be hard being an evolutionary mistake." My friends tried to be helpful, but there really isn't a solution. Then there's swimming, a sport worse than basketball. The shame of going to pool parties and showing my ugly thighs and fear of water to the world is equaled only by the bother of 8:30 am Aquatics 1 [a mandatory class for students who cannot swim] this semester. At least that's over, but I'll always be clumsy and slow and bitter.

Integrative summary

The participants describe their physical attributes as the origin of their discomfort in the gym. All four of them seem to blur together being overweight, being out of shape (lacking stamina or strength), and being clumsy, awkward or uncoordinated (even though these are independent and separable). The possibility that their bodily short-comings are on display to peers of any sex category is a source of embarrassment, shame, and heightened self-consciousness. All the tellers seem to imply that their body size and/ or lack of agility are enduring and unchangeable attributes. None of the tellers seem to hold themselves accountable for these attributes. At the same time (paradoxically?) none of the tellers hold onlookers morally accountable for disparaging women who are fat or unfit or for shaming them. For three of the four participants, the solution has been to avoid the gym (and athletic activities).

* You need to repeat the steps we have just described for every dimension under consideration. This will yield at least one and perhaps several files of stories pertaining to each of the dimensions. Each file will contain a group of related stories, along with an integrative summary describing what unites that group.

Verifying the analyses

Now you need to verify your work. This requires that you turn back to the full stories. For each integrative summary, you now focus on the group of stories that it summarizes. Read each story against the integrative summary with two questions in mind:

Does this story fit with the other stories that are summarized?
Does the integrative summary adequately capture the story?

It is likely that you will need to make some adjustments to your integrative summaries. For example, when you reread a story, you may find that the notes overlooked an element that you now see as crucial. Having read many stories, you now bring a more discerning eye to the stories you read earlier.

What to do if you are stuck

If you have read a set of notes and stories several times but you do not see any patterns, what can you do? One strategy is to pay attention to an extreme or dramatic story or one that is laced with hyperbole or blunt language. Trace out what this story tells you about your researchable question. This story may serve as a sensitizing device: that is, it may alert you to similar but less dramatic instances. You might ask yourself, "What is this instance an example of?" Answering this question moves your thinking toward a more abstract description. Then you can see whether there are other instances that fit the abstract description. For example, Katie's claim that onlookers think of her as an "evolutionary mistake" combines hyperbole and projection (i.e., her assertion about what others are thinking). It is an example of the speaker ascribing to herself a set of qualities – clumsy, unathletic, ugly, and ungainly – that render her monstrous and that are inherited and unchangeable. Imputing this judgment to others inflates its credibility and makes it less refutable. With this description in mind, Jeanne was able to see similar but less hyperbolic instances in other interviews.

Another strategy is to pick out a pair of strongly contrasting stories, for example, stories with distinctly different emotional registers or very different evaluative perspectives. Look closely at the whole stories to see if there are other differences between them. In analyzing young women's stories about their gym experiences, for example, Jeanne juxtaposed Jennifer and Lucy. Jennifer used morally neutral language when she described objectionable and distressing behavior of members of men's athletic teams. In contrast, Lucy offered a scathing indictment of team members.

A third strategy is more labor-intensive because it involves looking beyond the group you have chosen for study. You can identify people whose experiences are likely to differ from those of your study group and interview a few of them to serve as contrastive cases. Jeanne used stories from a small group of young men as contrastive cases. Comparing the women's stories to the men's stories made elements of the women's stories stand out. This helped Jeanne to see things that she had previously failed to notice in the women's stories.

Drawing the analyses together

Once you have completed analyzing the dimensions of the stories, you need to draw together what you have learned into a coherent whole. At this point, you have a set of integrative summaries that describe the main meanings that participants brought forward about each of the dimensions of a story that you have chosen to study. One way to bring the summaries together is to draw out their implications for the researchable questions. Let us give you two examples from Jeanne's analysis of gym stories. The first example concerns the Trouble, and the second example concerns participants' Theory of the Event.

Example 1

What did the analysis of Trouble say about the researchable questions?

When Jeanne sorted the stories, four files resulted, which encompassed four different meanings that the participants typically made in relation to Trouble. The integrative summaries for these four files made the following points:

1. In every story, Trouble concerned emotional or psychological states; no participant parsed the word "uncomfortable" to mean physical discomfort. Even when stories involved a physical injury or impairment (e.g., falling on a treadmill and requiring medical treatment; a severe bronchitis attack that halted a workout), the discomfort that participants talked about concerned their feelings (such as embarrassment, self-consciousness, or shame).
2. Although the participants had been asked to tell about "a situation," many stories (like nearly all the ones that you read above) instead told about ongoing or enduring negative feelings and habitual practices. Some stories (like Katie's) told about experiences that extended beyond gyms into athletic situations more generally and beyond their college years into earlier years of their lives.
3. Most participants substituted more specific emotion words in place of the term "uncomfortable." For the most part, the words that identified the Trouble conveyed intense negative feelings – feeling vulnerable, exposed, self-conscious, judged, out of place, stupid, intimidated, lonely, or even unsafe. For one woman, being observed while she exercised was "scary." For another, "[Having] guys staring you down . . . feels predatory."
4. A small minority of female participants used words that minimized the level of discomfort they felt. For example, they described themselves as "slightly" or "only a little" uncomfortable, or uncomfortable only "at first." Noting these exceptions allowed Jeanne to describe the full range of variation among the participants.

Now Jeanne asked what light these meanings of Trouble shed on the researchable questions. First, most of the women reframed the relatively innocuous term "uncomfortable" by using terms indicating intense negative feelings and thoughts. This speaks to the researchable question *Did participants experience barriers to using the facilities?* It suggests that uncomfortable experiences likely constituted a barrier to participants' use of the gym. Second, the negative feelings that the participants reported were always interpersonal in origin – feeling exposed, self-conscious, intimidated, judged, and so on. This speaks to the researchable question *What did participants say about their negative experiences?* Third, most of the women responded to the request for "an incident" by telling about a persisting state of affairs, a habitual practice, or a succession of negative events. This also speaks to the researchable question *What did participants say about their negative experiences?*

Taken together, the ways that participants told about Trouble suggested that the matter of unpleasant emotions and thoughts in relation to athletic settings or activities was highly salient. Furthermore, the Trouble involved heightened self-consciousness, feeling out of place, and feeling or being scrutinized and judged. The participants' feelings and thoughts largely concerned scrutiny or evaluation of their bodies mainly, though not exclusively, by their male peers. This speaks to the researchable question *What or whom did they hold accountable for those experiences?*

Example 2

What did the analysis of the participants' Theory of the Event say about the researchable questions?

Examining aspects of the Theory of the Event also sheds light on some of the researchable questions. One part of the analysis involved searching for similarities in plot. The plots of the stories varied in many ways, but Jeanne focused on elements that were relevant to the researchable questions: What were the events or circumstances that instigated the Trouble? Who or what was responsible for them? Were there indications that participants held anyone morally accountable for the events in the story?

Jeanne had already learned that Trouble nearly always concerned interpersonal relations, mainly men's scrutiny, judgment, or actions, whether actual, anticipated, or imagined. As she examined the notes and stories, she found two main sequences. In one plot sequence, it was the actions or manner of men that instigated the Trouble. Jennifer and Lucy, for example, both told how the presence (and collective behavior) of male athletic teams made them feel out of place, self-conscious, and so on. In the second plot sequence, the participant's physical deficiencies were the origin of the Trouble. That is, the teller described her body in derogatory terms – as fat, clumsy, awkward, inept, out of shape, sweaty, and so on. These shortcomings, which were on open display in athletic settings, invited negative judgments or possible ridicule. The Trouble – problematic feelings of self-consciousness, humiliation, or vulnerability – was a consequence. Katie and Maribeth, for example, told stories with plots of this kind.

The first of the two plot sequences speaks to the researchable question *Did the participants perceive gyms (or parts of gyms) to be male preserves? If so, what experiences brought about and sustained that perception?* The stories name certain actions and practices of men (and male athletic teams) that led participants to feel out of place. But these stories were not all the same. Jennifer, for example, described a high degree of emotional distress in response to men's actions. Lucy, by contrast, portrayed herself as only slightly discomfited and mainly annoyed. Furthermore, Jennifer did not register explicit criticism or disapproval of men's behavior. In contrast, Lucy offered relentless, blistering criticisms of male gym-users, masculine gym culture, and male athletic teams. This analysis helped Jeanne to answer the researchable question *What/ whom did they hold accountable for those experiences?*

In the other plot sequence, participants figured themselves as fat, ungainly, awkward, and/or inept. It was their flawed bodies that led to self-consciousness, shame, and sense of inferiority. In this plot sequence, participants represented these feelings as an inevitable concomitant of their flawed bodies. The part played by onlookers' critical scrutiny or derision was underplayed; negative commentary from onlookers was simply a matter of course and perhaps even deserved. This speaks to the researchable question *What/ whom did they hold accountable for those experiences?* Further, some participants framed their bodily inadequacies as permanent and even congenital (as Katie seemed to). This pattern of talk sheds further light on the question of accountability.

Although this is just a small portion of the analyses, it opens a window onto participants' negative experiences in the gym. For most of the participants, the gym was a place where women's bodies were on display. For many, it seemed to be beyond question that their bodies were flawed and thus deserved to be negatively judged by others. Although some participants raised objections to men who overtly ogled women or offered critical commentary, many seemed to regard men's evaluative scrutiny of women's bodies as an inevitable – albeit unpleasant – feature of the gym. Further, the stories suggested that participants accepted tacit "ownership" of the gym by men (especially male athletic teams) as a natural state of affairs: if the presence and actions of men made women uncomfortable, then women accommodated by avoiding the times when men chose to use the gym and the sections of the gym that men used. Or, women chose to avoid the gym altogether.

In this example, we have focused on brief and narrowly focused stories – essentially, critical incidents. You may, however, make use of similar analytical procedures to examine larger and more complex stories. For example, in the discussion below, we consider lengthier stories about a complex and more ambiguous life event, an episode of suicide-like behavior.

Exploring differences between groups of people

Tellers' perspectives shape their stories. Individuals in different social locations recount events differently. Comparing such differing accounts can tell researchers any number of things about, for example, social hierarchy and intergroup conflict or about mundane differences in the ways that people construe their life experiences. Consider the work carried out by Don Foster and his colleagues, who are social psychologists in South Africa (Foster, Haupt, & De Beer, 2005). Working in the post-apartheid period, the researchers gathered lengthy narratives from individuals who were perpetrators of violence during the intense armed struggle to overthrow apartheid, a struggle that persisted for nearly thirty-five years. The researchers gathered narratives from police officers, members of government intelligence services, members of liberation movements, and people involved in township conflicts. They contrasted the accounts provided by members of the different groups on such matters as the reasons for engaging in violence, the tellers' narrative strategies in accounting for violent acts, and the narrative strategies by which tellers deflected responsibility. The researchers also examined elements common to all the tellers such as the significance of masculinity and the power that group membership wielded over individuals' behavior.

As Foster and his colleagues did, you may design a project specifically to compare people drawn from different social groups. Or, as your analysis proceeds, you may discern a striking difference among the stories that leads you to divide the participants into groups in accord with the stories they told. You can then do additional analyses to examine whether the groups differ on other dimensions as well. Such analyses may enable you to paint a fuller picture of the participants you have chosen for study.

If you want to compare groups of participants, you should select a subset of dimensions that will help you to answer the researchable questions about the group comparisons. Then analyze the set of stories for each group of participants separately. When you have completed the analyses for both groups for all the dimensions, you will have separate sets of integrative summaries for each group. Comparing the integrative summaries enables you to examine differences between the groups.

To give you a flavor of what such group comparisons might yield, we give a few examples from a project that Jeanne and Chandanie Senadheera carried out involving teenagers in rural Sri Lanka. As you read in Chapter 2, Jeanne and Chandanie studied what they have called suicide-like acts – acts that involve deliberately swallowing poisons or overdoses without any intention to die. In the context of Sri Lanka, such acts are often impetuous responses to acute interpersonal conflicts; they rarely arise out of depression or mental illness. Although people of all ages engage in such suicide-like acts, they are particularly frequent among teenagers. At present, among teenagers, very few of these suicide-like acts (fewer than 1 percent) end in death. Nonetheless, Jeanne and Chandanie were troubled to observe that the previous decade had seen a 300 percent increase in the numbers of teenagers who engaged in such acts and they were also concerned that three quarters of the victims were girls.

Chandanie, who is a native Sinhala speaker, interviewed girls who had been admitted to a medical ward following a suicide-like episode. With the girls' agreement, Chandanie interviewed their mothers as well. By custom, it is female family members who attend to patients in hospital, providing personal care, meals, laundry, and otherwise managing their care. Furthermore, it is mothers (not fathers) who have the responsibility for nurturing and caring for their children. Mothers also have the crucial task of guarding the social reputations of their daughters once they reach puberty. Consequently, they knew that mothers would be deeply engaged in coming to terms with what had happened to their daughters and with figuring out the near-term arrangements following their daughters' discharge from hospital.

Chandanie began the interviews with the question "What happened?" This question signaled a request for a story but left it to the teller to decide what kind of story to tell, where the story should begin, what should be told, and how it should be told. When necessary, Chandanie prompted participants to continue the story and, as the interview drew to a close, to project what was likely to happen after the girl left the hospital.

As Jeanne and Chandanie read the mothers' and daughters' stories, they saw a number of differences between the two sets of stories. We briefly describe two of the dimensions on which they compared the stories. One of the dimensions is Trouble, as it was perceived by the mothers and daughters respectively.

Comparing daughters and mothers: what is the Trouble or problematic event?

For the girls, the opening question "What happened?" called forth an elaborate story about the events that led up to their suicide-like behavior. These events constituted the Trouble in the narratives. For most girls, the Trouble involved harsh scolding (not infrequently accompanied by beatings) by one of their parents, usually their mother. The scolding was often precipitated by a violation of the standards of feminine modesty and sexual respectability to which postpubertal girls in rural Sri Lanka were held. (Such violations included coming home late from school, loitering with girlfriends, being seen in the company of a boy, or receiving calls from a phone number that the parents did not recognize.) For other girls, Trouble involved other relational impasses in the family. One such frequent impasse concerned a father or elder brother whose drinking habits caused scandal in the community, thus jeopardizing the girl's future prospects for marriage. As the girls recounted it, being harshly scolded or a father's drinking led them to be disappointed, upset, saddened, and angry. In short, it was this set of occurrences, which the girls identified as the Trouble, that prompted the suicide-like act.

The mothers' stories in response to the same question ("What happened?") had a different focal point. Although their stories referred to the difficulties (e.g., infractions of the rules and scoldings) that preceded their daughters' suicide-like acts, the mothers pinpointed the suicide-like act itself as the Trouble. The mothers' stories emphasized how their daughters' suicide-like act had set off a cascade of difficulties that the mothers would now have to resolve. These difficulties did not concern the daughter's emotional condition, her psychological well-being, or even her physical health. Rather, the difficulties lay in the responses of the extended family network and the local community to the girl's suicide-like act. For example, some mothers anticipated that they would have to quell the anger of other family members toward the girl. Other mothers worried about finding a way to squelch rumors that would stain the girl's sexual reputation and jeopardize the family's good name. Many mothers were entertaining drastic measures to mitigate the daughter's disgrace and the family's loss of face. These included sending their daughter to live with a distant relative, forcing her into a hasty arranged marriage, or taking her out of school and keeping her at home. In this aspect, the mothers' stories diverged sharply from the girls' stories. Many, if not most, girls predicted that the suicidal act would have positive consequences. For example, they expected that their mothers would desist from harsh scoldings in the future or that their fathers would have "learned a lesson" from the daughter's act and would henceforth quit drinking.

Comparing mothers and daughters: taking a canonical narrative into use

In Sri Lanka, the routine and commonplace way of understanding suicide is that suicidal acts are fueled by anger. Suicidal acts are thought of as motivated by a desire to "take revenge" on a wrongdoer or to force another person to bow to one's will. This way of understanding suicide is pervasive and unquestioned in Sri Lanka: it circulates through the mass media, the professional medical literature, the lessons taught to children in school health classes, and the training curricula for lay counselors. Jeanne and Chandanie therefore deemed this to be a canonical narrative of suicide.

The researchable question that Jeanne and Chandanie asked was *How does this canonical narrative take shape in the stories that mothers and daughters tell about the daughter's suicide-like act?* In the mothers' stories about their daughters' suicide-like acts, the canonical narrative clearly seemed to serve directly as a template. One mother, for example, explained, "She became friendly with a boy and she is too young. I shouted at her over that and she became angry and drank kerosene." Another mother said, "She was annoyed [by her father's embarrassing drunken behavior] and so she crushed mosquito coils in kerosene and drank it." Another mother explained that her daughter drank insecticide because she was "in an angry mood" and "wanted to hurt me." A fourth described her daughter's suicide-like act as an act of "disobedience."

The daughters' stories of their suicide-like behavior offered a sharp contrast to the mothers' stories. The girls' accounts of the events that led up to the suicidal act were vivid, highly elaborated, and laced with references to feelings of hurt, outrage, and disappointment. However, there was an abrupt shift in tone and content when they came to describing the suicide-like act itself. These descriptions were laced with vague, passive voice, agent-less expressions. ("The poison got swallowed." "Pills got bought.") Many girls denied having any feelings at the time and denied even knowing what had happened ("I myself do not know what really happened. It is as if someone else forced me to do it"; "I can't remember how it happened"; "I didn't think"). They used adverbs of time that denoted impulsive behavior or snap decisions ("instantly," "immediately," or "without giving any thought"), even though this did not necessarily accord with other details they recounted. The girls' stories avoided mention of all feelings, including angry ones, as well as any motives, including vengeful ones.

These two comparisons helped Jeanne and Chandanie to answer two of their research-able questions. Let us turn first to the differences in the mothers' and daughters' "take-up" of the canonical narrative regarding suicide. The mother–daughter compar-ison casts the silences, denials, and vagueness in the girls' accounts in bold relief. Ultimately, Jeanne and Chandanie related the silences to gendered norms governing the girls' comportment and to societal prescriptions regarding deference to and respect for one's parents (Marecek & Senadheera, 2012). In short, avoiding direct mention of anger and vengeance helped the girls to paint a portrait of themselves as good girls.

Despite the frequency of suicide-like acts in Sri Lanka, no researcher had ever attempted to trace out the aftermath of such acts beyond possible physical health consequences. This topic was one of the knowledge interests that Jeanne and Chandanie had. The interviews during the girls' hospitalization could only reveal what the mothers anticipated, which might or might not be what later happened. Nonetheless, the analysis of the mothers' stories delineated an array of concerns about social repercussions for the girls, as well as for other daughters in the family, and for the family's standing in the community. These possible repercussions were the focal point of the mothers' interviews; only a few mothers voiced concerns about the circumstances that spurred their daughters' suicide-like act or about their daughters' mental health or emotional well-being.

Synthesizing the analyses

As you move forward to synthesize the results, the researchable questions can serve as the organizing framework: that is, considering how the results of specific analyses speak to the researchable questions should afford a means to tie those results into a coherent whole. Chapter 12 offers a fuller discussion of how to organize and write a written report.

10 Analyzing talk-as-action

As you already know, interviews are a form of conversation. That is, research interviews are not only occasions for gathering material pertinent to your researchable questions but also occasions in which two or more persons are interacting. The people interacting in the interview are always doing more with their talk than asking questions and giving answers. For instance, through their talk, people are also continually creating a relationship with their conversation partners; through what they say, they are often also creating relationships with people who are not present. Researchers have used several different terms to refer to these and other interactive functions of talk. Examples are "the action orientation of talk," "what people do with their talk," "talk-in-interaction," "texts and talk in action," and "talk-as-action." These different expressions do not have exactly identical meanings; they have their origins in different theoretical traditions. We have settled on one of these terms: *talk-as-action* (Edwards, 1997). Talk-as-action and its analytical possibilities are the focus of this chapter. We describe how studying talk-as-action can help you address your researchable questions and in some cases develop those questions further.

The analytical framework and procedures that we describe in this chapter bring into focus the interaction work that people's talk does beyond communicating facts, meanings, or opinions to listeners. For instance, if speakers want to persuade listeners of their opinion, they usually use explicit arguments in favor of that opinion. But they also tend to mold the form of their talk in ways that make it more persuasive. These ways may not appear to have anything directly to do with the topic.

The analyses that we describe concern what talk achieves in conversation and how those achievements are conditioned by the context in which the talk occurs. Some of the analyses examine the immediate interpersonal context of the talk, for example, who the conversation partners are. Other analyses focus on the socio-cultural context of the talk, that is, the larger societal setting in which the talk is taking place. The chapter begins with an example that illustrates talk-as-action. We then present the analytical framework for the chapter. Next we present a compendium of conversational features that are useful as entry points for analyses of talk-as-action. We illustrate each conversational feature with examples from our own research.

What is talk-as-action?

The expression talk-as-action refers to the idea that people are always doing more with their talk than communicating information. For instance, talk brings across the information that is communicated to the listener *in a certain way*. Talk also presents the speaker *in a particular light*. And talk may make a certain activity seem worthwhile (or not) to the listener. To illustrate talk-as-action, we have selected an excerpt from an interview in Eva's study of Nordic couples, which you read about in Chapter 2. In the couple who were being interviewed, Stina, the wife, did most of the housework and childcare. She told the interviewer that she was quite content with this situation, and that she and her husband Stephen never quarreled about housework sharing. She then continued:

STINA: That's something I think many other people perhaps squabble a lot [.] too much [.] about. You know: "Now it's your turn to do the cleaning!" We have friends who do [.]
INTERVIEWER: Things have to be the same?
STINA: They have to be as similar as possible.
STEPHEN: Because, "If you do this, then I get to do that. If you go there, then . . ."
STINA: We have never, *ever* talked like that!
STEPHEN: *No!*

If we look at the content of this brief conversation, we see that Stina and Stephen were telling the interviewer: (a) that many people disagreed about housework sharing; (b) that these people, including some of their friends, "squabbled" too much about housework sharing; and (c) that they themselves never resorted to bickering about petty issues in housework.

Let us consider this interaction in its context. This Swedish couple lived in a time and place in which the cultural ideal was for couples to share housework and childcare equally. That was the larger sociocultural and political context. The interviewer was a young woman, and she had been asking them several questions about the way they organized their everyday life – who did the dishes, who did most of the childcare, and so on. Many of these questions connected quite directly to gender equality issues. That was the local context, which is also distinctly related to the larger context. Stina and Stephen could not have been unaware of either the larger or the local speaking context. Moreover, by this point in the interview, they may well have realized that they had presented numerous examples of their own unequal sharing patterns. This may have made Stephen and Stina apprehensive about placing themselves in a bad light before the interviewer.

Let us now consider what this couple's talk may have been *doing* in the excerpted interaction. Stina's initial depiction of strivings for equal sharing as "squabbling" connected gender equality with disagreements and possibly quarrels. In the original Swedish, the later descriptions of their friends' squabbles ("Now it's your turn to do the cleaning!"; "If you do this, then I get to do that") made their friends' discussions seem akin to bickering about millimeter justice in the nursery. Further, Stephen and Stina's insistence that they never squabbled about equal sharing ("We have never, *ever* talked like that!") effectively set them apart from the friends who "squabbled." To summarize, their talk performed the following actions: it connected striving for gender equality with quarreling; it made debates about gender equality seem childish; and it positioned Stephen and Stina as different from (and better than?) couples who squabble about gender equality.

What can a researcher learn by taking into account interactional aspects in conversations? In the case above, did a focus on such aspects in this particular couple's conversation help Eva address her researchable questions – which of course go beyond this couple? For Eva, the answer was yes. In the description of this study of Nordic couples in Chapter 2, we listed three of its researchable questions. The first asked about the cultural understandings and ideologies about issues such as femininity, masculinity, and parenthood that could be discerned in the talk of the men and women. The second asked about variations among the couples in how they related to dominant cultural understandings. The third question developed out of the analyses of the first two questions. These analyses had led Eva to an interest in what different forms of talk achieved in the interview conversations. The third question asked about how the partners in each couple "used" talk in specific interactions in the interviews. Insight into such uses helped to address the other researchable questions (including several additional ones beyond those mentioned in Chapter 2).

In Stina and Stephen's conversation, one focus for analysis was the relational goals that their talk may have accomplished. Another focus was the image of themselves as a couple that they communicated to the interviewer through their talk. In order to examine what went on in this piece of interaction and make it useful for further analysis of her researchable questions, Eva entertained questions such as these:

– What might the local speaking situation in the interview have meant for this conversation?
– What might the contemporary gender politics of Swedish society have meant for the conversation?
– Were there other couples in the study who talked in similar ways about gender equality? If there were, could some conclusions be drawn across the couples concerning this kind of talk-as-action?
– If there were other couples who talked in similar ways, did these couples have anything else in common with Stina and Stephen, such as demographics or features of their housework or childcare arrangements?
– Further, did these couples talk in this way only when they talked about gender equality and housework, or were there other topics for which similar kinds of talk-as-action occurred?
– Finally, what could it have meant that the members of the couples were interviewed together, rather than separately: would their accounts have been different if they were interviewed separately?

This example gives you a flavor of the analytical procedures we take up in this chapter. However, before we move to analytical procedures, you need to be familiar with the analytical framework for them.

Analytical framework

Context always matters. This claim is at the foundation of the general framework for this book. When analyzing interviews, context has to be taken into account, whether it be the interpersonal context of a conversation or the larger sociocultural context of a country. In this section, we consider what the centrality of context implies for how to conceive of individual thinking, reasoning, and talking. We draw especially on the work of Michael Billig, a British critical social psychologist, along with ideas of other researchers. Our purpose is not to give a full representation of these ideas but to acquaint you with those aspects that we have found particularly helpful.

Rhetoric

The word *rhetoric* is always used in reference to persuading or convincing others. You have probably heard the label "empty rhetoric" applied to an utterance made up mainly of tricks meant to sway the listener's opinions in the speaker's direction. It is not surprising that rhetoric has been called "the art of persuasion." Much has been written about this art. Writers on rhetoric in classical and early modern times divided the rhetorical knowledge necessary for good speakers into esthetic and pragmatic dimensions. The esthetic dimensions concern rules for elegance and eloquence. The pragmatic dimensions concern how speakers might best succeed in persuading their listeners. For the purpose of this chapter – studying talk-as-action – it is the pragmatic aspects of rhetoric that are of interest.

The pragmatic aspects of rhetoric concern listeners' psychology: a speaker who wants to influence listeners needs to know what is most likely to change opinions in the type of audience he or she is addressing. To be effective persuaders, speakers therefore study their audiences and note what effect their words have on them and what turns of speech seem most effective. On formal occasions such as political speech-making, such scrutiny is expected of the speaker and, of course, his or her speechwriters. But rhetorical scrutiny is also a feature of everyday conversations. For instance, most people plan ahead before they embark on a difficult conversation. Also, most people have found themselves thinking back on a conversation that went awry. What, they wonder, went wrong? What was it I said that made my attempt at persuasion fail?

The term "rhetoric" is most often used about interactions in which a speaker is deliberately setting out to persuade somebody else. However, all interactions have a rhetorical character. It is, for instance, a near-universal characteristic of talk that it is tailored to a specific audience and takes the speaker's knowledge about that audience into account. In the next subsection, we follow Michael Billig's line of thinking in considering speaking, and, by implication, thinking, as fundamentally social and therefore rhetorical.

Talking, thinking, and rhetoric

It is easy to see that *speaking* is rhetorical: it takes characteristics of its audience and the audience's possible reactions into account. Speaking, after all, is directed to others, often in immediate give-and-take with them. It may take a bit more reflection to accept that *thinking* is also rhetorical. Put another way, people usually think in ways that are analogous to speaking to others. Consider how children learn to think. They learn through interactions in which they are spoken to by others. Eventually children learn not only to speak but also to think within the framework that is provided by the speakers' words and categories. This means that both thinking and talking are fundamentally social activities: they both began, after all, in interactions with others. The rhetorical aspect of talking and thinking does not vanish when children grow up, though it may be less overt as people grow older and become better able to keep their thoughts to themselves. As you read the rest of the chapter, we urge you to keep in mind what Michael Billig calls "the irreducibly argumentative aspects of thinking" (1996, p. 113; see also Billig et al., 1988).

Language, categorization, and argumentation

All languages provide their users with more than one way to talk about and think about the world and what happens in that world. In fact, a person's language usually provides a wide variety of ways to talk about any specific situation or event. Our experience readily tells us that two observers of the same event will describe it differently. They use different words to describe the same phenomenon, and in so doing categorize that phenomenon in different ways. Think of Stina and Stephen, who talked about sharing housework as something that causes disagreement and conflict in everyday life. Their talk placed sharing in a negatively charged category – a category of marital "risk factors," perhaps? There were also a number of other couples in the study who talked about sharing housework as something that helped them to avoid disagreement and conflict in their everyday life. Their talk placed sharing in a positively charged category – a category of marital "peace factors," perhaps?

People are generally aware that several ways of categorizing a phenomenon are possible. In the case of the couples in the study, they had access to the same language, and that language enabled them to place the phenomenon of sharing housework in different categories. People also generally know the arguments of more than one side of an issue: they know the arguments for their own preferred categorization and also, though perhaps in less detail, the arguments for other categorizations. In the case of the Nordic couples, all of them knew the range of views about sharing housework because such issues were widely debated in the Nordic countries.

If we had brought together Stina and Stephen with Kalle and Kristina (a couple who had emphasized the great merits of sharing housework equally), each couple could have argued *for* their own position. But they would also have been able to argue *against* the other couple's position. That is, both couples likely would know enough about the arguments *for* the other position to find ways of arguing *against* those arguments. Without any knowledge of the other side, no argument would be possible. People would be able only to announce their own position, but not to take issue with arguments for the other position. Knowing the arguments of the other side is what makes people able to oppose other people's arguments effectively, that is, to negate.

People's ability to negate makes rhetoric both possible and inevitable in human interaction (Billig, 1996).

The words "arguments" and "argumentative" as we use them here should not be taken as referring exclusively to situations where there is disagreement or where speakers are angry at one another. We use these words to indicate the argumentative character of much ordinary conversation where there is no disagreement or ill will. Consider the three-way conversation that Stina, Stephen, and the interviewer had, which you read at the beginning of this chapter. No criticism of Stina and Stephen's position had been broached in that situation, yet something "argumentative" certainly occurred in their talk. What happened was that, even though no criticism of their position had been voiced, Stina and Stephen nonetheless justified their own position. They did this by *criticizing* other people's position. In conversation, people often justify their own position even when it has not explicitly been called into question and even when they do not expect any counterargument.

Writers on rhetoric suggest that criticism (of others' position) and justification (of one's own position) are central to all kinds of argumentation and also that criticism and justification are closely connected. As the philosopher Chaïm Perelman put it: "Every justification presupposes the existence or eventuality of an unfavourable evaluation of what we justify" (1979, p. 138). We can put it more starkly: people do not justify their actions and opinions unless they hear, or expect to hear, some criticism of those actions or opinions. What they expect the criticism to be depends on the context in which the argumentation occurs.

Rhetorical contexts

Words and phrases do not have fixed meanings; therefore, what a particular utterance means cannot be fully understood without taking its *rhetorical context* into account. The rhetorical context is fundamentally social (Billig, 1991, 1996). There are two senses in which this is so, both of which are of interest to interpretative researchers. To begin with, the topic of a discussion often relates to societal issues; that is, larger social values and norms are at least indirectly part of the discussion. Therefore, by arguing in favor of one position on an issue, a speaker may be put in a morally compromised position in the eyes of the other speakers. This first dimension of the rhetorical context, then, includes social relations between the speakers and the listeners.

Let us look again at the brief interaction between Stina, Stephen, and the interviewer with the first dimension of the rhetorical context in mind. We can see that they were talking about a topic that was potentially highly charged in their cultural setting and explicitly related to social values and norms: gender equality in the home. The social values that will be brought into such a conversation are not necessarily determined beforehand, though. There is the value of equality, of course. However, you will recall that Stina and Stephen also brought in the values of harmony and freedom from conflict or strife in their marriage. In the interview, Stina and Stephen, having agreed to tell a stranger about their daily life, were in an unusual social situation. The interviewer, being an interviewer, did not interject her opinions about the competing merits of peace at home versus equal sharing. However, considering many of the topics in the interview, it is likely that Stina and Stephen presumed that the interviewer was in favor of gender equality in the home. This may have made them apprehensive about being placed in a morally compromised position. Or not: they may have felt that it was the presumed position of the interviewer that was morally compromised.

Now we turn to the second way in which the rhetorical context is social. This concerns the opinions that the speaker is arguing for and the counter-opinions that the speaker is explicitly or implicitly criticizing. The counter-opinions are part of the rhetorical context within which the speaker is speaking. Note that this is true whether or not the listeners who are present hold the counter-opinions and whether or not they express them.

If we look at Stina and Stephen's interaction with this second dimension of the rhetorical context in mind, we see that their talk can be read as an argument *for* the value of keeping the peace and avoiding quarrels. But it can also be read as an argument *against* sharing housework equally. That is, they argued that it was their friends' desire to share equally that led to squabbles. Reading their conversation from this perspective enables the researcher to draw some inferences about the argumentative landscape within which Stina and Stephen operated.

The rhetorical context of interview interactions

From a rhetorical perspective, participants' talk in interviews does more than answer questions. When participants are responding to interview questions, they are also continually creating their relationship to the other people who are part of the interview (such as the interviewer). Often they are also creating a relationship to absent people who are mentioned in the interview conversation (such as "other couples" in the example of Stina and Stephen). Through their talk, the partici-pants are enacting what it means to them to be members of the categories that are made salient in the interview (such as "couples who do not share housework equally"). Finally, the participants are enacting what the topics of the conversa-tion mean to them (such as "the value of sharing housework"). How can research-ers study such a complicated melee of relationships? This is the focus of the rest of this chapter.

Analytical procedures

Here we present a selection of features of talk-as-action and we describe what you can learn from studying them. Researchers have come to the study of talk-as-action from different theoretical perspectives and with different analytical goals; consequently, they have focused on different features of talk. There is a substantial literature about the action properties of talk, including different theoretical perspectives on them. Here, however, it is not our purpose to enter into theoretical debates.

Talk-as-action and the researchable questions in a study

Let us set the stage for our presentation of analytic procedures. The analyses of talk-as-action that we describe are set within the larger framework of the researchable questions of a project. This means that the purpose of these analyses is not to study specific instances of talk-as-action for their own sake. We focus instead on how the analysis of talk-as-action can help address the researchable questions that a researcher has. As a rule, therefore, researchers do not choose beforehand to analyze one specific type of talk-as-action rather than another.

Identifying pieces of talk to study

Identifying the pieces of talk to analyze is not always easy, but the work of previous researchers can serve as your guide. They have found that certain forms of talk often signal that some conversational work that is pertinent to the researchable questions in the project may be ongoing. We refer to these forms of talk as *conversational features*. You can use these conversational features to guide you to the pieces of talk that are worth a close look. These are the pieces of talk that you will excerpt from the interview material. Note that there is no one-to-one relationship between a certain conversational feature and a certain type of conversational work. We therefore reiterate the advice of pioneer researchers: researchers should learn to recognize as many conversational features as possible. Familiarity with these features enables the researcher to identify them when they occur and to use these occurrences as starting points for their analysis (Antaki, Billig, Edwards, & Potter, 2003).

In what follows, we describe a selection of conversational features that researchers have identified as indicating that some significant conversational work may be under way. We also describe the types of conversational work to which the features may contribute.

As always in interpretative research, when you select excerpts of talk for analysis, your excerpts should be ample. That is, you should include enough of the ongoing conversation to indicate the immediate rhetorical context.

The phases of the analysis

The analytical procedure has three phases. The first phase consists of identifying and excerpting instances of conversational features to study. The second phase consists of analyzing the work that a particular occurrence of a feature does within the rhetorical context of the excerpted text. The third phase consists of relating the analyses to the researchable questions in your study.

In each of the subsections that follow, we describe what the second phase of analysis can encompass by using examples from our research interviews. These excerpts had already been identified in the first phase of the analysis. How researchers proceed in this second phase varies depending on the type of interaction, the type of conversational feature, the researchable question that is being addressed, and the overall purpose of the study. Therefore, we cannot provide an exact set of steps that would always be appropriate. The third phase of analysis also typically varies between researchers. In this phase, the task is to relate the "local" action in a specific interaction to the larger issues in a study. All told, then, it is not possible to lay out detailed, universal, or routine steps for analyses of talk-as-action. The examples we provide are meant to give enough substance for beginners to start the second phase of analysis of their material. We have chosen this strategy for presentation because the best way for beginners to learn how to do these kinds of analyses is by reading other researchers' analyses and by doing analyses of their own material. As in all interpretative analyses, it is quite common for researchers to move back and forth among the phases of analysis.

A note about transcription and listening. The transcription procedures and the notation system that we recommended in Chapter 7 are likely to be detailed enough for many analyses of talk-as-action. However, sometimes it may be useful to have information about simultaneous talk, interruptions, voice inflection, etc., which is not recorded in the transcription. In such cases, once you have identified a piece of interaction to study, a good strategy is to listen again to that section of the interview. You can either make notes of specific characteristics that may be of relevance or you can amend the original transcription by adding more detail (Taylor, 2001).

Analyzing conversational features

"Witcraft" – statements plus justifications

When a speaker makes a statement and immediately follows it with a justification of that statement, this is an indication that something of analytical interest may be going on. Perhaps an opinion has been questioned or doubted by somebody else, and the speaker is making a counterargument for his or her own position. It also frequently happens that speakers fortify their statements with justifications even when no disagreement is present or seems forthcoming. Such instances are examples of what Michael Billig has called *witcraft*. To quote him: "witcraft involves reasons being framed cunningly to answer, and thereby contradict, other reasons" (1996, p. 115). That is, when speakers give reasons for their own standpoints, they frequently smuggle in arguments against other contradictory standpoints, often without mentioning the contradictory standpoints.

For the researcher who is analyzing talk-as-action, locating such instances of witcraft can help to identify issues that are controversial in a particular social setting or personally troublesome for a speaker. The portions of talk in which witcraft occurs may therefore merit close analysis. Let us give an example from one of Eva's studies in which she did one-on-one interviews with women about daily life at work and at home (Magnusson, 1998). Barbara, one of the participants, told Eva that she demanded a lot of herself in the household; she had to have everything "just so." Eva then asked if this meant that she saw herself as a "conscientious housekeeper."[1] Barbara answered: "Yes! I mangle our clothes [.] I don't clean house a lot. I mangle and iron everything except

---

[1] The Swedish expression was *noggrann husmor*, which does not have direct English translation. *Husmor* denotes a woman who is in charge of the household, but is not necessarily a full-time housewife. Such was Barbara's situation: she worked full-time in an office job.

underwear! [laughs] And some have stopped doing all such things. But it [.] I do it for my own pleasure, because I want it that way!"

After her initial "Yes!" in this excerpt, we see that Barbara mentioned a few of her many time-consuming housework practices as illustrations. At the end of the extract, she gave her reason for doing these tasks: her own pleasure in the results. These two utterances combine a statement ("I mangle and iron everything except underwear") with a justification ("But it [.] I do it for my own pleasure, because I want it that way").

When the researcher has identified such a combination during the first phase of the analysis, the second phase consists of considering it in the *rhetorical context* within which the participant is speaking. In this case, there was first the interview context: Eva had not asked Barbara about her reasons for wanting to be a "conscientious house-keeper" nor expressed any opinions or arguments to do with housework. However, it is likely that the topics of the interview would have led Barbara to see Eva as someone in favor of equality measures.

The second context was the larger society, including norms and values. The time when the interview was done was a period of intense political debate in Sweden about many kinds of gender equality, including sharing housework in the family. A hint about how Barbara saw herself in relation to this larger context can be found in her observation "And some have stopped doing all such things." This observation indicates that she was aware that housework chores such as mangling and ironing all the laundry had become obsolete for an undefined number of women captured by her word "some." Perhaps she, then, could be seen as old-fashioned compared to them.

The third rhetorical context consists of the opinions that the speaker is arguing for, and the counter-opinions that the speaker is explicitly or implicitly criticizing. In the excerpt, Barbara argued *for* the opinion that "mangling and ironing everything except under-wear" is a valuable pursuit. She ended her account, after all, by saying, "I do it for my own pleasure, because I want it that way." Words such as "pleasure" and "want it" certainly give the impression that these chores were of value to her. What, if any, counter-opinions was she criticizing? As we can see, her account contained no explicit arguments against counter-opinions. Might there have been implicit ones? As a Swedish woman in her mid-forties, Barbara was certainly aware of existing counter-opinions, such as that women who did these chores were trapped in outmoded traditions and conventions, or were even "oppressed." It is possible that some of these counter-opinions were on her mind when she mentioned women who had stopped doing these chores. If so, the immediately following "But it-" that began her final sentence, along with her emphasis on "my own pleasure" and "wanting it that way," may have been her implicit way of criticizing those counter-opinions. She was saying that the counter-opinions did not apply to her: she did these things because she wanted to.

What can you learn about analysis from this example? There are four key points: (1) Spontaneous justifications may signal that participants feel that something they said could provoke counterarguments; (2) by providing immediate justifications – for example, in the form of reasons for an action – participants may be preempting counter-arguments; (3) instances of statements-plus-justifications in interviews probably indicate points of controversy or conflict for a participant; and (4) such instances may be especially informative for researchers who are interested in the ideals, cultural meanings, or opinions in their participants' surroundings.

Expressions of disagreement

Expressions of disagreement in interviews are likely to signal issues that are important for the participants. These may be disagreements between the people in the interview room, but it may also be that a participant expresses disagreement with someone who is not present. In an example from Eva's couples study, one of the men, Lars, told the interviewer that he picked up the children from daycare once a week or so. His wife, Lene, immediately contradicted his statement by exclaiming, "You don't pick up the kids once a week!" She went on to claim that, in fact, he never did. There followed what sounded like a brief negotiation that ended in a joint recollection of a short period of time during which Lars had picked up the children from daycare fairly regularly. At present, however, he did not. Through this negotiation, the couples' initial disagreement was resolved into a new joint version of Lars's record of daycare duties. The new version agreed better with the initial description that Lene had presented than his original statement had.

How might you analyze disagreements such as this in an interview? In the first phase of analysis, the researcher identified and described an instance of disagreement. The second phase then begins with a focus on content. What important issues might the disagreement (and in the case of Lars and Lene, its resolution) be signaling? For instance, are there indications in other parts of the interview that picking up the children from daycare was an inflammatory issue for this couple? And are there indications that the husband and wife in this couple lived with many discordant versions of how daily responsibilities were distributed between them? In that case, what were the other areas of daily life about which their versions diverged?

The next thing to do in the second phase of the analysis is to explore how the disagreement "works" in its local rhetorical context. For Lars and Lene above, the context was the interview. The researcher could learn more about the meaning of this particular disagreement for Lars and Lene by studying it in relation to what else took place during the interview. For instance, if the researcher were to find that this was the only instance of disagreement in the interview, it is likely that the matter that they disagreed about had some significance that was worth pursuing further. Alternatively, if Lars and Lene disagreed repeatedly in the interview, and they disagreed about many different topics, then the matter of this particular disagreement might not be significant. Instead, the researcher might be interested in comparing this couple with other couples who rarely disagreed in the interview context.

A further analytical use of instances of explicit disagreement is as sensitizing devices. That is, they may open your eyes to parallel, but perhaps less explicit, instances of disagreement in other interviews. Participants often express disagreement in indirect ways that are difficult to detect unless the researcher's attention has been sharpened by the more explicit instances. If you identify disagreements in other interviews, it is a good idea to look across the study group to see if participants disagree about similar topics. If you find that certain topics are especially likely to evoke disagreement, it is probably worthwhile to examine those topics more closely.

To get a fuller picture of what a particular disagreement may mean to participants, it is a good idea to study how they report about disagreements – their own and others' – that have occurred outside the interview. For instance, Eva found that many couples (like Stina and Stephen) emphasized that they rarely or never disagreed about anything, and that they "never, *ever*" quarreled with one another. The same couples also spoke disparagingly – often almost in the same breath – about couples who did disagree openly. Other couples told the interviewer about disagreements and quarrels that they had had in the past. Yet other couples told about ongoing disagreements. When Eva followed up these different ways of talking about disagreements, she found a pattern: the couples who emphasized that they never quarreled were the ones who did not share housework and childcare equally, whereas the couples who talked about explicit disagreements were the ones who shared housework and childcare more equally. Eva used these differences in patterns of speaking about disagreements as the starting point for the third phase of analysis in her study.

Contrasting and extreme cases

Contrasting is a conversational feature that brings into a conversation a threatening or particularly unattractive alternative to a situation, point of view, or way of being that the speaker presents as normal, good, or taken for granted. By depicting the alternative ideas or practices in negative ways, the speaker makes his or her favored practices or ideas appear superior. Recall how Stina and Stephen, in our first example, talked about other couples who "squabbled." In another interview, Johan, a Swedish man, replied, when he was asked what made his wife Jessica a good person to live with: "Neither one makes unreasonable demands on the other. I think many relationships split up because of that: people keep demanding lots of things of each other. After all, we are two single individuals . . . One sees families where it doesn't work our way [as flexibly as in their family]. And I would never be able to live like that." Johan then described how the women in these other families demanded that their husbands come home from work at a set time each day, thus preventing the men from coming home whenever it suited them. Johan's contrasting is evident in his choice of words. He used expressions that conjured up unpleasantness and trouble (such as "unreasonable demands" and "keep demanding lots of things of each other") when he talked about the other couples whose lifestyle he would not be able to stand. And he used words that convey valued qualities, such as "flexibility" and "individuals," when he talked about the arrangements in his own family.

In talk that contrasts practices or ideas, speakers often use *extreme case formulations*. Extreme case formulations are expressions that describe phenomena in ways that bring to mind the outer edges of the range of possible judgments (Pomerantz, 1986; Edwards, 2000). An extreme case formulation may contain superlatives, such as best, worst, most, or biggest, or extreme adverbs such as always, never, or absolutely, or exaggerations such as "everybody has the same problems" or "nobody likes him." Johan, for instance, used the expression "unreasonable demands" and the phrase "I would never be able to live like that."

Locating extreme expressions and phrases in interview talk is a strategy for identifying instances of contrasting that merit further analysis. For instance, in Eva's couples study, Ulla argued that for the sake of their children, her husband Ulrik should not be absent from home so often. Ulrik answered that he did not think that he was away so often that it was bad for the children. He continued, "Just look at other children – look at X, her daughter grew up practically without a father, and there is nothing wrong with her!" He ended his argument, "so, if I am not home until after their bedtime a couple of nights a week, I really don't think that will hurt them." By conjuring up the extreme case of X's daughter and her absent father, Ulrik made his own less extreme absences look acceptable, at least to himself. When speakers use extreme case formulations in a conversation, it is a likely indication that something contentious or conflictual is under way. So it proved in this couple: they had a long discussion in the interview about prioritizing one's work or one's children, finally telling the interviewer that this was an issue about which they had not been able to agree. Here we see that this analysis touches on the previous section about disagreements. You may therefore want to return to that section for suggestions for further analysis.

Metacommunication in interviews

It is not unusual that participants in interviews comment on their own stories or statements or on what is happening in the interview situation. Such comments are called metacommunications. The comments can be of many different kinds, such as disclaimers, evaluative remarks, or reflexive comments, but they all relate to something that is or has been going on in the interview. A participant may express astonishment about what he or she has just told the interviewer, as when a participant in one of Jeanne's studies said, "I can't believe I'm telling you this!" after expressing criticism of her professional colleagues. It also may happen that a participant comments on the interviewer, as when a participant in one of Eva's studies exclaimed, "It is so terribly easy to talk to you!" And sometimes, the participant's comment summarizes and evaluates a previous account. Such was the case when Birgitta, a participant in one of Eva's studies, exclaimed, "Yes, in our house things are completely traditional, so that all professional women would go crazy if they heard it!" (Magnusson, 1998, p. 186). She made this comment after she had described who did what daily chores in her home.

Metacommunications in interviews are potentially interesting to the researcher because they may signal that the participant is managing some kind of interactional issue or trouble related to the topic of the talk. It may be trouble in relation to some group or person outside the interview setting (such as the profession, in the first example above), or it may be trouble of some kind in the interview setting. Researchers are therefore well advised to analyze metacommunications closely. As always, such analyses should take into account the local and larger rhetorical contexts in which the metacommunication appears. To illustrate, let us look closer at Birgitta's statement above.

To begin with, Birgitta's metacommunication can be taken as a summary of how she had just described the details of the distribution of housework in her family ("completely traditional"). Summarizing like this is a fairly common content-oriented function of metacommunication in interviews. Participants often comment on what they have just said in order to summarize it and perhaps also emphasize an especially important aspect.

Metacommunications, however, usually also do some interaction work in the interview setting. This was the case in Birgitta's statement. Its first part portrayed her as a traditional housewife ("in our house, things are completely traditional"). Its second part referred to "all professional women," who, Birgitta said, would be aghast at her traditional household arrangements ("would go crazy"). Birgitta's expression "professional women"[2] had not been used earlier in the interview. Did it therefore carry some special significance at this point? And what, if any, interaction work did Birgitta's metacommunication do?

To begin to answer questions such as these, the researcher needs to take into account the rhetorical context. What was the rhetorical context in Birgitta's case? The first dimension of the rhetorical context concerns the social relations between the participant and the interviewer within the larger setting of the gender equality debates in contemporary Swedish society. The second dimension of the rhetorical context was the questions and opinions about sharing housework that had been discussed in the interview. In this case, the interviewer (Eva) was an academic researcher and a psychologist; it is likely that Birgitta regarded her as one such "professional women." Therefore, when Birgitta exclaimed, "all professional women would go crazy if they heard it!" did she perhaps imply that Eva would also "go crazy" about the lack of equality in Birgitta's household? Did Birgitta's utterance perhaps function as an excuse for having an unequal sharing situation in her home? That is one possible interpretation. Are other interpretations possible? Certainly. For instance, what if her exclamation about "all professional women" was instead a way to distance herself from the opinions that she ascribed to these women? If that interpretation is correct, Birgitta's metacommunication might actually, via the detour of referring to professional women, be voicing a disagreement with Eva. Birgitta might be telling Eva that she did not share the set of values about gender equality in the home that she ascribed to "all professional women," implicitly including Eva. In that case, Birgitta's metacommunication might have been an instance of disagreement with the interviewer and could be treated analytically as such (*cf.* the earlier section about disagreements).

Variability in accounts: when participants contradict themselves

Researchers almost invariably find that people sometimes contradict themselves while being interviewed and that they often do so without acknowledging that contradiction. Sometimes the contradictions are evident, such as when a participant makes statements

---

[2] The Swedish word that we translated as "professional women" is *yrkeskvinnor*, a word that signifies a woman who has a high education and a fairly responsible position at work. Birgitta herself had a high school education and about a year of college. She worked in a position as a secretary to a high official in a government office.

about a certain issue that clearly contradict one another. Often, though, participants do not state contradictions outright but show *variability* in their accounts. For example, participants may use words with distinctly different meanings in different parts of the interview. Such variability will usually on closer scrutiny prove to contain or imply one or more contradictions.

Let us exemplify. Think back to the section about statements and justifications, in which Barbara said, "Yes! I mangle our clothes [.] but I don't clean house a lot. I mangle and iron everything except underwear! [laughs] And some have stopped doing all such things. But it [.] I do it for my own pleasure, because I want it that way!" In this account, Barbara emphasized that the reason why she did this type of housework, though others had stopped doing it, was that *she* enjoyed the results. Fair enough. Then, six lines further down in the interview transcript, Barbara said, "because [.] they can come and visit whenever they want to [.] the place won't be messy. And I think that that would be harder for me, you know." In this second account, she brought in "they" who might come unannounced to visit her but who, because of her tidiness, would not find the house messy. If "they" had found the house messy, she said, it would have been worse ("harder") for her than doing the work to keep the house tidy. So, now we are faced with two reasons why Barbara was a conscientious housekeeper: her own pleasure and her fear of other people's judgments. The reasons seem contradictory: she first says that she keeps her house tidy because she wants to, and then that she does it because she feels pressure from others.

What can the researcher learn from contradictory statements and variability in interviews? That depends on the researchable questions that are in focus. The researcher might be interested in the register of different meanings and contradictory meanings of an issue that a participant uses while talking about the issue. Further, the researcher may be interested in the register of meanings available to the whole group of participants in a study. In that case, the researcher may want to analyze all the interviews for how participants use particular meanings in relation to a certain topic. Additionally, the researcher may be interested in how participants relate to the different *rhetorical contexts* evoked in an interview. For instance, participants may vary the meanings they give to a topic between different rhetorical contexts, and by doing so *position* themselves or others in specific ways in different parts of the conversation (Magnusson, 1998).

Emphasizing consensus and corroboration by others

Emphasizing consensus is a way for speakers to give an aura of legitimacy to an opinion by presenting it as something that is agreed upon by a large number of people. Emphasizing consensus can also be used to convey a sense of objective existence to a claim, for example, by describing it as corroborated by independent observers.

Let us give an example from Eva's study of Nordic couples. Mogens and Mette described their sharing of housework as very traditional, with Mette staying at home to take care of their children and the housework. Immediately after this description, Mogens said that he saw parallels to their arrangement in many other couples: "there is a tendency that the sex role pattern is more divided again. [.] It's to be father who works and mother who takes care of the children." Mette agreed with him, saying: "Yes, I can see among my female friends, that they take care of the children, and then the father comes home late from work." Mette and Mogens, through their references to "the sex role pattern," to "a tendency," and to "my female friends," portrayed their own house-work distribution as part of a larger social change back to a traditional pattern and not just their personal preference. When reading this exchange, you need to know that this couple's "traditional" arrangement went directly against the ideal in contemporary Danish society. It may be, therefore, that Mette and Mogens felt that they needed to justify their household arrangements by describing them as widely shared.

For the researcher, identifying instances where a participant recruits others for support is often a fruitful way of locating issues that are in some way troublesome for that participant. Such issues may be worthy of closer analysis. Mette and Mogens's assertion of the increasing social consensus about unequal sharing led Eva to look for similar instances in other interviews and eventually to do detailed analyses of the various rhetorical strategies and conversational features that couples with traditional household arrangements used when arguing against the value of equal sharing of housework (Magnusson, 2006, 2008a).

Reported speech in interviews

Interview participants sometimes bring absent others into the conversation by quoting them verbatim or seeming to do so. The term for this is *reported speech*. An instance of reported speech is often a sign that something worthy of closer analysis may be going on. For instance, speakers often use reported speech by authoritative persons to corroborate their own opinions. Another common practice is to use reported speech as an indirect means of offering an opinion for which the speaker does not want to be held accountable. Yet another use of reported speech is for speakers to vivify an assertion that they have just made. May, for example, who was a participant in a study of organization change that Eva did, told Eva that she was irritated because her work colleagues expected her to take care of most of the social functions in the workplace. She then exclaimed: "Just fancy, they take it for granted: 'Why, she will fix it' [..] Yes, you hear that a lot: 'May will fix that. We can take it easy.' " By inserting these quotes from her work colleagues into her talk, May is offering their talk as testimony that her assertion ought to be believed. These pieces of reported speech by May, who was a low-level office worker, gave Eva some of the initial material and analytical ideas for a study of the intertwining of social class and femininity in workplaces (Magnusson, 1997b).

In other cases, reported speech is used to highlight or emphasize disagreement about some contentious point. Paulina, who had taken part in Eva's couples study, told the interviewer that it was important to her that she and Petri, her husband, both took independent initiatives and had equal responsibilities in the home. She then contrasted their practices with those of other couples, in which "somehow the woman has all the threads in her hands and keeps giving advice to her husband about everything he ought to do, how he should feed the children, and so on. I don't think I do that [quotes the other woman]: 'Now it's dinner time for the kid, you have to go and feed her!' We have nothing like that." Immediately after this instance of reported speech, Paulina and Petri jointly emphasized that it was of value for them that they were equally proficient on all household and childcare tasks. Paulina's use of reported speech to disparage traditional couples led Eva to ask how the couples with the most equal sharing patterns talked about themselves in relation to their social surroundings. It turned out that it was common to talk in terms of distance and contrast, and sometimes to talk about being seen as avant-garde or odd or even deviant (Magnusson, 2006).

You may have noticed that the examples of reported speech above also contain some contrasting and extreme case formulations. This is to be expected; speakers often combine conversational features in their accounts.

Descriptions and facts

An important function of many conversational features is that they contribute to depicting a speaker's account as factual, objective, and trustworthy, and therefore not merely the speaker's personal opinion. This function of talk-as-action is called *fact construction*, because it makes a speaker's account appear anchored in something (i.e., facts) outside the speaker's mind or opinions (Edwards & Potter, 1992; Speer, 2005). Facts, after all, are external to the speaker; they are not the speaker's opinions, nor are they assertions fabricated by the speaker. Of the conversational features we have described above, two – contrasting and what we have called consensus and corroboration – are often used to construct "facts," sometimes in combination with appeals to outside authority. If you look back to the excerpt from the interview with Mette and Mogens, for instance, you will see that they stated as a fact – that is, something not based on their opinions – that many other couples had, like themselves, reverted to a traditional family pattern.

Researchers have identified several techniques or strategies that people regularly use to construct facts in their talk. If a researcher is studying a controversial topic, it is useful to identify instances in which these techniques are in use. This is so because speakers commonly use forms of speech that make an account seem factual when they are arguing about controversial or morally contentious issues. Below we introduce some of the many techniques of fact construction that researchers have identified. Identifying instances when these techniques are used may be helpful as pointers to further analysis.

Descriptions and vivid descriptions

To describe a phenomenon or event is one way to give it a fact-like character. When a speaker describes something, he or she does so in ways that appear neutral and objective. The resulting description is made to appear as if it were "outside" the describer's own opinions and values and, therefore, a fact. However, when speakers describe something, they necessarily do so in a specific rhetorical context and from a specific speaking position. Therefore, when speakers describe events and phenomena, their descriptions may simultaneously create an impression of how responsibility, agency, and power were distributed in the described situation. In this way, a description may, for instance, suggest who is to be blamed and who is to be praised for a particular outcome in the situation or event that the speaker described (Edwards & Potter, 1992; Speer, 2005).

Vivid descriptions entail describing an event or a situation with many contextual details and incidents. By giving a vivid description a speaker can create a particularly strong impression of authenticity and factuality, almost like saying "I was there." Speakers sometimes enhance vivid descriptions with reported speech, that is, quotes, or alleged quotes, from participants in the events that are recounted (Buttny, 2003). Vivid descriptions can be used to talk about problematic or controversial events or other phenomena about which people disagree.

In an example from Eva's couples study, Lars, a Danish man, argued that his son and daughter were fundamentally different because they belonged to different sex categories, not because they were being brought up differently: "Now, we have a boy and a girl, and you can't believe how different they are just because they are of different sexes! You may say that boys cry less because people have told them 'You mustn't cry! Be a man!' But I don't think that's how it hangs together." He followed his argument with a vivid description of his three-year-old son: "if you give him a sword, then you can really see how two thousand years of masculinity comes out: He squeezes his eyebrows together and lifts his sword!"

Systematic vagueness in descriptions

Rich and vivid descriptions carry a risk: too much detail may provide the listener with material for contestation. A speaker may take the opposite strategy and offer descriptions that are replete with vague and global expressions. Such descriptions make it difficult for listeners to latch on to concrete points to question. At the same time, such a vague account may be enough to create the sense of factuality that the speaker wishes to create. If you refer back to the conversation between Stina and Stephen at the beginning of the chapter, you can see such an instance in their vague reference to "other couples."

Empiricist accounting in descriptions

Empiricist accounting is the term used for descriptions in which facts and phenomena are presented without a narrator being involved. This strategy makes phenomena appear as if they were actors that more or less force themselves on the describer (Gilbert & Mulkay, 1984). The describer is either "deleted" from the account (for instance, by using passive voice constructions) or treated as a passive recipient of events (Edwards & Potter, 1992). Although empiricist accounting is more common in research reports than in conversations, it occurs in ordinary conversation as well, where it often points to topics and issues that are contentious.

In Eva's couples study, empiricist accounting was used by some men who argued for the necessity or naturalness of dividing housework and childcare according to a traditionally gendered pattern. Such accounts featured genes, nature, or "motherliness" as the agents. For example, John, one of the Finnish men, explained that the uneven distribution of housework and childcare in their family had come about naturally. This meant that the distribution was a consequence of biological differences between him and his wife. He recruited genetic arguments such as "But I think it has something to do with the female and male genes, that it lies – I could try, but it [the responsibility for childcare] lies closer to – [Jenny, his wife]." Later in the interview, John further explained why he did not take as much a part in caring for their children as Jenny did. He referred to what he saw as fundamental differences between himself and his wife: "but perhaps it is still that mother –, the 'mother thing' is perhaps more a – It is more an instinct that is more innate, I think, sort of stronger."

John here recruited "female and male genes," "the 'mother thing,' " and "an instinct that is more innate" as the causes of his and his wife's different behavior in the home. By doing so, he moved the issue of gender equality in the home away from being about ideology and justice to being about genetic differences. Explaining the uneven distribution of housework and childcare as a result of genes and instincts makes such a distribution seem natural and not the speaker's "fault." The distribution may even seem to be a fact of nature that presses itself upon the speaker.

Category entitlement

Speakers often bolster the truth of a description by referring to their membership in a particular category of people who are assumed to be especially knowledgeable about the issue under discussion. When speakers identify themselves as members of such a category, this may lead people to assume the veracity of what they say. It is as if membership in the category is all that is needed (Potter, 1996). Another type of category entitlement comes from having had some unusual experience, such as being present at a road accident or a natural disaster. Being a first-person witness entitles a speaker to stronger feelings than being a listener to a story about the accident (Sacks, 1992).

The purposes of analyzing talk-as-action

As we conclude this chapter, we remind readers that the purpose of the types of analysis we have described here is not to produce a list of conversational features that were used by the participants in a study. Rather, the purpose of analysis is always (as in the examples) to address the researchable questions or sub-questions that motivated the search through the interview material for conversational features. Identifying the conversational features enables the researcher to locate portions of an interview in which difficult matters were being talked about or where the interaction was conflicted.

11 Analyzing for implicit cultural meanings

In this chapter we describe an analytical framework and two types of analytical procedures for studying how people's talk and meaning-making relate to sets of meanings that are shared either locally or more broadly. The analytical procedures that we describe require that researchers pay close attention to language and language use, as well as to features of the local context and the larger culture. The researcher also needs to pay close attention to the relation of these larger cultural features to individual meaning-making.

We describe two kinds of analytical procedures. One kind focuses mainly on how people take shared sets of meanings into use in their talk and meaning-making. The second kind focuses mainly on how shared sets of meanings encourage certain ways of understanding oneself and others and discourage other ways. The procedures we describe treat interviews and other kinds of conversations as necessarily part of a larger social world beyond the immediate context in which the words are said. Thinking about conversations in this way moves the researcher's attention to what we call *implicit cultural meanings* – that is, meanings about some area of life that members of an interpretive community share and take for granted.

We begin with an overview of the analytical framework for the procedures for analysis we describe in this chapter. After that, we describe analytical procedures that enable a researcher to discern the implicit cultural meanings that a group of people share and to discern how they take those meanings into use. In the final section of the chapter, we describe analytical procedures that enable researchers to study individual meaning-making; these procedures concern how implicit cultural meanings may inform or restrict how people understand themselves and others.

Analytical framework: implicit cultural meanings

The general theoretical framework of this book holds that personal meanings and meaning-making are not idiosyncratic. Personal meanings are always fashioned within the network of possible meanings that are available in the interpretive communities of which the person is a member. People always understand events, other people, and themselves against a background of shared meanings. We use the expression *implicit cultural meanings* to denote meanings about some issue or area of life that are shared and taken for granted by the members of a particular social group or that are commonplace in the culture at large.

An example may clarify what we mean: In the mainstream culture in many societies, it is taken for granted (i.e., commonly understood) that if nothing is said to the contrary, a person can be assumed to be heterosexual. This meaning of "a person" as somebody who is heterosexual is *cultural* in the sense that it is shared by members of the mainstream in many societies. And the meaning is *implicit* because it is usually not voiced, that is, made explicit. Everybody in such interpretive communities "knows" that one should presume that people are heterosexual unless there is reason to think otherwise. One "knows" this even if one has never been told outright to make that assumption. It is likely that people in these cultural settings do not consciously decide to make the assumption of hetero-sexuality every time they make a new acquaintance. Instead, it is as if the assumption has been made *a priori*: it is a preconception that is culturally shared. Such "knowing" that people are heterosexual unless specifically known to be otherwise is kept alive by daily experiences that seem to confirm this unvoiced assumption.

Implicit cultural meanings could be thought of as elements of shared tacit knowledge that enable members of a particular social group to negotiate their daily lives in mutually compatible ways. The shared meanings smooth people's navigation through the social landscape of daily life. Members of a certain culture or of a local interpretive community have access to the same sets of implicit cultural meanings and to the same sets of expressions and words that are anchored in these cultural meanings. These cultural meanings and expressions are the resources that are available for composing their accounts and stories. You could say that the implicit cultural meanings of a particular culture or interpretive community are the main resources that the members have for making themselves understandable to one another and to themselves. In fact, being a competent member of a particular cultural or subcultural group means having at hand the implicit cultural meanings shared by members of that group. When a set of implicit cultural meanings has been shared over time, people do not have to refer explicitly to a particular meaning for it to be invoked. Rather, in their talk, people typically use fragments of arguments, idiomatic expressions, or culturally familiar forms of talk to do the invoking (Wetherell, 1998).

Implicit cultural meanings often can be quite powerful. An implicit cultural meaning, if it is dominant, may make certain ways of seeing oneself, expressing a feeling, experiencing an event, or linking an effect to a cause seem to be expected, normal, or even natural. The analytical procedures that we describe in the second half of this chapter are informed by this feature of implicit cultural meanings, which emphasizes their power to guide people's meaning-making along particular channels.

Another perspective on implicit cultural meanings stresses that the activity of perso-nal meaning-making is inventive. Although people use already-existing pieces of language, culture, and history to make meaning in their lives, they often assemble these pieces in ways that make meanings that did not exist before. Viewed from this perspective, speakers may be seen as recruiting a particular cultural meaning in their talk in order to achieve a specific purpose, such as persuading listeners or presenting themselves in a favorable light. Speakers use the same cultural meaning in different ways, depending on differences in the rhetorical context, including differences in the speaker's intentions. Speakers can also refer to different cultural meanings, depending on differences in the rhetorical context. This perspective on implicit cultural meanings is the focus of the analytical procedures that we describe in the first part of the chapter.

The two perspectives on implicit cultural meanings that we briefly outlined in the two previous paragraphs originate in divergent theoretical and epistemological traditions. There is a theoretical divide between conceiving of people as active and voluntary "users" of implicit cultural meanings for their own purposes versus conceiving of people as "responders" who are influenced and constrained by implicit cultural meanings. This divide has given rise to considerable debate among interpretative researchers (see, for instance, Edwards et al., 1995; Parker, 1990a, 1990b; Parker and Burman, 1993; Potter et al., 1990; Potter and Wetherell, 1992). Our standpoint is that which of the two perspectives on implicit cultural meanings a researcher should choose ought to depend on the knowledge interest and researchable questions that the researcher has for a particular study. Some researchers have worked to devise ways to encompass both perspectives within a study (see, for instance, Wetherell, 1998).

Terminology in this chapter

You may have noted that the description of implicit cultural meanings in the previous section is similar to definitions of such terms as discourses, interpretative repertoires, and interpretative resources. And you may wonder why we do not use one of those more commonly used terms. We have several answers to this query. Our first answer is that the research literature contains a profusion of different definitions of those terms and different uses of these definitions. Consequently, learners often find themselves thoroughly bewildered about which definition to take up and how to put the chosen definition into analytical use. We hope to avoid causing such bewilderment by using a clearly defined term here. We also wanted a term that is clearly located within the larger theoretical framework for the book. Our second answer is that any choice of a particular definition of a term such as discourse or interpretative repertoire would draw you into the fray of debates and positionings among researchers. This we felt was unnecessary for a learner's guide. Our third answer is that in reports about empirical research, the actual uses of these different terms often boil down to the two general aspects of implicit cultural meanings that we have described in the previous section. We therefore decided to use the term "implicit cultural meanings."

We are aware that experts in one or another of the fields we write about may find that our term does not capture precisely their use of various terms. That cannot be helped. We have found that, as a way to help learners move into the analytical territory that we describe in this chapter, the strategy we take has often been helpful.

The analyses that we describe in this chapter are commensurate with some forms of discourse analysis in the social sciences. However, consistent with our choice of terms above, we do not use "discourse analysis" for these analyses. The reason is that the term is used to refer to many different types of analysis, which have many different theoretical bases and analytical goals. Invariably, this confuses learners. In an effort to avoid some of that confusion, we have decided to use a term that stays within the theoretical framework of our book.

ANALYTICAL PROCEDURES

(A) Group-focused analysis of implicit cultural meanings

In this section, we describe a way to analyze interviews when your main interest is to elucidate the most common ways of making sense of a particular topic or issue in a specific setting and how people in that setting take them into use. For instance, it is by using certain cultural meanings to inform their talk, and using those meanings in certain ways, that members of a social group demonstrate their membership to themselves and to others. Usually, a speaker does not have to make a particular cultural meaning explicit for this to happen; rather, certain key words or brief indirect references are enough.

The analyses we describe here share some characteristics with the types of analysis we described in Chapter 8 (both concern patterns of shared meaning-making) and Chapter 10 (both focus on how people "use" talk). However, the analyses that we describe here take a turn different from those that we describe in Chapter 8 and Chapter 10. They focus specifically on how common understandings, and the ways people may use them, are located in the cultural surroundings of the speaker. Often, researchers want to find out if and how people use culturally shared meanings when they give their accounts about a topic or issue. Also, researchers often want to identify the options for action that are opened up or closed down when speakers use certain culturally shared meanings.

The first step: selecting the material to analyze

As is always the case in interpretative research, the initial phase of this analysis is to become familiar with the interview material. The researcher reads through the whole set of interviews with the knowledge interests and researchable questions in mind. The next, and more structured, phase of the analysis also looks much like some of the other types of analysis we describe: searching through the interview material for pieces of talk that relate to the researchable questions. As you locate such pieces of talk, you copy them into new excerpt files, with a separate file for each researchable question or sub-question. As in other types of interpretative analysis, it is common for researchers to develop new questions as they read the transcripts. For any such additional questions, you should create another excerpt file for the new excerpts. As is also typical of this phase of interpretative research, as you go through more and more interviews, you will discover new facets of your researchable questions. You may want to use these new facets of the questions to complement or revise the initial version of the question. If you make such changes, you need to go back and reread material that you have already excerpted to make sure the excerpts still fit. You may also need to go back to the full transcripts to see if more interview material fits with the revised versions of the researchable questions.

While you are selecting excerpts for the excerpt files, it is useful to annotate the excerpted pieces of talk with short labels, questions, or other comments related to your analytical interests. This will make it easier to locate relevant pieces later in the analysis.

The initial phase of the analysis that we have just described has two purposes: first, to select the material that the researcher intends to analyze; and second, to get the material sorted by researchable questions or topics, rather than by participants. This re-sorting of material is essential to the type of analysis we describe here, because the purpose of the analysis is not to classify individuals, but to identify and study the use of implicit cultural meanings related to a certain topic or question.

What we have just described may at first glance appear identical to the analyses that we described in Chapter 8. However, although there are similarities in the early parts of the procedure, the later parts differ. In the analyses we described in Chapter 8, the purpose is to identify patterns of individual meaning-making about some question or issue across a group or groups of participants. Therefore, the researchable questions, and the criteria for selecting portions of the interview to excerpt, are focused on how the participants understand a question or issue. In the type of analysis we describe in this chapter, the aim is to identify the implicit cultural meanings that speakers make use of in their accounts. The researchable questions in these analyses, therefore, are focused on meanings that are shared by a group or subculture and on the participants' ways of "using" these meanings. These characteristics of the researchable questions determine the criteria for selecting pieces of talk to excerpt. We illustrate the remaining steps of the procedures with an example taken from one of our research projects.

The second step: from researchable questions to group commonalities

We use excerpts from Eva's study of Nordic couples as the material to illustrate group-focused analysis for implicit cultural meanings. In that study, identifying and studying differences between couples in how they talked about sharing housework and child-care was part of the original researchable questions. For that purpose, Eva sorted pieces of such talk into three separate excerpt files: one file for couples who shared housework equally, one for couples who did not share, and one for the couples whose sharing patterns fell in between. Reading through these files, Eva noticed that there were many aspects of their talk that differed among the three groups. One aspect was that in the couples with the most unequal sharing of housework and childcare, virtually all the men gave accounts that explicitly described and justified their low level of participation in ways that made this low level seem to be taken for granted. There were also a few instances of similar talk by the men in the in-between group. As would be expected, there was no such talk by the men in the equally sharing group. Eva was interested in finding out more about the accounts the men gave, especially about the implicit cultural meanings that the accounts were based in. Eva was also interested in how these accounts "worked" in the conversation. Below is a selection of accounts:

> As Johan compared his own situation at home with that of male colleagues who prioritized their families' needs on a par with their wives, he stated: "I don't know if I myself would like to do it that way. I think [.] I get so enormously engrossed. I get absorbed in my work." He expanded on this statement by

describing his attitude toward work: "I'm a bit of a career person. [.] So things have to become more difficult, tougher, more responsibility all the time. Otherwise it's no fun."

Lars told about the reason why he hardly ever shopped for food for his family: "I am so bad at shopping for food [.] even when Lene has made a shopping-list, I forget half of it. Yes, I am hopeless."

This is what Bengt said about his wife Britta and their unequal distribution of housework and childcare: "I think she knows that there are certain chores that she can't make me do." He also declared that he could not possibly imagine staying home with the children on parental leave.

When Valdemar and his wife Vivi discussed what would happen if she were to start working full-time, he said: "It would mean that I would also have to do some reorganization [of my work schedule]. But I really don't know if I'm prepared to do that. One should realize one's personal ambitions, and I can't see how I could do that if I were to work part-time. That's just how it is."

When Malin and Mattias talked to the interviewer about their unequal distribution of most of the housework and childcare, Mattias gave his view of how this distribution had come about: "I guess it's about that threshold [i.e., who first sees and feels the necessity of doing a chore] that [.] well, I don't care that much."

Torben declared that he kept out of all kinds of housecleaning: "Well, I have always bowed out of such things. Cleaning [.] that's not me. I like to have things orderly, but I'm not the kind of person who can be bothered to scrub the floor."

Carl explained why he did less housework than his wife: "No, I guess I'm not very domestic. [.] I don't make such things a priority."

Peter told his wife in the interview: "You have to go on shopping for food, because I can't be bothered to do that. I hate shopping for food. [.] I hate shops [.] things like standing in line and the like."

Ulrik had been fond of cooking, but that was before they had children. He said: "If I'm to cook at all, I need to have half a day to spend just looking at and thinking about the ingredients." If he could not spend that amount of time, he was not prepared to do the cooking: "Cooking spaghetti Bolognese is not for me. It's a bit too simple."

Mika said about housecleaning (for which his wife Minna had the main responsibility): "Well, no, I guess I am more in favor of a *laissez-faire* style on that question."

In the accounts listed above, the men stated two things either directly or indirectly: that they *did* not perform certain tasks and that they *would* not perform them. A characteristic of these statements that Eva noticed was that the assertions that they did not and would not perform the tasks were phrased in seemingly non-problematizing and self-evident ways. It was as if the statements needed no justifications or explanations. What cannot be seen in the short excerpts, but which Eva had noted down when reading through the interview transcripts, was that most of the wives of these men did not criticize either their husbands' minimal levels of housework sharing or their statements that they would not perform certain tasks. The only women who voiced any criticism of their husbands were in the in-between sharing group, and their criticisms were mild. Eva wondered therefore how it could be that the men's assertions seemed to be uncritically accepted by their wives.

Eva found that thinking in terms of *implicit cultural meanings* was helpful for her analyses. Implicit cultural meanings are commonalities of meaning on a "larger," cultural, scale compared to the meanings that we identified in the previous paragraph (such as that all the non-sharing men stated that they would not do certain tasks and that their wives did not object). Within the analytical framework of this chapter, implicit cultural meanings are what make it possible for some specific content to be common to a certain interpretive community.

We should note here that the specific analytical strategies in this phase may vary across studies, depending on the type of project and the type of researchable questions (such as whether those questions focus on identifying implicit cultural meanings or focus on how they are being deployed). Not surprisingly, therefore, researchers and textbook authors have found that the analytical phases cannot be described as a series of steps to be followed in every case. Researchers usually learn how to do these kinds of analyses through taking part in other researchers' studies or reading about the details of others' studies. We hope that the descriptions here will furnish enough material for such learning.

The third step: from group commonalities to implicit cultural meanings

The analytical step that moves from the commonalities of meaning in a group to implicit cultural meanings is one that often baffles learners. We use Eva's study to illustrate this step. How could Eva find out what implicit cultural meanings the men in the non-sharing couples made use of when they talked about their minimal contributions to housework and childcare? Because implicit cultural meanings are "cultural" and not individual, Eva had to widen her gaze beyond her interview material and then to develop a strategy for interpreting the patterns she had identified in the interviews in the light of the cultural commonalities that the speakers were likely to share.

Widening the researcher's gaze beyond the interviews first requires taking into account the cultural and societal settings of the participants in the study. For Eva, this meant learning as much as she could about the cultural settings of the Nordic countries and the ongoing political and other debates about gender equality and house-work sharing. Because she was part of the same larger culture as the couples in the study, Eva could draw on her own experiences and cultural competence to identify potentially relevant issues. One such issue was that in these countries, equal sharing of housework and childcare was put forth as desirable and good in national politics and policies (e.g., shared parental leave). This meant then that the men in Eva's study who proclaimed their unwillingness to share were positioning themselves as being at odds with national ideals. Given this discordance, the seemingly non-problematizing and self-evident accounts that the men gave became even more intriguing and worthy of further study.

Widening the researcher's gaze beyond the interviews also requires consulting other research. Eva also drew on earlier research as an aid to refine and develop the researchable questions. Much research has shown that housework-sharing in hetero-sexual couples is closely entangled with gendered power issues. On the basis of this research, Eva asked whether meanings of gender might be included among the implicit cultural meanings to which the men had recourse. She formulated this general research-able question: *What implicit cultural meanings, especially meanings related to masculinity, were in the background when the men in non-sharing couples described and justified their non-sharing in housework and childcare?* Eva also wanted to explore what work the presence of these implicit cultural meanings did in the interviews. A second researchable question therefore was: *What did the non-sharing men's talk about their refusal to share housework achieve in the interview context?*

Returning to the interview excerpts to look for implicit cultural meanings. How do you find implicit cultural meanings in people's talk after you have selected pieces of talk to scrutinize in detail and after you have widened your gaze? To begin with, you are not likely to "find" such meanings in explicit form in the content of people's talk. For instance, if you were to reread the interview excerpts we gave above, you would not "find" implicit cultural meanings spelled out there. They are *implicit* in what is said, and they are part of what members of a culture or an interpretive community use to explain themselves. Because the set of meanings has been shared over time, speakers do not need to refer explicitly to a particular cultural meaning in order for that meaning to be invoked. Speakers use recurring idiomatic expressions, fragments of well-known argu-ments, or habitual forms of talk to do the invoking (Edley & Wetherell, 1997; Wetherell, 1998). Listeners who are members of the same interpretive community will pick up implicit meanings from these utterances. For the members of the community, the idiomatic expressions and the implicit cultural meanings they invoke are often so taken for granted that they will not be seen as "meanings" or as ways of making sense. They are simply the way things are. To find implicit cultural meanings, you therefore need to unpack "the way things are."

Unpacking taken-for-granted meanings in the interview talk. As we have pointed out, interpretative researchers argue that people use recurring expressions and forms of talk to invoke implicit cultural meanings. This means that if the researcher identifies such recurring expressions or other patterns of talk in a group of speakers, it makes sense to assume that the patterns indicate that one or more implicit cultural meanings are being invoked. Let us illustrate with material from Eva's excerpts earlier in this section.

We have already noted that all the men whose excerpts were selected stated that there were certain tasks that they did not do and would not do. Those statements were the ones that Eva selected for closer analysis and that you read a few moments ago. The statements are similar on the manifest or "content" level. The task now is to look once more at the statements to see if they have other characteristics in common, such as key expressions, recurring ways of talking, or choices of words. As we said above, such common characteristics might point to a certain shared cultural meaning.

A common characteristic that Eva noticed in the excerpts was that the men consis-tently referred to characteristics or traits of themselves, or in a few cases to strong personal beliefs. A few of the men used somewhat more indirect references to themselves, but all the men in one way or another brought themselves into their accounts. We have copied the self-descriptive pieces here for easier reference:

Johan: "I'm a bit of a career person . . . I get absorbed in my work." Lars: "I am so bad at shopping for food." Valdemar: "I really don't know if I'm prepared to do that." Mattias: "I don't care that much." Torben: "I'm not the kind of person who can be bothered to scrub the floor." Carl: "I'm not very domestic." Peter: "I can't be bothered to do that [shopping]. I hate shopping for food. I hate shops." Ulrik: "cooking spaghetti Bolognese is not for me. It's a bit too simple." Mika: "I'm more in favor of a *laissez-faire* style on that question." Mattias: "Well, I don't care that much." Bengt said, a little more indirectly than the others, "I think she knows that there are certain chores that she can't make me do."

Some key expressions in these excerpts were "I'm," "I don't care . . .," "I can't be bothered . . .," that is, self-referring and self-descriptive phrases. Another common feature of the excerpts was that the speakers brought forward these self-descriptive statements as reasons for, and justifications of, their low level of involvement in housework and childcare. Eva coined the expression "the 'That's Just Who I Am' stance" as a shorthand for this pattern.

The women in these couples did not object to the self-describing justifications. This points to another feature of the talk we are studying: the men's utterances seemed to "work"; that is, they were not followed by challenge or questioning. In fact, these utterances seemed to put a stop to discussion. Hardly any talk about the topic followed the men's self-descriptive utterances. This was in contrast to other parts of the interview interactions, in which prolonged discussions often ensued.

Having come this far in the analysis, the researcher should consider whether the patterns of talk that have been identified are specific to the speakers whose talk has been scrutinized, or whether they are more widespread and appear elsewhere in the interview material. When Eva read through the interviews of the other couples in the study, she found that the use of self-descriptions to justify not doing housework was practically nonexistent among the other couples. While both men and women in the other couples made references to their own traits and characteristics in various contexts, they did not use such references rhetorically as justifications, as the men in the excerpts above did. This means that using self-descriptions such as "That's Just Who I Am" as justifications for not performing certain tasks appeared unique to men who did not share housework equally.

Let us now summarize the characteristics that we have so far pointed out in the talk of the men in the excerpts. What ideas about implicit cultural meanings can we get from the characteristics of the talk? A recurring expression that the men used was "I'm," which was part of the self-descriptions that were central to their arguments. The self-descriptions were placed so that they justified the speaker's refusals to do certain tasks. This is what Eva called the "That's Just Who I Am" stance. This stance, which occurred only in the talk of these men, seemed to set fairly narrow and self-defined boundaries for what these men were prepared to do at home. In the interviews, this stance was paired with the absence of objections to it by the men's wives. This absence can probably be read as a signal that this kind of talk "worked."

Referring back to the researchable question. In our example, the researchable question was: *What implicit cultural meanings, especially meanings that relate to masculinity, were in the background when the men in non-sharing couples described and justified their non-sharing of housework and childcare?* This question reminds us that these men were married to women, and that the tasks that were being talked about were mainly tasks that have traditionally been associated with women. Therefore, we might juxtapose the characteristic speech patterns with the traditional gender-specific division of household labor and childcare. The distinct characteristics that these men's talk projected about themselves were: having great personal latitude; being able to realize and pursue one's own interests without having to take others' interests and needs into account; not being easily influenced by others (perhaps especially not by a woman?); and being able to set down and enforce limits on what one will or won't do.

What does this set of characteristics allow us to conclude about the implicit cultural meanings on which these men's talk was based? One thing they have in common is that they point to some of the key ingredients of traditional masculinity, perhaps especially a career-oriented masculinity that is common in Western high-income countries. Eva's provisional conclusion therefore was that the men in the non-sharing couples formulated their justificatory accounts on the basis of the implicit cultural meaning "traditional masculinity."

Toward drawing conclusions: bringing in the larger picture of the study to verify ideas

At this stage, conclusions about implicit cultural meanings should be seen as provisional. When the researcher has identified one or more implicit cultural meanings and suggested how they are taken into use by some participants, it is time to reread the interviews to see if these preliminary conclusions obtain within the larger material of the study.

In the case of Eva's study, she asked whether the use of "traditional masculinity" as justification was specific to the men in the non-sharing couples. She found that it was. Traditional masculinity was referred to by other men in the study; however, when these other men invoked it, they always used negative terms and immediately distanced themselves from it. Therefore, men in non-sharing couples were not the only men who had access to the implicit cultural meaning of "traditional masculinity," but they were the only ones who made use of it to justify their choices and behavior in everyday family life. Further, the men in equally sharing couples who referred negatively to "traditional masculinity" invariably explicitly named it as such before taking exception to it. In contrast, the men in non-sharing couples never referred explicitly to "traditional masculinity." They confined themselves to the key expressions and speech forms that we saw above.

At this stage, the researcher has identified and briefly explored the uses of one or more implicit cultural meanings that may be central to the people who are being studied. In our illustration, we wanted to keep the analysis reasonably easy to follow and we therefore have described an analysis related only to one implicit cultural meaning. However, it is much more common that a researcher would study several implicit cultural meanings in parallel.

Whether or not the analysis ends at this point depends on the general knowledge interest of the researcher. If identifying and describing active implicit cultural meanings was the goal, the analysis is finished. Sometimes, however, identifying implicit cultural meanings leads the way to further questions.

Toward synthesizing and drawing conclusions

As you move toward synthesizing the results, you should begin by using the researchable questions in your study as the organizing framework. This means that you will consider how the results of specific analyses speak to the researchable questions. Eventually, you need to tie the results together into a coherent whole. Much of this work will be done while you are writing your report about your project. Chapter 12 offers more specific information about how to organize and write your report.

Outline of the steps in the analysis

1. Selecting the material to analyze
2. From researchable questions to group commonalities
3. From group commonalities to implicit cultural meanings
   Widening the researcher's gaze beyond the interviews
   Returning to the interview excerpts to look for implicit cultural meanings
   Unpacking taken-for-granted meanings in the interview talk
   Referring back to the researchable question
4. Toward drawing conclusions: bringing in the larger picture of the study to verify the results

ANALYTICAL PROCEDURES

(B) Studying an individual's meaning-making in a cultural context

The analytical procedures that we describe in this part of the chapter focus on the restricting and productive aspects of implicit cultural meanings. Both these aspects can be inferred by studying an individual's accounts in the light of the local and larger cultural contexts in which that person lives.

Cultural settings provide their members with resources for meaning-making, among them implicit cultural meanings. Implicit cultural meanings function both to enable and restrict the meanings of an event or experience that are available to members of a setting. As a result, certain meanings will be more self-evident or natural-seeming than others. Particularly well-established cultural meanings come to be taken as the way things are, not as one of many possible ways of understanding things. Which implicit cultural meanings dominate in a setting is a matter of negotiations, perhaps recent or perhaps not. A cultural meaning may have been established long ago and now be taken as "natural." It no longer seems to be the result of negotiation.

In many interactions in daily life, people are placed in positions of unequal power to influence ongoing meaning-making and decisions. Such different *subject positions* and the access to power that is associated with them are often corollaries of salient social categories, such as sex category, social class, ethnic group, age, or a combination of them (Wetherell, 1998). Membership in these categories is often enduring, but such membership has a different impact in different interaction settings.

There are many ways to analyze for implicit cultural meanings in people's individual accounts and stories. The literature in the fields of critical discourse analysis and critical discursive psychology provides many similar but not identical ways to carry out this type of analysis. As in the other analysis chapters in this book, we present analytical procedures that exemplify and illustrate some basic aspects of the approaches encompassed by these fields. The procedures we have chosen are fairly easy for a learner to follow.

The analysis example

To illustrate the analytical procedures for studying implicit cultural meanings in an interview account, we provide a step-by-step outline of procedures and illustrate it with a research example. We use material from Eva's study of women in the Swedish civil service, carried out during a three-year period of thoroughgoing organizational change in their workplaces (Magnusson, 1997a; 1998). Eva was interested in how the women, whom she selected to represent the different hierarchical positions in the organizations, experienced and dealt with the challenges they confronted during this period. She interviewed the participants twice a year during the project period. The initial analyses of the interviews were done using procedures similar to those we described in Chapter 8. Those analyses focused on the women's accounts of their experiences in their daily lives at work and at home during the three years. The analyses yielded a wide range of variation in how the women experienced and reacted to demands and expectations from their surroundings, and in how they reflected on and understood themselves as women in their local settings.

Eva also wanted to explore how her participants' ways of being women were channeled by local and larger implicit cultural meanings in their everyday worlds. Specifically, she was interested in how the women's ways of understanding themselves and their worlds were enabled by or restricted by certain implicit cultural meanings. Eva thus shifted her analytical focus on the perspectives of the individual participants in the first set of analyses to a focus on how these perspectives were constituted by the cultural surroundings in which the women lived. The analytical focus thus shifted to implicit cultural meanings.

The women Eva interviewed were living through a time of changing and sometimes contradictory organizational "messages" about what was the best way of being a female civil servant. Traditionally, women in the civil service had worked as mainly secretaries, lower-level clerks with routine tasks, and receptionists. These positions were associated with certain types of subservient feminine behaviors. These had been the expectations that most of the women had encountered when they entered the workplace one or more decades earlier. During the period of study, the expectations were changing: the messages now were that employees were supposed to be "modern," strategic, and career-oriented. The expectations for women outside the workplace had also changed in Swedish society; in many parts of society, there was a strong emphasis on gender equality and on questioning traditional ways of being a woman. It was likely, then, that the women in Eva's study were surrounded by many conflicting cultural meanings of "being a woman" both at work and in their family lives. The analysis that we describe below gives one example of how Eva explored the implicit cultural meanings connected with being a woman which formed the background for one participant's interview accounts. This analysis addressed aspects of one of the researchable questions in Eva's study. The example is chosen from an interview with Birgitta, whom you already met in Chapter 10.

Birgitta, her husband, and the professional women

One of the researchable questions in Eva's study was how the women in the study – given the culturally expected ways of being a woman – understood situations where gendered power might be at large. The excerpt from one of the interviews with Birgitta speaks to this researchable question. Eva had two reasons for choosing this excerpt. First, she chose it because in it there seemed to be some conflict that was relevant to the researchable question. This meant that there were textual characteristics, especially contradictions, in the excerpt that made it seem as if it would be illuminating to analyze. Second, Eva chose the excerpt because parts of the narrative resonated with material in the interviews of many other participants.

How to select excerpts for analysis

There are four key characteristics of talk to consider when selecting excerpts for analysis:

- *A pertinent topic*: a general criterion, which should always be satisfied, is that the topic of the talk should be pertinent to at least one of the researchable questions in the study.
- *Representativeness*: sometimes, the researcher selects a piece of talk by a participant because that piece resembles what goes on in the talk of several other participants.
- *Contrast and deviation*: sometimes, a researcher selects a piece of talk by one participant because it deviates from the talk of most participants in some way that is relevant to one of the researchable questions. Such a piece of talk may illustrate a phenomenon that was not present in the talk of other participants.
- *Characteristics of the talk*: researchers often select a piece of talk from among several equally representative (or deviant) ones because it contains potentially interesting contradictions or inconsistencies. Contradictions and inconsistencies often signal that conflicts between implicit cultural meanings have been activated, perhaps in analytically interesting ways.

At the time of the interview, Birgitta was about forty-five years old. She had an advanced high school diploma and worked as a secretary to a manager who held a high organizational position. She was married but had no children living at home. Just before the selected piece of the interview began, Eva had asked about the distribution of housework in her family. Birgitta had told Eva that in her family, housework was very traditionally distributed. She was very pleased with this situation, she said, and continued: "Yes, in our house things are completely traditional, so that all professional women would go crazy if they heard it!" Directly afterward, Eva asked her how decision-making was done in their family. Her answer to this question was as follows:

EVA: ... who makes the decisions?

BIRGITTA: It's actually really me, though he thinks he does. [.] That's how it's done, you see. [.] Food and that kind of thing [.] I decide about those. [.] I have got to know him so well that – it's sort of a question of planning your strategy. [.] And that means that if I want something to happen, then I begin at an early stage to talk around it. And then I have talked so much "around" that he thinks it's he who has come up with the suggestion! [.] And then that's called, in military-speak, that he has made a decision! So then, when we are visiting – [Birgitta here alluded to social situations in which her husband told others about an activity as completely his own idea and decision.]

/ It's like a life-form, you see, so if I want to have that particular goal, then- And it's not possible to change direction along the way. [.] you have to talk slowly about it [.] because it isn't possible to say it outright. Once I have gotten in along one road, then I can't change direction [.] because, you see, then he is on that road! [.] Therefore I know already when I begin [.] what I want. But it takes its time, you know. And then I get my way, though he may not really understand that I do get my way. On the contrary, he thinks he is the one who came up with the suggestion. And I let him think so.

/ I only present the suggestions that I want to have discussed! [Here Birgitta comments on a story that she had just told about decision-making for a vacation trip.]

/ But really, I would never take it on my conscience to trick him into something that I know would be bad for him. / And [.] but I could never do him any harm, or trick him into anything.

/ it's probably I who am the most active. But now and then he makes his own decisions, sort of [.] I mean, he is very [.] he is like this: if he says no, then it is NO! Then you get nowhere!

/ At work he is known to be a very good leader, can make decisions, be very straightforward, gets very good evaluations [at work] and such things. But at home he is a completely different man.[1]

---

[1] Note that this excerpt is translated from the original Swedish. The translation focuses on maintaining the meaning of what was said, rather than on translating the conversation word for word. We mention this, because, even though Eva has worked through the translation several times, she still does not think that it gives quite the same overall impression as the Swedish original does. Note also that the *analysis* was done in Swedish, using the original Swedish version of the interview transcription.

Reading and reflecting: the preliminary step

As always when analyzing talk for its meanings, a preliminary step when analyzing for implicit cultural meanings is to read through the excerpt carefully several times and note down your reflections and associations to the meanings that the participant seems to be communicating in the piece of talk.

In this case, Eva noted down what Birgitta seemed to want to tell her about the situations that she described and what kind of sense these situations seemed to make. Eva inferred that Birgitta was telling her that it was she who made the decisions in her family. Eva also inferred that the experiences and situations that Birgitta talked about seemed to Birgitta herself to cohere. That is, they were not presented as a bundle of contradictory events. Eva also observed, however, that the story was not wholly smooth; there were some inconsistencies.

Subjects and verbs: beginning to identify the action in Birgitta's account

The analysis now moves toward identifying the implicit cultural meanings that form the background of the conversation. The general assumption in this phase of the analysis is that one or more implicit cultural meanings bring in, inform, or influence at least parts of what is said in a conversation.

The specific assumption in the case of Birgitta's interview is this: in a historical situation where old and new cultural meanings about how to be a proper married woman and a proper married man are in play, conversations about related topics will contain traces of old and new norms and of the conflict between them. Of course, norms and meanings cannot be actors in a conversation. It is people who speak and do things. The influence of implicit cultural meanings therefore is channeled through the things that people say and do, that is, through the *action* in the text.

To begin to target the presence and influence of implicit cultural meanings, the researcher looks for the action in a conversation: what it is that happens there and what events are being talked about. Grammar helps the researcher to find the action. *Verbs* carry the actions – to talk, to write, to scream, to discuss, and so on. Grammatical *subjects* bring about the actions. In a text, subjects such as I, you, we, a man, or a woman do things like talking, writing, screaming, discussing, making decisions, and so on.

In the type of analysis we describe here, the researcher assumes that the same *physical* subject (person) can appear to be speaking as more than one *textual or grammatical* subject, that is, speaking from more than one textual *subject position*. To illustrate: in a conversation, a woman may speak as the daughter of her parents, as the mother of her children, and as a worker in a workplace – three different textual subjects within the same physical person.

Identifying textual subjects. In what follows, we show how Eva identified the textual subjects in the excerpt from Birgitta's interview. We also describe how Eva reasoned about the textual subjects within the framework of the interview. Eva used pronouns and nouns (such as "I," "He," "Friends") to denote physical subjects. She then added numbers (e.g., "I 1" and "He 2") to point out the different textual subject positions that a physical subject was placed in or assumed in different parts of the conversation. Eva also gave short names or labels to each textual subject. Such labels should be selected with care, and the researcher should be prepared to change them as she learns more while doing the analysis. Eva also provided short quotes from Birgitta's talk to document how she arrived at each textual subject.

Widening the researcher's view. The information to which Eva had access when she did the original analysis was the whole interview text and her knowledge about Birgitta from other interviews, combined with her knowledge about Birgitta's social situation and about the political and social situation in Sweden when this study was done. Such knowledge should be taken into account when analyzing for implicit cultural meanings. The analysis for implicit cultural meanings in a piece of talk cannot be limited to an analysis of what goes on in that piece of talk. It always has to include at least parts of the larger social and cultural contexts.

Textual subjects in Birgitta's story

I no. 1 – the powerful wife who makes the decisions. This textual subject talks about herself as the one who is really making the decisions in their house. She also talks about herself as the one who drives changes and takes initiatives, while pointing out that this is not how things appear to her husband or to their friends. To document how Eva arrived at this textual subject, we repeat the pieces of talk that led her there: "It's actually really me [who makes decisions], though he thinks he does. [.] That's how it's done, you see"; "And then I get my way, though he may not really understand that I do get my way"; "he thinks he is the one who came up with the suggestion. And I let him think so."

I no. 2 – the traditional housewife. She decides about food and other practical things in the house; she also carries out the work that these practical matters entail. ("Food and that kind of thing – I decide about those.") Elsewhere in the interview, Birgitta had told Eva that she took care of all the indoor chores, and her husband did the outdoor work.

He no. 1 – the husband who thinks he makes the decisions. Although it is not so, he believes that he is the one who comes up with ideas and suggestions and who makes the decisions in their family. ("That's called, in military-speak, that he has made a decision!"; "He thinks he is the one who came up with the suggestion.")

I no. 3 – the strategist who knows her husband. She is so well acquainted with her husband that she knows what to do to get her own way. She also makes sure to know from the very beginning what it is she wants to accomplish. And she is prepared to plan well in advance and allow time to pass. ("If I want something to happen, then I begin at an early stage to talk around it. And then I have talked so much 'around' that he thinks it's he who has come up with the suggestion!"; "I only present the suggestions that I want to have discussed!"; "I know already when I begin [.] what I want. But it takes its time, you know.")

We – the couple who present a united picture of their marriage. When they are in the company of friends, Birgitta and her husband tell about their choices and decisions in ways that feature him as the decision-maker as well as the person with the good ideas ("When we are visiting . . ." – an allusion to social situations when her husband tells others about an activity as if it was completely his own initiative and decision).

Friends and acquaintances: their circle of acquaintances who expect a family life pattern in which the husband makes the big decisions. This "subject" can be inferred from Birgitta's talk, although there are no explicit utterances tied to it.

Her conscience. Birgitta talks about her conscience as keeping her from abusing her power over her husband: that is, it stops her from tricking him into doing things that might be bad for him. ("Really, I would never take it on my conscience to trick him into something that I know would be bad for him.")

He no. 2 /"him" – the husband who needs protection. This is Birgitta's husband as an object of her actions, rather than an active subject. He no. 2/him is central to her story. Birgitta told Eva that she had a responsibility to protect her husband and not trick him into doing things that would be bad for him. ("Really, I would never take it on my conscience to trick him into something that I know would be bad for him.")

He no. 3 – the unbending and impervious man. It is completely impossible to shake her husband when he has made a decision, but equally so as soon as he has set out on the road toward a particular decision. This is so, even if it is a decision that was "planted" by Birgitta. ("Once I have gotten in along one road, then I can't change direction [.] because, you see, then he is on that road!"; "Now and then he makes his own decisions, sort of [.] I mean, he is very [.] he is like this: if he says no, then it is NO! Then you get nowhere!")

I no. 4 ("you") – the powerless wife. Once her husband has made up his mind about something, there is nothing she can do about it; she must go along with his decision. ("If he says no, then it is NO! Then you get nowhere!")

In this list of textual subjects, the physical subjects Birgitta and her husband have become "unpacked" such that each of them seems to be speaking from several positions. It is perhaps not surprising that they can be "unpacked" in this manner, given the topic: it is to be expected that there will be several opinions in relation to topics about which there is political debate and conflict. At the time when this interview was done, there was much debate in Sweden about power and decision-making in heterosexual couples.

One initial thing to note in Birgitta's talk is that all the different textual subjects seemed to be able to coexist in the story she told in the interview. She made no comments about explicit conflicts between the textual subjects that she had been activating. Even so, it seems likely that some subjects would coexist more easily with one another than others would. It also seems likely that the researcher might learn something from looking at the smooth coexistences and the disagreements. Close consideration of the lines of conflict and agreement between textual subjects is therefore common in analysis for implicit cultural meanings. Note, however, that the lines of conflict and the analysis lines of agreement tell the researcher different things. We begin with the disagreements.

Identifying textual subjects that seem to disagree

We should keep in mind here that it is the researcher who discerns disagreement and conflict between subjects. Birgitta did not explicitly point out any such disagreements or conflicts, nor did she implicitly refer to them. Whether she saw some conflicts but preferred not to mention them, we cannot say. In Birgitta's transcript, Eva located lines of conflict between the following subjects:

(a) *I no. 1* – the powerful wife who makes the decisions – vs. *He no. 1* – the husband who thinks he makes the decisions.

(b) *I no. 1* – the powerful wife who makes the decisions – vs. *Friends and acquaintances*.

(c) *I no. 1* – the powerful wife who makes the decisions – vs. *I no. 4* – "you" the powerless wife.

(d) *I no. 1* – the powerful wife who makes the decisions – vs. *He no. 3* – the unbending and impervious man.

(e) *He no. 2* – "him" who is an object of Birgitta's actions – vs. *He no. 3* – the unbending and impervious man.

(f) *He no. 2* – "him" who is an object of Birgitta's actions – vs. *I no. 4* – "you" the powerless wife.

This list indicates that several parts of Birgitta's narrative are potentially in conflict with one another. The fact that Birgitta did not point them out as being in conflict may lead the researcher to speculate about what her intentions were – both in the situations she was describing and when she told Eva about those situations. If we look closely at the list, we see that there were two different kinds of misalignments in Birgitta's account, *contrasts* and *contradictions*. Items (a), (b), and (d) above involved contrasts between two or more physical subjects who had different ways of describing reality. Items (c) and (e), instead, involved contradictions between two textual subjects located in the same physical body. Item (f) is less easily categorized, because it seems speculative to ascribe any explicit motives to "him"; we do not have enough information about "him" to do so.

Finding this number of lines of conflict in a piece of talk is typical. What the lines of conflict in this case indicate is that in the types of situations that Birgitta talked about there are likely to be (at least for her) both the possibility of disagreements between physical subjects (persons), and the possibility of "internal" contradictions or conflicts between textual subjects (within the same person). Where these lines get drawn and whether they seem to be mainly "external" or "internal" should be kept in mind in the next step of the analysis – locating the agreements between the textual subjects.

Textual subjects that seem to agree: on the way to identifying cultural meanings

The previous step in the analysis identified several disagreements in Birgitta's talk, but there are also several agreements in it. It is these agreements that hold Birgitta's talk together as *a story*, instead of a scattered mass of contradictory utterances. After all, even if *we* find that Birgitta's talk is shot through with disagreeing textual subjects, *she* does not dwell on the disagreements. And it is her story, and how her story is constituted, that we are interested in learning about. The next step of the analysis therefore looks for the agreements. It does so on the assumption that utterances or textual subjects that are in agreement are likely to draw on the same implicit cultural meanings.

There are two steps in the analysis of agreements: first, identifying textual subjects that agree with one another and grouping them together; and second, describing the characteristics of each group with the aim of arriving at implicit cultural meanings.

Identifying textual subjects that agree

The first step of the analysis is to identify textual subjects that seem to agree about one or more of the issues that are brought forward in a participant's talk. It is Eva who has discerned the agreements between the textual subjects; Birgitta did not explicitly point them out. When Eva scrutinized Birgitta's narrative for agreements between textual subjects, she discerned four clusters of textual subjects that seemed likely to agree on the central issues in the story. (Other clusters could perhaps be identified; the ones here are the ones most relevant to the researchable questions.) The clusters were as follows:

(a) *I no. 1* – the powerful wife who makes the decisions + *I no. 3* – the strategist who knows her husband + *He no. 1* – the husband who thinks he makes the decisions (+ possibly *He no. 2* – "him" who is an object of Birgitta's actions).

(b) *The conscience* + *He no. 2* – "him" who is an object of Birgitta's actions (+ possibly *I no. 2* – the traditional housewife).

(c) *He no. 1* – the husband who thinks he makes the decisions + *We* + *Friends and acquaintances* + *He no. 3* – the unbending and impervious man (+ possibly *I no. 2* – the traditional housewife).

(d) *I no. 3* – the strategist who knows her husband + *He no. 3* – the unbending and impervious man + *I no. 4* – "you" the powerless wife.

If we were to imagine that the textual subjects in each of the clusters could speak, we would expect their utterances to agree with one another, given the context of Birgitta's storytelling. We can imagine such utterances because the textual subjects have an existence beyond Birgitta's story. That is, these textual subjects all have some anchoring in the local context or the larger surrounding culture within which Birgitta tells her story. Presumably, people who share Birgitta's cultural context would recognize these textual subjects. To take two examples, people would recognize "the traditional housewife" and "the strategist who knows her husband." And as a consequence of their larger existence, the textual subjects in a cluster – if they could speak – would speak within the frame of the same implicit cultural meaning.

From agreeing textual subjects to implicit cultural meanings

In the second part of this step, the researcher begins by thinking about and making notes about what it is that the textual subjects in each cluster "agree" about. The researcher then uses these notes to describe the clusters of agreeing subjects in order to be able to infer the implicit cultural meanings around which they cluster. Each cluster is assumed to identify one implicit cultural meaning. Below are the associations and descriptions that Eva produced at this point in the analysis of Birgitta's story. The associations and descriptions were based on the textual subjects within each cluster, the general tenor of Birgitta's story, and Eva's knowledge about Swedish society and ongoing debates at the time of the interview.

(a) This cluster conjures up notions of secrecy and perhaps an image of women as manipulating behind the scenes. This image fits sayings such as "the woman behind it all …" The images and the kind of power that is conjured up do not seem to be compatible with a modern view of "gender equality." Historical parallels can perhaps be found in old counterarguments against women's suffrage, such as claims that women had much greater opportunities to wield power by indirectly influencing their husbands at home than by voting in elections. The textual subjects in this cluster coalesce into an implicit cultural meaning that Eva named "Women's hidden power."

(b) This cluster conjures up the idea that it would be Birgitta's fault if anything bad were to happen to her husband because of what she decided. There are resonances, for instance, with the tendencies to "blame the mother/woman" that have been prevalent in psychiatry, education, and child psychology. The textual subjects in this cluster coalesce into the implicit cultural meaning "The responsible woman."

(c) This cluster is based in traditional patriarchal views of marriage, in which the husband makes the big and important decisions and is the one who represents the family to the outside world. This had earlier been a pervasive masculine ideal in Swedish society. The textual subjects in this cluster coalesce into the implicit cultural meaning "The strong (perhaps unbending) man."

(d) This cluster exemplifies the conditions necessary for a powerless person to influence a superior person. Any possibilities of having such influence require detailed knowledge of the superior person. This knowledge makes it possible to predict the superior person's actions and whims and eventually to surreptitiously introduce one's own ideas disguised as his. The textual subjects in this cluster coalesce into the implicit cultural meaning "The manipulator from below."

Discussing the implicit cultural meanings

Up to this point in the analytical procedure, the kinds of analyses we have described claim that certain utterances have something in common that seems to be connected to larger cultural patterns (i.e., they share the same implicit cultural meaning or culturally shared pattern of talking). So far, so good. It seems possible to substantiate such claims by combining the scrutiny of the talk with the researcher's knowledge of larger socio-cultural patterns. However, sometimes implied in that claim is another claim, namely that these implicit cultural meanings have a deeper meaning for the person whose talk is being analyzed. Sometimes a researcher might also want to argue that the implicit cultural meanings that have been identified could in one way or another motivate a person's utterances or actions.

When a researcher considers making such motivational claims, he or she needs to be careful not to fall into circular reasoning. We especially warn against the circularity of using implicit cultural meanings that the researcher has identified in a person's talk to *explain* utterances (or implied actions) in that same piece of talk (see also Antaki, Billig, Edwards, & Potter, 2003). Such claims cannot be substantiated solely by scrutinizing the interview talk and combining it with knowledge about sociocultural patterns.

Let us look into Birgitta's story again, keeping the warnings about circularity in mind. First, let us remind ourselves of the researchable question that formed the background for the analysis: *How did the women in the study – given the culturally expected ways of being a woman that they were accustomed to – understand situations in which gendered power might be at large?*

The analysis up to this point had led to the claim that Birgitta's story was informed, or influenced, by the four implicit cultural meanings in the list above. This claim seemed reasonably well substantiated by the researcher's cultural knowledge and the scrutiny of Birgitta's talk. The implicit cultural meanings also seem to be connected to culturally expected ways of being a woman; therefore, the analyses were germane to the researchable question. So far, so good. How can we move the analysis further? Can we make any claims or draw any conclusions that go beyond this point?

Overt and hidden power. To explore possible further claims while keeping in mind the caveats regarding circularity that we discussed above, we begin at the moment when Birgitta told Eva that she could influence her husband only so long as he was unaware that she was wielding any influence ("you have to talk slowly about it [.] because it isn't possible to say it outright"). We had earlier identified this utterance as being one of those that invoked the implicit cultural meaning "Women's hidden power." In contrast, when Birgitta talked about her husband, he came across as able to influence her when she was aware that decisions were being made. That is, when her husband decided to wield power explicitly ("Now and then he makes his own decisions."), he could not be challenged ("If he says no, then it is NO! Then you get nowhere!"). Such utterances had earlier been identified as invoking the implicit cultural meaning "The strong (and perhaps unbending) man."

Beyond his power to make explicit decisions when both were aware of it (which Birgitta lacked), Birgitta told Eva that her husband also could abstain from making decisions initially. If at some later point, he wanted to make a decision or change one of her decisions, he could do so. Birgitta's conscience ensured that it was safe for him to refrain initially. ("I would never take it on my conscience to trick him into something that I know would be bad for him.") This utterance was among those that invoked the implicit cultural meaning "The responsible woman." It seemed as if her husband was able to assert power whenever he wanted. But for Birgitta, things seemed different. If she initially refrained from exerting her (hidden) power, she could not take it for granted that her husband would later take her wishes and needs into consideration ("If he says no, then it is NO! Then you get nowhere!"). This was in contrast to what her conscience demanded of her, which was to take his needs into account when she made decisions.

Birgitta's claims to be able to influence her husband did not seem groundless. When she told Eva that she repeatedly got her husband where she wanted him, she appeared to be talking about real decisions, real changes, and consequently real influence. The prerequisites for her influence were that it had to be gradual ("I begin at an early stage to talk around it") and that she had to decide on her goals well in advance ("I know already when I begin [.] what I want"). It thus seemed as if she saw herself as getting her own way only when she acted in accordance with the implicit cultural meaning "Women's hidden power."

Birgitta's story thus contained two distinct strands: in one strand, Birgitta succeeded in getting her way by indirect means; in the other strand, she was powerless to get her way (when her husband had made a decision and when there were open negotiations about whose will should prevail).

Power and women's responsibility. At this point Eva brought into consideration the researchable question about accepted ways of being a woman and the relation of those ways to power in a heterosexual couple. She focused especially on the common conflation of power and responsibility in women's daily lives. It has until recently (and perhaps still is in some settings) been common to mistakenly label women's *responsibility* for the details of their families' everyday life as "*women's power* in the family*."* Could it be that this conflation of power and responsibility was operating in Birgitta's story?

An indication of such a conflation was that Birgitta talked about her power as closely coupled to responsibility. She invoked her conscience as compelling her to use her power responsibly. ("I would never take it on my conscience to trick him into something that I know would be bad for him." "And [.] but I could never do him any harm or trick him into anything.") These utterances invoked the implicit cultural meaning "The responsible woman," which seemed prominent for Birgitta, especially when she talked about her own power.

If Birgitta associated her own decision-making above all with responsibility and concealment, perhaps *her* power had different implications for her than *her husband's* power had for him? For instance, could it be that when she made decisions, she interpreted them in accordance with the implicit cultural meaning "The responsible woman" (where "blame the woman" might loom)? (And could it conversely be that when her husband made decisions, no such "responsibility" was conjured up?)

Birgitta's descriptions of how she protected her husband from awareness of her decision-making indicated another possible responsibility she placed on herself: she may have worried that her husband would be offended or have his self-esteem bruised if he were to uncover her stratagems and notice that she really made decisions. ("It's actually really me [who makes decisions], though he thinks he does"; "he thinks he is the one who came up with the suggestion. And I let him think so.")

Decision-making and femininity. It seems likely, in the setting we are talking about, that if Birgitta were found to be making decisions, whether explicitly or covertly, she would be violating the cultural expectation that it was her husband who made the decisions. What might be the consequences for her if such a violation were uncovered? Here we can only speculate, and we have to take care to avoid circular reasoning. Our speculations can be aided by the common observation that when an individual is found to violate powerful cultural rules or expectations, there will be penalties of some kind for that individual. One relevant cultural "rule" or expectation in Birgitta's case was femininity: the culturally expected and accepted ways of being a woman. This brings us back to the researchable question that motivated this analysis: how the women in the study – given the culturally expected ways of being a woman that they were accustomed to – understood situations where gendered power might be at large.

To speculate about femininity and decision-making in Birgitta's life, we have to move outside the interview material that was analyzed here. First, we need to bring in any available specific knowledge about cultural patterns related to femininity in the location where the interview was done. Second, we have to bring in other information about Birgitta, if any. Eva had done several interviews with Birgitta over the three years of the study, and they provided additional material. Eva had, for instance, observed in the other interviews with Birgitta that she was among the few women in the group of participants who spoke forthrightly about themselves as being feminine. The meanings of "feminine" that she invoked included being nicely dressed and coiffed, being good at housework, and having abundant social graces. As a secretary, she worked in a position that was heavily coded as traditionally feminine. The meanings that Birgitta ascribed to femininity in her various stories did not seem to encompass decision-making and power. Thus, the kind of femininity that Birgitta spoke of as ideal might lead us to speculate that if she were to be visible as a decision-maker in the couple, she would run the risk of having her femininity called into question. She could also run the risk, as we discussed above, of injuring her husband's self-esteem – and this in itself might be seen as another blot on her femininity.

Toward synthesizing the results

The analysis of Birgitta's story has helped us to address parts of the researchable question "How did the women in the study – given the culturally expected ways of being a woman that they were accustomed to – understand situations where gendered power might be at large?" The section "Discussing the implicit cultural meanings" lays out three of the possible answers. However, this analysis concerned one woman's story, albeit in the light of larger cultural patterns in the country where she lived and her local cultural setting. This analysis needs to be complemented by similar analyses of the stories by other women in the study. There are also several other possible avenues for following up and augmenting an analysis such as this, for instance, by analyzing other kinds of material from the same time and place.

As the researcher moves toward synthesizing the results, the researchable questions in the study can serve as the organizing framework. That is, by considering how the results of specific analyses speak to the researchable questions, the researcher will be able to tie those results into a coherent whole (*cf.* Taylor, 2001). Much of this work will be carried out during the process of writing about the project. Chapter 12 offers more specific information about how to organize and write a written report.

Outline of the steps in analysis of individual excerpts for implicit cultural meanings

1. Selecting excerpts for analysis
2. Reading and reflecting
3. Subjects and verbs: beginning to identify the action
   Identifying textual subjects
   Widening the researcher's view
4. Identifying textual subjects that seem to disagree
5. Textual subjects that seem to agree: on the way to identifying cultural meanings
   Identifying textual subjects that agree
   From agreeing textual subjects to implicit cultural meanings
6. Discussing the implicit cultural meanings
7. Synthesizing the results

12   Reporting your project

In this chapter, we turn to the matter of composing the final research report. We focus mainly on composing reports about students' projects (such as doctoral dissertations, master's theses, or undergraduate theses) and manuscripts intended for scholarly journals. The focus here is on how to write a report. However, writing is not confined to the end of a project. As you have learned, an interpretative research project involves writing from the very first stage of the research process. Put simply, writing is part of the research process and cannot be separated from it. This is why we have urged you to keep a research journal from the beginning and to write notes and reflections in it at every stage of your project. You will have been doing two kinds of writing: the first kind comprises the notes, reflections, and hunches in your research journal, and the second has involved writing down summaries of and notes about the results that you produced as you carried out your analyses. The latter includes the documentation of your interpretations in the form of descriptive notes, integrative summaries, and the like.

There are a number of benefits to recognizing that writing is a continual process that is integral to carrying out every phase of a project. First, by writing continually, you continually compel yourself to clarify your thinking. Second, writing notes about your process, as well as noting down the intermediate steps by which you arrived at the results of your analyses, provides a thorough record of the judgments and decisions that you made at each step of the project. Third, the notes afford a source of evidence that your work has been done with care and thoroughness. There is a fourth reason behind the writing you have done. This one is pragmatic, and you are now at a stage to capitalize on it: Many parts of the writing you have done can serve as the basic material for parts of your report.

If you have been writing throughout the project, you will have many resources at hand as you begin to compose your report. These include your notes about the relevant literature; your list of researchable questions and sub-questions; your notes about the considerations that guided you in selecting and composing the group of participants; notes about the final composition of the group of participants; the interview guide; the transcriptions of the interviews; the "raw" excerpt files; and the notes, integrative summaries, and other writing that served to document the analyses as you did them. You may also have made some notes in your journal concerning possible ways of synthesizing or drawing together some of the results of your analysis.

Writing a research report is an endeavor that involves a number of different tasks. You conducted your research because you wanted to answer a set of questions. Presumably those questions were of some importance both to you and to a wider audience, such as other members of your academic discipline, practitioners, or policy-makers. Your overarching task in writing the research report is to put forward the answers you now have. But you have several other tasks as well. For instance, you must help your readers to see the answer to the question "So what?" Why does your research matter? Now that you are nearing the completion of your project, what do the results say that is original and important? The answer to this question may seem obvious to you. But count on it: It will not be obvious to many of the readers of your work. You must tell them. Another task you have in writing your report is to depict the particular world and set of people that you have studied for readers who likely will have little or no direct knowledge about them. And your report must also explain how your results and conclusions relate to the research literature. That is, how do your results comment on, expand upon, or take issue with the concepts and theories that pertain to your topic? And how does your report expand on or take issue with the body of empirical findings in the literature?

This chapter contains two sections. The first section discusses what a report should contain. We discuss the main sections in a typical report of interpretative research and we give a road map for writing each of these sections. The second section takes up several matters concerning language, style, and ethics in report writing.

What the research report contains

A research report centers on a single main argument or thesis. Before you begin writing, you need to decide upon this argument. The argument sets the frame for the report; the frame enables you to determine what belongs in the report and what does not. A research report is not merely a depository for an assortment of unfiltered and randomly ordered "findings." Such a report would not make a contribution to knowledge. Once you have in mind the argument that you want to put forward, this will guide you in selecting the subset of findings that are pertinent to that argument. Note that selecting a subset of findings that pertain to an argument is not the same as suppressing findings that do not confirm a hypothesis, nor is it the same as "cherry-picking the data" in order to rig a certain conclusion.

As you begin writing, you also need to give careful thought to your intended reader-ship. Knowing the audience that you are addressing can help you to make the right choices about content and style. For example, if you have an audience in mind, you can consider how you might need to gear your vocabulary toward that audience. You can also weigh the question of how much explication and justification of the methods of study might be needed for your readers to understand what you have done.

The sections of a typical report of an interpretative research project include Title, Abstract, Introduction, Methods, Results and Discussion, and Conclusion. We strongly advise against beginning your writing with the Introduction. It is better to begin in the middle – with the Methods section and the Results and Discussion section. After you are satisfied that the Results and Discussion section says what you want it to say, you should turn to the Introduction and the Conclusion. These latter two sections require that you take a step back from the details of the project in order to place your findings in a larger framework. It is much easier to do this after you have a firm grip on the material in the Results and Discussion section. The Abstract and Title can be composed last.

The Methods section

This section contains three kinds of information: (1) information about the participants and how you selected and recruited them; (2) information about the structure and content of the interview and about how you carried out the interviews; and (3) information about the procedures that you used to analyze the interview material. The information in the Methods section should include the rationale for your choices of methods and procedures. Keep in mind that an important goal in writing the Methods section is transparency: that is, this section should show readers as clearly as possible the steps you actually took to gather and analyze your material. Below we give an overview of what should be included.

(1)   About the participants

What was the nature of the set of people that you studied?

How did you decide on that group of people? (That is, why did they seem suitable for your project?)

How did you locate, contact, and recruit the participants?

How did you handle matters of confidentiality and anonymity during this stage of the study?

What were the actual conditions of anonymity, consent, assent, and so on in the project?

What was the number of individuals who participated?

What was the demographic composition of the group?

How many people were invited to participate but declined?

(2)   About the interview

Give a brief overview of the topics in the interview guide.

Describe the contents and sequence of the items in the interview guide, and, if possible, provide the full guide in an appendix or as supplementary material.

What formats did you use to ask questions? (E.g., semi-structured interviews? Open-ended questions? Group interviews?)

What considerations guided your choice of formats?

Describe how the interviews were conducted. (For example, how long did a typical interview last? Where were the interviews held? How were they recorded?)

Describe the transcribing procedures and the notation system you used.

(3)   About the procedures for analyzing

Give a detailed description of the analytical procedures you used. It is not sufficient merely to drop the name of a procedure or method because, in interpretative research, such names rarely refer to a single formulaic way of treating interview material.

Describe why you chose that analytical procedure. If possible, draw a connection back to the researchable questions: Why was this analytical procedure best suited to those questions?

Give a detailed description of the steps you took when you were following the chosen analytical procedure. (For example, what steps did you employ to verify that your interpretations were supported by the material?)

The Results and Discussion section

We suggest combining the Results and Discussion into a single section. This is common practice in interpretative research because the results cannot be understood without commentary and discussion. When you are writing this section of the report, you are not only reporting the analyses that you have completed; you are also engaging in the final stage of analysis. To wit, you are synthesizing the findings. Typical steps in this synthesis, which order and integrate the results, are included below:

1. In preparation, remind yourself of the researchable questions of your project and the main arguments that you want to put forward in your report.
2. Then assemble the specific parts of your finished analyses, that is, your *results*, that seem to bear on those arguments.
3. Think about how to order the results in a way that is easy for the readers to follow. This is the order in which you will present the subsections within the Results and Discussion section.
4. As you write each subsection, you should bring in verbatim interview material as illustrative examples. The following outline may be helpful when you are writing:
   a. State the point of the subsection. This orients readers' attention to the relevant feature of the example(s) to be presented.
   b. Supply the context needed to understand the example (e.g., who was the participant, what was the topic of the conversation, and perhaps what was spoken about previously in the interview).
   c. Give the illustrative excerpts as examples. Choose excerpts that are straightforward and easy for the reader to understand. The range of examples should exemplify nuances in the ways that participants expressed themselves. You should limit yourself to a few examples. In the next section, we address how to modify an excerpt to be used as an illustrative example.
   d. Give your analytical commentary. The purpose of the commentary is to tell readers what each example contributes to the argument you are building. In the commentary, you therefore tell readers what it is you want them to see in the

example. You can do this by pointing to certain features of the example and then elaborating on their meaning in relation to the topic of the subsection. This means that simply paraphrasing what the participant has said is not enough as an analytical commentary. To put it even more bluntly: the commentary never should merely restate what the participant said. To analyze is always to go beyond each participant's statements and tell readers how you, the researcher, have interpreted what the participant says.

The next two sections to write, the Introduction and the Conclusion, require that you take a step back from the procedures and results that you wrote about in the Methods section and the Results and Discussion section. That is, both the Introduction and Conclusion are written at some remove from the actual project. It is helpful to write them in tandem because, in some ways, the two look toward each other. If you have written "promissory notes" in the Introduction, they need to be paid off in the Conclusion. For example, if the Introduction promised that the project would have "policy implications," then the Conclusion should discuss such implications. If the Introduction promised that the project would yield "new theoretical developments," then the Conclusion should include a section that speaks about such developments. As you might guess, researchers often find themselves making adjustments in these two sections to fit them together and to make sure they complement each other.

Before we finish this section, we enter a caveat. Oftentimes, interpretative researchers are instructed by reviewers or editors to report the percentages of participants who have given each kind of response. As a rule, however, this is not appropriate because it misleads readers. There are two compelling reasons not to report such percentages. First, the groups that interpretative researchers study are typically quite small. This makes percentages largely meaningless. Second and more important, reporting percentages easily leads readers to misinterpret the results as claims about the general population (such as all Americans). As you know, such general claims are not the goal of interpretative research, nor could they be substantiated by such research.

The Introduction

This section introduces readers to the project. It establishes the topic of the study and its relevance to prior empirical findings, theories, practical issues, or policies. The Introduction should include four broad parts:

1. The argument of your report should be put forward in the first part of the Introduction, preferably in few sentences. The statement of the argument is important information for the readers because it gives them a frame of reference for what follows.
2. The second part of the Introduction situates the research topic with respect to the scholarly literature. This involves discussing relevant theories and concepts from the scholarly literature and it also involves reviewing the current state of knowledge. This discussion should be selective and to the point; your task is not to summarize or describe all the literature pertaining to your knowledge interest. Your task is to select

and recount the literature that bears on your argument. In addition to orienting the reader to your project, this selective recounting should also help the reader to see what makes your project important. Why is the question that you are asking important? For example, will your project help to resolve a theoretical debate or to clarify murky thinking? Or will it shed light on a body of inconsistent or contradictory findings? Or will it counter misinformation?

3. The third part introduces readers to the setting and the particular set of people that you have studied. As you sketch a portrait of the world of the participants, you will also begin to share with readers the thinking that guided your choice of this setting and these individuals. That is, why was this group of individuals appropriate for your study?

   In some cases, it may seem better to present Section (3) before Section (2). That is fine; however, you should not mix the two together.

4. The Introduction should end with a formal statement of the questions that you will discuss in the Results and Discussion section. Presenting them in the form of an ordered list or an outline is a good way to help the reader to keep them clearly in mind.

The Conclusion

The Conclusion places the results of the study in perspective. In doing so, it picks up on ideas that appeared in the Introduction. We suggest that you begin the Conclusion with a very brief summary of the results. Next, we suggest that you scan the following list of questions, which we have termed "So what?" questions. You should always address the first three questions. The remaining three (which are marked with asterisks) may be relevant to some projects but not to others. You should select the ones that are pertinent to your project.

1. What does your work say about the state of theoretical knowledge about your topic? This question asks you to place your findings within the network of relevant theory and theoretical constructs. Do your findings suggest places where theories or concepts should be expanded, revised, or discarded? Do your findings suggest that some theoretical constructs should be redefined?

2. What light does your work shed on previous empirical findings? How do your results extend, confirm, clarify, or dispute the pertinent body of empirical findings? If there are discrepancies, why does your study provide a more accurate portrait than others?

3. Why should readers care about these results? More specifically, why should the readers whom you are addressing care about these results?

*4. Are there any practical implications to be drawn from your study? Or any policy implications? Do your results speak to a social issue or a societal concern?

*5. As you reflect on your data-gathering and data analysis procedures, can you offer any suggestions that would improve research on this topic in the future?

*6. What topics for further research are opened up by this project?

Language, style, and ethics in scientific writing

It takes many drafts to produce a finished piece of writing. You should expect to revise and edit your report several times before you are satisfied with it. Writers develop different strategies for transforming their writing from a heap of notes about the results into a finished report. You may benefit from reading about the writing strategies of experienced academic writers (see, for instance, Becker & Richards, 1986; Emerson, Fretz, & Shaw, 2011; Turabian, 2007). When you are revising and editing, you will also benefit from asking your supervisors and colleagues to read drafts of your work. Ask them to read with as critical an eye as possible. Their job is to point out portions (whether words, sentences, paragraphs, or entire sections) where they cannot follow your train of thought. You are not seeking bland praise from these readers and you should make that clear to them. Their comments will make it easier for you to get your report into good shape before it leaves your hands to be graded by a committee or reviewed for publication.

In what follows, we give general advice on suitable writing styles for academic publications. We advise thesis writers to check the style guidelines for their university. If you aim to publish in a scholarly journal, you should check its style guidelines and read through several articles in the journal to observe the style of writing that the authors use.

Using material from your interviews in your report

To do your analyses, you scrutinized a large amount of interview material and you may have selected and sorted out a large number of excerpts from the interviews. When you come to write your report, however, you need to choose just a few of those excerpts to appear in the report as illustrations of the main points that you had brought forward during the analysis. The quoted material that appears as illustrations in your report must be easily understood by your readers, who will not be familiar with the details of the topic or the people you have studied. To make these illustrations meaningful, it is likely that you will need both to add detail and to remove detail.

Let us first consider what to add. You may need to add material that provides readers with the context necessary to understand the illustration. This can be a brief context-setting description that appears just before you present the illustrative material. You may also need to add brief explanations to the quoted material itself. These explanations can be inserted into the material in square brackets. For example: "Marvin [the participant's dog] and I go for long walks on the beach every day."

Now let us consider what you might need to remove or alter. One principle is that you should eliminate details of the talk that carry no meaning and that may distract or confuse readers. You need to exercise your judgment about what to keep and what to remove. For example, when speakers habitually insert repetitive expressions such as "um," "you know," and "like," those expressions may carry no meaning and can be removed. However, for speakers who seldom use such expressions, the occurrence of such an expression may signify that the speaker is struggling to find the right word or pausing to put a complicated thought into words or weighing what to say. In these cases, you should let the expressions stand in the quoted material.

You ought to omit extraneous material from excerpts that you want to use. That is, if the speaker has wandered off the topic and talks about things that have no relation to the reason why you chose the excerpt, you can omit the off-topic portions of the material. You should indicate that you have omitted material by using ellipses, that is, a string of three periods separated by spaces (. . .).

In an effort to impart the flavor of a participant's speech, some researchers attempt to reproduce accents, local dialects, and mispronunciations in quoted material. You should think carefully before you opt to do this. One drawback is that if you revert to phonetic spellings in order to capture accents or dialects, you are placing heavy demands on the reader to figure out what is being said. This may lead readers to skip past the quoted material. Another drawback is that such efforts to mimic participants' speech patterns can easily seem condescending, ridiculing, or possibly tinged with racial, ethnic, or class prejudices.

Avoid formal language

As a general rule, you should avoid overly formal, stilted, and pompous language in your report. For instance, avoid abstract words when more ordinary words can get your message across. Avoid intricate sentence structures and very long sentences. Try to keep most of your writing in the active voice, with the grammatical subject of the sentence as the doer of the action. Use passive voice constructions sparingly (e.g., avoid statements like "The participants were contacted by the researcher"). Steer clear of agent-less constructions such as "It was thought that . . ."

At the same time, you should also avoid writing prose that is chatty or breezy. Avoid personal asides, slang, and loose grammar. These may be acceptable in spoken language; however, in a written research report, such elements are unprofessional. They quickly become irritating to the reader.

Using the first person ("I," "me," "my," and so on) to refer to yourself is the accepted (and sometimes mandated) usage in most academic journals. Using the first person ("I") is far preferable to agent-less constructions such as "It was thought that . . ." or "It was decided to . . ." However, do not refer to yourself as "we" unless you are royalty.

Avoid imprecise or misleading terms borrowed from other fields

You should avoid terms that were devised for other fields and that therefore are misleading when used in interpretative research reports. Two examples are as follows:

− The participants in interpretative research are usually not referred to as "subjects." They are more often called participants, respondents, informants, or interviewees.
− The words "sample" and "sampling" are as a rule inappropriate for interpretative research reports because these words are usually used to denote random selection

procedures. It is rare that interpretative research projects use random samples of participants. Instead, interpretative researchers purposively select their groups of participants. Consequently, a term such as "the group of participants" or "the study group" is more precise. There is another related reason for avoiding the term sample. Drawing a random sample from a population is a step in a procedure aimed at making general statements about a population (often as wide as humankind). Interpretative research does not make such claims. Words like sample and sampling, therefore, inadvertently lead readers to misread your conclusions.

Avoid discriminatory language

You should think through the ramifications of all the terms you use to describe the people you have studied and the social arrangements and customs in which they take part. Below is a list of some particularly contentious issues to consider. Depending on the topic of your study and the group you have studied, there may be other issues to consider as well. See also Braun and Clarke (2013) for useful suggestions.

– When you refer to people in general, you should avoid the traditional usage "he," "man," or "mankind." Use neutral words like "people" or "humans" or "persons." In some languages, there are neutral terms; use them when possible.
– If you study members of a marginalized group, you should use the terms they use about themselves when you write your report. However, sometimes even those terms may be controversial. As an example, transgender activists have offered challenging critiques of everyday ways of speaking about sex categories and also of style guidelines that have been designed to be nonsexist (*cf.* Ansara & Hegarty, 2014).
– If issues of ethnicity or race are salient in your study, you should use precise and culturally specific words to describe your participants' identities. The ways in which these issues are described and thought about vary greatly between countries, and you need to take this into account. You should, for instance, consider whether the local designations used in the setting in which your study was done might be misunderstood by your readers or be offensive to some of them. You may need to incorporate a brief discussion of word usage into your text.
– If your study concerns people who have some condition or illness, you should use care when you choose the words to describe those people and their conditions. As a general rule, you should avoid expressions like "an anorexic" or "a paraplegic." It is usually better to say "people with . . ." (Do not, however, alter direct quotes of participants if they use such language.)
– Avoid designating societal arrangements that are common or typical as "normal." The word "normal" inevitably implies that other arrangements are "abnormal." Using words like "normal" brings into your text an implicit normative and evaluative dimension that you likely do not intend.

Safeguard the anonymity of your participants and their communities

When you write about individual participants in a report (for instance, if you give information to contextualize an interview excerpt), be cautious about how many specific details you mention and what those details are. You should divulge only enough to elucidate the issues that are at stake and no more. That is, you need to consider which categories of identity, personal details, etc., are necessary to bring your interpretations across. If your research concerns a group that is easily identified, and especially one whose individual members would be easy to identify, you need to take extra care to limit or disguise the descriptions you give in your report. If the group is small and easily recognizable in society, it may be almost impossible to give details about individual members without jeopardizing their anonymity. If that is the case, you may have to avoid giving any details about individuals in your entire reports.

A further question concerns ethical responsibilities that may go beyond the individual participants. What if the results of your project paint a damaging and demeaning portrait of the site of your study or of the community from which your participants were drawn? Often, it is not difficult for insiders to guess the location of your research or the specific community from which you drew your participants. The standard ethical requirements for research focus only on concealing the identities of individual participants. However, you might do well to consider whether you have an obligation to conceal the identities of locales, institutions, or communities.

Languages and writing styles

No single writing style is appropriate everywhere. The academic world contains many disciplines, all with their own traditions of style and writing (Sword, 2012). Also, research is done in many different countries and by people who speak different languages. Academic traditions and writing styles differ across language boundaries. Styles also differ among countries that use the same language. For instance, the English language styles that are deemed acceptable in the UK and the USA are not identical; the accepted spelling and diction varies, and so do elements of expository style. Therefore, you should consult style guides that are "close to home" both as regards your discipline and the language in which you are writing.

When you move between languages

In the social sciences, a large proportion of published research appears in English language publications, regardless of the author's native language. This means that a substantial number of researchers do not publish in their native language. This situation often creates some difficulties. One problem is that these researchers often are at a disadvantage because they are less adept at producing the accepted style of writing than are researchers whose native language is English. This problem can be partly taken care of by employing translators or "language checkers." Unfortunately, however, these experts seldom have knowledge of the special terminology and theoretical apparatus that is used in scientific publications. Therefore, the results of their work are often unsatisfactory. If you use translators or "language checkers," you must therefore check their work carefully to ensure that special terminology and concepts have been translated correctly.

Another problem that crops up when researchers do not write in their own language is perhaps unique to interpretative research. If the research interviews were done in a language other than that of the final report, researchers have to think carefully about how to incorporate excerpts of participants' talk in the final report. The analyses should, of course, be done in the original language. For the report, however, the pieces of talk that are used to illustrate results need to be translated. This translation should focus on the meaning of what was said, rather than exact lexical translations of individual words. It is also a good idea to point out to readers that the analyses were done in the original language.

Plagiarism

Plagiarism refers to representing others' work or others' data as one's own. This includes both quoting the exact words of others without attributing them properly to the authors and paraphrasing others' words or ideas extensively without attribution. Plagiarism is a form of academic dishonesty and it is never acceptable in academic work. In the academic world, the penalties for engaging in plagiarism are substantial.

Authorship

Questions about who will be listed as the authors of a publication and in what order the authors' names will be listed often become contentious. In principle, it is good to decide these matters as early as possible. In practice, however, the distribution of effort often changes dramatically over the course of a project for reasons that could not be anticipated. In such circumstances, early decisions about authorship may need to be modified. The American Psychological Association's *Ethical Principles of Psychologists and Code of Conduct* (APA, 2003/2010) contains principles for assigning authorship credit (and other forms of credit such as acknowledgments) to the researchers who have participated in a project.

Where to publish

Getting your work into print is not just a matter of producing a high-quality product. That, of course, is necessary, but it may not be sufficient. You also need to direct your writing toward the right audience and the right publishing outlet. A starting point is seeking advice from experienced interpretative researchers about the journal for which your particular study is best suited. In addition, you should scan the literature that you have reviewed. The journals that are heavily represented in your literature review will have published work similar to yours and therefore are likely to be suitable venues for your work. Another good strategy is to read through several issues of the journals you are considering. If those journals have not published articles akin to your work (either substantively or methodologically), you might do better to look for a more hospitable venue.

Epilogue

In this epilogue, we offer our reflections on several features of interpretative research. We begin by considering how interpretative research is situated in relation to other scientific research. All scientific research is guided by theory, which gives the researcher a set of concepts and previous findings for thinking about the topics that are being studied. All good social research uses systematic methods of selecting participants for study, systematic methods for gathering material from them, and systematic and transparent procedures for analyzing that material. Also, there are common ethical standards for conducting a study and common standards for reporting the results of research.

Beyond the commonalities, each approach to research has distinctive features that are determined by its overarching framework. Let us briefly recap the overarching framework of interpretative research. To begin with, interpretative researchers think of people as always located in social contexts and as continually engaged in making sense of their experiences. Interpretative researchers seek to understand the meanings that people give to particular events and actions. They also want to know how those meanings arise in the cultural and social settings in which people live – how people arrive at meanings through their interactions with others and how they then make those meanings their own.

To accomplish their goals, interpretative researchers employ several distinctive procedures. These procedures set their research apart from, for instance, experimental research and survey research. We have found that some beginners are puzzled by certain procedures of interpretative research. We discuss four such procedures here: the use of semi-structured interviews, the use of purposive selection for composing study groups, the use of open researchable questions instead of *a priori* hypotheses, and the practice of refining and augmenting the researchable questions as the research unfolds.

Using semi-structured interviews

To learn about people's meaning-making, interpretative researchers rely on interviews in which they ask participants to tell about real-life relationships and situations. They ask participants to tell about their thoughts, intentions, reactions, and reflections, and how and for what reasons they made choices about how to act. When people agree to take part in such research interviews, they shoulder the task of explaining themselves to the interviewer – of making themselves understandable to an outsider who lacks local knowledge. Such interviews are therefore likely to be dense with clues about the participants' ways of seeing the world.

Semi-structured interviews, which you learned about in Chapters 5 and 6, depart in two important ways from the close-ended questions and scales that are used in experiments and surveys. First, semi-structured interviews do not require the participant to choose from a small set of responses that have been predetermined by the researcher. The open-ended format of the interview questions allows participants to bring forward their own ideas, perceptions, beliefs, and reactions. This enables the researcher to learn about a wide range of experiences and meanings related to the topic, including new or unexpected things. Second, in order to learn as much as possible from each participant, the interviewer adjusts the order and flow of interview questions as the interview unfolds, rather than adhering to a uniform preset order.

Some beginners look askance at such a flexible approach to data gathering. They may be accustomed to the idea that researchers must treat all participants alike or else the results will be biased. But for interpretative researchers, the rationale is clear: The goal is to create conditions that enable each participant to contribute his or her own material to the study. Because people are different, these conditions will not be the same for everyone. Therefore both the shape and specific content of the interviews need to vary across participants.

Selecting research participants purposively

Different types of research entail different principles for composing groups for study. Newcomers to interpretative research sometimes worry about the usefulness of research that is not based on random samples. Such worries reflect a misunderstanding of the overarching framework of interpretative research. This misunderstanding could lead one to impose the standards of other types of scientific research onto interpretative research. Let us clarify matters.

Interpretative research focuses on experiences that arise in specific contexts or that pertain to specific occurrences. Researchers seek to learn how those experiences vary; unusual experiences are as important to study as typical ones. Therefore interpretative researchers purposively select a set of participants who have had as wide a variety of experiences as possible, not just the typical or modal experience. To achieve this variety, interpretative researchers might, for instance, seek out individuals from different social class backgrounds, age groups, or educational backgrounds. Or they might compose a study group that consisted of participants who occupy different positions or roles within an organization or community.

The goals of interpretative researchers would not be served by drawing a set of participants at random from the general population. In fact, random selection would be counterproductive. By the very nature of random selection, a random group of research participants will necessarily have many people with typical experiences, whereas people with unusual or atypical experiences will be few in number or excluded altogether. Capturing the full variety of experiences is an integral goal of interpretative research, and so selection procedures that enlist people with both uncommon and common experiences are necessary.

In this book, we have avoided words like "sample" and "sampling" when referring to the groups of participants that interpretative researchers study. In place of those words, we have used words such as "study group" and "purposive selection" of participants for study. This was a considered choice on our part. "Sampling," as in the expression "random sampling," is usually used to denote procedures that ensure that research participants are drawn at random from a defined population. Such words therefore mischaracterize the selection procedures of interpretative researchers.

Formulating open researchable questions

As you have read in Chapter 3, the researchable questions in interpretative research have an open format; they are not if-then hypotheses or theoretically derived predictions. Newcomers to interpretative research sometimes wonder about the implications of this open format. Because the connection between the type of research question and the type of research design is often unclear to learners, we take a moment to explore this connection.

In hypothesis-testing research, the researcher begins by formulating one or more hypotheses that will be tested and then designs a study that is tailored to test these hypotheses. When designing the study, the researcher determines the categories, variables, meanings, statistical tests, and interpretations that the study will address. In this type of research design, hypothesis-testing statistics are applied only to the questions (i.e., the hypotheses) that the researcher posed at the outset of the study. Altering or expanding the original hypotheses once the study is under way, and testing those alterations by hypothesis-testing statistics, is not permitted.

In interpretative research, the researcher begins by formulating one or more open researchable questions and then designs study procedures that can expand and refine knowledge beyond the categories, understandings, and questions that were determined at the outset of the study. That is, the researcher does not regard the original categories, questions, and understandings as hypotheses to be tested, but as ideas to be elaborated and refined in the course of the study.

Refining and augmenting the researchable questions as the research unfolds

As researchers engage in interviews with participants, they usually uncover important matters that they had not anticipated. That is, participants may bring forward new meanings, new points of view, and unforeseen facts that lead the researcher to change his or her original way of thinking about the topic of study. The researcher may come to see that the original researchable questions were insufficient or perhaps misdirected. In response, he or she may devise additional researchable questions or modify the initial ones. Some of the original researchable questions may even turn out to be entirely beside the point; they will be discarded. Furthermore, as the researchable questions are refined, the researcher may well see that new items or even new topics need to be added to the interview guide. The researcher may further decide that it would be useful to interview additional types of people who can offer additional viewpoints about the topic. An apt aphorism for this process of continually refining and expanding the scope of the project as it proceeds is one coined by the sociologist Howard Becker (1998): *thinking about your research while you are doing it.*

References

Anderson, K.L. and Umberson, D. (2001) Gendering violence: Masculinity and power in men's accounts of domestic violence. *Gender & Society*, 15, 358–380.

Ansara, Y.G. and Hegarty, P. (2014) Methodologies of misgendering: Recommendations for reducing cisgenderism in psychological research. *Feminism & Psychology*, 24, 259–270.

Antaki, C., Billig, M., Edwards, D., and Potter, J. (2003) Discourse analysis means doing analysis: A critique of six analytic shortcomings. *Discourse Analysis Online*. www.shu.ac.uk/daol.

American Psychological Association (2003/2010) Ethical principles of psychologists and code of conduct. Retrieved on January 14, 2015 from www.apa.org/ethics/code/principles.pdf.

Becker, H. (1998) *Tricks of the trade: How to think about your research while you're doing it.* Chicago: University of Chicago Press.

Becker, H. and Richards, P. (1986) *Writing for social scientists: How to start and finish your thesis, book, or article.* Chicago: University of Chicago Press.

Billig, M. (1991) *Ideology and opinions: Studies in rhetorical psychology.* London: Sage.

Billig, M. (1996, 2nd edn.) *Arguing and thinking: A rhetorical approach to social psychology.* Cambridge: Cambridge University Press.

Billig, M., Condor, S., Edwards, D., Gane, M., Middleton, D., and Radley, A. (1988) *Ideological dilemmas: A social psychology of everyday thinking.* London: Sage.

Braun, V. and Clarke, V. (2013) *Successful qualitative research: A practical guide for beginners.* London: Sage.

Bruner, J.S. (1986) *Actual minds, possible worlds.* Cambridge, MA: Harvard University Press.

Bruner, J.S. (1990) *Acts of meaning.* Cambridge, MA: Harvard University Press.

Bruner, J.S. (1991) The narrative construction of reality. *Critical Inquiry*, 18, 1–12.

Buttny, R. (2003) *Social accountability in communication.* London: Sage.

Capps, L. and Ochs, E. (1995a) Out of place: Narrative insights into agoraphobia. *Discourse Processes*, 19, 407–439.

Capps, L. and Ochs, E. (1995b) *Constructing panic: The discourse of agoraphobia.* Cambridge, MA: Harvard University Press.

Cohen, J., Marecek, J., and Gillham, J. (2006) Is three a crowd? Clients, clinicians and managed care. *American Journal of Orthopsychiatry*, 76, 251–259.

Cronon, W. (1992) A place for stories: Nature, history, and narrative. *Journal of American History*, 80, 1347–1376.

Currie, D., Kelly, D., and Pomerantz, S. (2006) "The geeks shall inherit the earth": Girls' agency, subjectivity and empowerment. *Journal of Youth Studies*, 9, 419–436.

D'Alwis, M. (1995) Gender, politics and the "Respectable Lady." In P. Jeganathan and Q. Ishmail (Eds.) *The politics of identity and history in modern Sri Lanka* (pp. 137–157). Colombo, Sri Lanka: Social Scientists' Association.

Davidson, L. (2003) *Living outside mental illness: Qualitative studies of recovery in schizophrenia*. New York: New York University Press.

Davidson, L., Stayner, D.A., Lambert, S., Smith, P., and Sledge, W.H. (1997) Phenomenological and participatory research on schizophrenia: Recovering the person in theory and practice. *Journal of Social Issues*, 53(4), 767–784.

Davidson, L., Stayner, D.A., Chimney, M.J., Lambert, S., and Sledge, W.H. (2000) Preventing relapse and readmission in psychosis: Using patients' subjective experience in designing clinical interventions. In B. Martindale (Ed.) *Outcome studies in psychological treatments of psychotic conditions* (pp. 134–156). London: Gaskell Publishers.

Davidson, L., Haggled, K.E., Stayner, D.A., Rakfeldt, J., Chinman, M.J., and Tebes, J.K. (2001a) "It was just realizing... that life isn't one big horror." A qualitative study of supported socialization. *Psychiatric Rehabilitation Journal*, 24, 275–292.

Davidson, L., Stayner, D.A., Nickou, C., Stryon, T.H., Rowe, M., and Chinman, M.J. (2001b) "Simply to be let in": Inclusion as a basis for recovery from mental illness. *Psychiatric Rehabilitation Journal*, 24, 375–388.

Dottolo, A. and Stewart, A. (2008) "Don't ever forget now, you're a Black man in America": Intersections of race, class and gender in encounters with the police. *Sex Roles*, 59, 350–364.

Edley, N. (2001) Analysing masculinity: Interpretative repertoires, ideological dilemmas, and subject positions. In M. Wetherell, S. Taylor and S.J. Yates (Eds.) *Discourse as data: A guide for analysis* (pp. 189–228). London: Sage.

Edley, N. and Wetherell, M. (1997) Jockeying for position: The construction of masculine identities. *Discourse & Society*, 8, 203–217.

Edwards, D. (1997) *Discourse and cognition*. London: Sage.

Edwards, D. (2000) Extreme case formulations: Softeners, investment, and doing literal. *Research on Language and Social Interaction*, 33, 347–373.

Edwards, D. and Potter, J. (1992) *Discursive psychology*. London: Sage.

Edwards, D., Ashmore, M., and Potter, J. (1995) Death and furniture: The rhetoric, politics and theology of bottom line arguments against relativism. *History of the Human Sciences*, 8, 25–49.

Emerson, R.M., Fretz, R.I., and Shaw, L.L. (2011) *Writing ethnographic fieldnotes*. Chicago: University of Chicago Press.

Farvid, P. (2010) The benefits of ambiguity: Methodological insights from researching "heterosexual casual sex." *Feminism & Psychology*, 20, 232–237.

Foster, D., Haupt, P., and De Beer, M. (2005) *The theatre of violence: Narratives of protagonists in the South African conflict*. Oxford: James Currey Press.

Galletta, A. (2013) *Mastering the semi-structured interview and beyond: From research design to analysis and publication*. New York: New York University Press.

Geertz, C. (1973) *The interpretation of cultures*. New York: Basic Books.

Gilbert, N. and Mulkay, M. (1984) *Opening Pandora's box. A sociological analysis of scientists' discourse*. Cambridge: Cambridge University Press.

Gold-Steinberg, S. (1994) Personal choices in political climates: Coping with legal and illegal abortion. In C.E. Franz and A.J. Stewart (Eds.) *Women creating lives: Identities, resilience, and resistance* (pp. 263–271). Boulder, CO: Westview Press.

Herman, D. (2009) *Basic elements of narrative*. New York: Wiley-Blackwell.

Howitt, D. (2010) *Introduction to qualitative methods in psychology*. Harlow: Prentice Hall/ Pearson Education.

Jefferson, G. (2004) Glossary of transcript symbols with an introduction. In G.H. Lerner (Ed.) *Conversation analysis: Studies from the first generation* (pp. 13–31). Philadelphia: John Benjamins.

Kirschner, S.R. and Martin, J. (Eds.) (2010) *The sociocultural turn in psychology: The contextual emergence of mind and self.* New York: Columbia University Press.

Lafrance, M. (2007) The bitter pill: A discursive analysis of women's medicalized accounts of depression. *Journal of Health Psychology*, 12, 127–140.

Lynch, C. (1999) The "good girls" of Sri Lankan modernity: Moral orders of nationalism and capitalism. *Identities*, 6, 55–89.

Magnusson, E. (1996) "Jag har faktiskt aldrig lidit av att vara kvinna." ["I have actually never suffered from being a woman"]. *Kvinnovetenskaplig tidskrift* [*Swedish Journal of Women's Studies*], 17(1), 30–46.

Magnusson, E. (1997a) Talking about gender equality: Swedish women's discourses on the home front. *NORA: Nordic Journal of Women's Studies*, 5, 76–94.

Magnusson, E. (1997b) Att vara en riktig kvinna på kontoret: När kvinnor skapar trivsel, skapar trivseln samtidigt kvinnor. [Being a real woman in the office: When women create cosiness, the cosiness simultaneously creates women.] In: G. Nordborg (Ed.) *Makt och kön: Tretton bidrag till feministisk kunskap.* [*Power and gender: Thirteen contributions to feminist knowledge*] (pp. 71–92). Stockholm: Symposion.

Magnusson, E. (1998) *Vardagslivets könsinnebörder under förhandling: om arbete, familj och produktion av kvinnlighet* [*Everyday negotiations of gender: Work, family and the production of femininity*]. PhD Dissertation, Umeå University, Sweden.

Magnusson, E. (2005) Gendering or equality in the lives of Nordic heterosexual couples with children: No well-paved avenues yet. *NORA: Nordic Journal of Feminist and Gender Research*, 13, 153–163.

Magnusson, E. (2006) *Hon, han och hemmet: genuspsykologiska perspektiv på vardagslivet i nordiska barnfamiljer* [*She, he, and their home: Gender, psychology, and everyday life in Nordic families with children*]. Stockholm: Natur & Kultur.

Magnusson, E. (2008a) The rhetoric of inequality: Nordic women and men argue against sharing housework. *NORA: Nordic Journal of Feminist and Gender Research*, 16, 79–95.

Magnusson, E. (2008b) Conflict, danger and difference: Nordic heterosexual couples converse about gender equality and fairness. In E. Magnusson, M. Rönnblom and H. Silius (Eds.) *Critical studies of gender equalities: Nordic dislocations, dilemmas and contradictions* (pp. 161–179). Göteborg: Makadambok Publishers.

Magnusson, E. and Marecek, J. (2012) *Gender and culture in psychology: Theories and practices.* Cambridge: Cambridge University Press.

Marecek, J. (2006) Young women's suicide in Sri Lanka: Cultural, ecological, and psychological factors. *Asian Journal of Counseling Psychology*, 13, 63–92.

Marecek, J. and Kravetz, D.F. (1998) Putting politics into practice: Feminist therapy as feminist praxis. *Women & Therapy*, 21, 17–36.

Marecek, J. and Senadheera, C. (2012) "I drank it to put an end to me": Sri Lankan girls narrate suicide and self-harm. *Contributions to Indian Sociology*, 46, 53–82.

Miller, P.J., Wang, S., Sandel, T., and Cho, G.E. (2002) Self-esteem as folk theory: A comparison of European American and Taiwanese mothers' beliefs. *Parenting: Science and Practice*, 2, 209–239.

Morée, M. (1992) *Mijn kinderen hebben er niets van gemerkt: Buitenshuis werkende moeders tussen 1950 en nu* [*"My children never noticed anything": Working mothers between 1950 and now*]. PhD Dissertation, University of Leiden, NL. Utrecht: Jan van Arkel.

NOSOSCO (2011) *Nordic Statistical Yearbook 2011*. Copenhagen: Nordic Council of Ministers. www.norden.org/nsy2011.

Ochs, E. (1979) Transcription as theory. In E. Ochs and B. Schieffelin (Eds.) *Developmental pragmatics* (pp.43–72). New York: Academic Press.

Ochs, E. (2005) Narrative lessons. In A. Duranti (Ed.) *A companion to linguistic anthropology* (pp. 269–289). New York: Wiley.

Oransky, M. (2002) *Doing boy: Adolescent boys' constructions of masculinity.* Unpublished thesis, Department of Psychology, Swarthmore College, USA.

Oransky, M. and Marecek, J. (2009) "I'm not going to be a girl": Masculinity and emotions in boys' friendships and peer groups. *Journal of Adolescent Research*, 24, 218–242.

Parker, I. (1990a) Discourse: Definitions and contradictions. *Philosophical Psychology*, 3, 189–204.

Parker, I. (1990b) Real things: Discourse, context and practice. *Philosophical Psychology*, 3, 227–233.

Parker, I. and Burman, E. (1993) Against discursive imperialism, empiricism and constructionism: Thirty-two problems with discourse analysis. In E. Burman and I. Parker (Eds.) *Discourse analytic research: Repertoires and readings of texts in action* (pp. 155–172). London: Routledge.

Perelman, C. (1979) *The new rhetoric and the humanities. Essays on rhetoric and its applications.* Dordrecht: D. Reidel/Springer.

Phoenix, A. (2008) Claiming livable lives: Adult subjectification and narratives of "non-normative" childhood experiences. In J. Kofoed and D. Staunaes (Eds.) *Magtballader* [*Adjusting Reality*] (pp. 178–193). Copenhagen: Danmarks Pædagogiske Universitetsforlag.

Pomerantz, A. (1986) Extreme case formulations: A way of legitimizing claims. *Human Studies*, 9, 219–229.

Potter, J. (1996) *Representing reality: Discourse, rhetoric and social construction.* London: Sage.

Potter, J., Wetherell, M., Gill, R., and Edwards, D. (1990) Discourse: Noun, verb or social practice? *Philosophical Psychology*, 3, 205–217.

Quinn, N. (Ed.) (2005) *Finding culture in talk: A collection of methods.* New York: Palgrave Macmillan.

Sacks, H. (1992) *Lectures on conversation, Volumes I and II.* Edited by G. Jefferson. Oxford: Basil Blackwell.

Sannetorp, K. (2012) *Upplevelser av att vara icke-heterosexuell i arbetslivet.* [*Experiences of being non-heterosexual in the workplace*]. Unpublished Master's thesis, Department of Psychology, Umeå University, Sweden.

Senadheera, C., Marecek, J., Hewage, C., and Wijayasiri, W.A.A. (2010) A hospital-based study of trends in deliberate self-harm in children and adolescents. *Ceylon Journal of Medicine*, 55, 67–68.

Shweder, R. (1991) *Thinking through cultures*. Cambridge, MA: Harvard University Press.

Speer, S. (2005) *Gender talk: Feminism, discourse and conversation analysis.* London: Routledge.

Stewart, J.E. (2013) *Living with brain injury: Narrative, community and women's renegotiation of identity.* New York: New York University Press.

Sword, H. (2012) *Stylish academic writing.* Cambridge, MA: Harvard University Press.

Taylor, S. (2001) Locating and conducting discourse analytic research. In M. Wetherell, S. Taylor and S.J. Yates (Eds.) *Discourse as data: A guide for analysis* (pp. 5–48). Milton Keynes: Sage and Open University Press.

Thompson, B.W. (1994) *A hunger so wide and deep: American women speak out on eating disorders*. Minneapolis, MN: University of Minnesota Press.

Turabian, K. (2007, 7th edn.) *A manual for writers of research papers, theses, and dissertations*. Chicago: University of Chicago Press.

Wetherell, M. (1998) Positioning and interpretative repertoires: Conversation analysis and post-structuralism in dialogue. *Discourse & Society*, 9, 431–456.

Wetherell, M. (2001) Debates in discourse research. In M. Wetherell, S. Taylor, and S.J. Yates (Eds.) *Discourse, theory and practice: A reader* (pp. 380–399). Milton Keynes, UK: Sage and Open University Press.

Wetherell, M. and Potter, J. (1992) *Mapping the language of racism: Discourse and the legitimation of exploitation*. New York: Harvester Wheatsheaf.

Index

Printed in Great Britain
by Amazon

22228140R00110